Anthropology and community in Cambodia

Anthropology and community in Cambodia

Reflections on the work of May Ebihara

edited by John Marston

Monash University Press
Caulfield

Monash University Press
MAI, Building H
Monash University
Victoria 3145, Australia
www.monash.edu.au/mai

All Monash University Press publications are subject to double blind peer review

National Library of Australia cataloguing-in-publication data:

Title: Anthropolgy and community in Cambodia : reflections of the work
of May Ebihara / ed. John A Marston.

ISBN: 9781876924744

Series: Monash papers on Southeast Asia ; 70

Notes: Bibliography.

Subjects: Ebihara, May.

          Anthropology—Cambodia.

          Women anthropologists.

          Anthropologists' writings, American.

          Festschriften.

          Cambodia—History—20th century.

Other Authors/Contributors:

          Marston, John A.

Dewey Number: 306.09596

Cover design and photograph by Jenny Hall.

Printed by BPA Print Group, Melbourne, Australia - www.bpabooks.com

Acknowledgments

John Marston

In a number of important ways this book has been the product of a sort of 'committee' including David Chandler, Charles . Keyes and Judy Ledgerwood, in addition to myself. The book grew out of our discussions as a group. Initial decisions about who might write articles and what publishers might be contacted were discussed among us, and Chandler, Keyes and Ledgerwood played major roles at several crucial junctures in our search for a home for this manuscript. A special debt is owed to Chandler, who initially 'assigned' me the task of editing the book, and who at one point went over all of the articles checking for basic copyediting errors; he also, for a couple of chapters, engaged contributors directly in discussion about content. The interview with May and the timeline were both his suggestions, and he played a key role in facilitating communication with Monash Asia Institute. My three 'committee colleagues' have shown an unflagging dedication to May Ebihara, and this at times has helped buoy my own motivation. They have also been a source of information about her.

I would like to extend my special thanks to Yohko Kirsch for supplying the article by Thomas Kirsch and for her continuing support of this book.

I would also like to express my thanks to the Center for Asian and African Studies of El Colegio for its ongoing support of my involvement in projects of this kind and the computer and secretarial support I have been able rely on. My own involvement with Cambodian studies has been supported by a vital community of scholars and Cambodian intellectuals, including, in addition to the contributors to this book, Elizabeth Guthrie, Caroline Hughes, Penny Edwards, Anne Hansen, Chan Sambath, Un Kheang, Yin Luoth, Prak Sonnara, Chean Men, Mony Pol Vann Chaom, Boramy Sou, Sotheary Duong and Chhuon Hoeur. At a personal level, I would also like to express my gratitude for the support of my mother, Lucy Marston, my sister, Mem Lloyd, Lien-tan Pan and Manuel Moises.

Note on the representation of Khmer words

I have elsewhere (Marston and Guthrie 2004: ix-x) discussed the ins and outs of different ways of representing Khmer words in the Roman alphabet. The two most common alternatives at the present time are the system devised by Saveros Pou (Lewitz 1969) and what is known as the 'Franco-Khmer Transcription System'. The Pou system has the advantage of being more scientific—it is truly a transliteration system—with a one-to-one correspondence between the Khmer writing system and the transliteration. Some scholars have been reluctant to use it because, given certain anomalies of the Khmer alphabet, it sometimes results in transliterations that are misleading as a representation of pronunciation.

For this volume, partly because it was closer to the system most of the contributors were already using, I have chosen the 'Franco-Khmer Transcription System'. The linguist Franklin Huffman, who in different contexts used a number of different systems to represent Khmer words, devised this system in 1983 in an attempt to chart the system used by the French during the colonial period in such a way as to capture systematically Khmer vowel distinctions. He insisted that it should not be considered a transliteration system. What it does generate is a representation of Khmer words that approximates well the pronunciation.

I believe the first volume to use this system was Ebihara, Mortland and Ledgerwood's Cambodian Culture since 1975 (1994). However, at that time Judy Ledgerwood, in implementing the system, discovered that the extensive use of diacritics would create type-setting problems, and she was forced to eliminate all diacritics except for 'a' with a circumflex (that is, â). The use of the system without diacritics has been followed in a number of other volumes. Given the variety of fonts now readily available on any computer, I have decided to re-instate the diacritics in the original Franco-Khmer Transcription System.

The one symbol that Huffman used that is still difficult to reproduce is a letter 'a' with both a circumflex and a breve diacritic above it. I have chosen to represent this by a circumflex above and a dot below (that is, ậ).

In a few cases, where representing a final silent letter would be confusing, I have dropped the final letter. I have decided that the word 'wat' has already entered the English language in that spelling (from Thai) and I represent it in the text as such without italics, even though the representation of the Khmer word would be vatt according to the system. Similarly, certain Buddhist terms, such as sangha and vinaya are known to English users as such, and I have not tried to represent them as they would be pronounced in Khmer.

Ebihara, May, Carol Mortland and Judy Ledgerwood (eds) 1994, *Cambodian culture since 1975: homeland and exile*, Cornell University Press, Ithaca.

Lewitz, Saveros 1969, 'Note sur la translittération du Cambodgien', *Bulletin de l'École Française d'Extrême-Orient* 55.

Marston, John and Elizabeth Guthrie (eds) 2004, *History, Buddhism and new religious movements in Cambodia*, University of Hawai'i Press, Honolulu.

Contributors

David Chandler is Emeritus Professor of History at Monash University in Melbourne, Australia, where he taught from 1972 to 1997 and was also a research director of its Centre of Southeast Asian Studies. He worked in the US Embassy in Phnom Penh in 1960–1962. Early in his academic career, he was one of several historians who jointly authored the seminal book *In search of Southeast Asia: a modern history*. His other books include *A history of Cambodia* (4th edition, 2008), *Voices from S-21* (1999), *Facing the Cambodian past* (1996), and *The tragedy of Cambodian history: politics, war and revolution since 1945* (1991).

Soizick Crochet received her doctorate in social anthropology from Paris X-Nanterre University in 2001. She was a social and medical worker in refugee camps on the Thai–Cambodian border in the early 1980s and in Phnom Penh in 1984–85. She conducted doctoral research between 1995 and 1997 on how lay women (traditional midwives, mothers) were working in the same models as more specialised healers (*kru*). She has also conducted research on Aids-related issues. She is the author of *Le Cambodge* (Paris, Karthala, 1997). Her recent articles include 'La sante au Cambodge: histoire et defis' (2008) in *Cambodge contemporain* (Alain Forest, ed) and '"They do not get angry": notes on the speeches of HIV positive women contaminated by their partners' (2010) in *The trade in human beings for sex in South East Asia* (Pierre Leroux, Jean Bafffie and Gilles Beullier, eds). After 18 years in Cambodia, Thailand and Malaysia, she recently moved to the United States.

Kate Frieson received a PhD in politics from Monash University in 1992. Her dissertation, 'The impact of revolution on peasants in Cambodia', examined the relationship between Khmer Rouge revolutionaries and rural society during the civil war period of 1970 to 1975. She taught Southeast Asian history and politics for five years at the University of Victoria, Canada, and has worked in the areas of human rights, gender and development, and natural resource management for the past 15 years with the United Nations and other international institutions in Bosnia-Herzegovina, Cambodia, and Viet Nam. She is based in Phnom Penh, Cambodia.

Jane Richardson Hanks is the doyen of female anthropologists who have carried out research in Southeast Asia. Born in 1908, she took her PhD in anthropology at Columbia University in 1938. After early work on Blackfoot native Americans in Canada, her husband Lucien Hanks's wartime experience in Burma led both of them to turn their attention to Southeast Asia. In 1951, they were invited to join a project focused on the impact of modernisation in central

Thailand. Some of Jane Hanks's most influential work, such as 'Reflections on the ontology of Rice' (1960), were based on this work. In the 1960s Jane and Lucien began their last major ethnographic project in the highlands of northern Thailand. Hanks had a strong influence on May Ebihara.

Alex Hinton is Executive Director of the Center for the Study of Genocide, Conflict Resolution, and Human Rights, and Professor of Anthropology and Global Affairs at Rutgers University. He is the author of *Why did they kill? Cambodia in the shadow of genocide* (California, 2005) and six edited or co-edited collections, including *Transitional justice: global mechanisms and local realities after genocide and mass violence* (Rutgers, 2010) and *Genocide: truth, memory, and representation* (Duke, 2009). He is currently working on several other book projects, including an edited volume, *Genocide and mass violence: memory, symptom, intervention,*and a book on the politics of memory and justice in the aftermath of the Cambodian genocide. The American Anthropological Association selected Hinton as the recipient of the 2009 Robert B Textor and Family Prize for Excellence in Anticipatory Anthropology.

Charles Keyes, Professor Emeritus of Anthropology and International Studies at the University of Washington and past-president of the Association for Asian Studies, has since the early 1960s carried out extensive research in Thailand, Vietnam, Laos, and Cambodia on Buddhism and modernity, ethnicity and national cultures, and culture and 'development'. He has written, edited or co-edited 14 books, monographs or special issues of journals and published over 80 articles, among them: *The golden peninsula: culture and adaptation in mainland Southeast Asia* (reprinted, 1995); 'Northeastern Thai ethnoregionalism updated' in *Anthropological traces: Thailand and the work of Andrew Turton*, Nicholas Tapp (ed, 2010); and '"The peoples of Asia": science and politics in ethnic classification in Thailand, China and Vietnam', *Journal of Asian Studies* (2002).

Sedara Kim holds a masters in cultural anthropology from the Northern Illinois University, where he studied with a Fulbright Scholarship. In 2005–10 he conducted doctoral studies in development and political science at the School of Global Studies, Gothenburg University. Since 2001 he has been a Senior Research Fellow with the Cambodia Development Resource Institute. His PhD dissertation is titled 'Democracy in action: decentralisation reform in post-Cambodia'. His current research focus is governance and public sector reforms in Cambodia.

A Thomas Kirsch was Professor of Anthropology and Asian Studies at Cornell University from 1970 until his death in 1999. He conducted fieldwork in Thailand, beginning in the northeast in the early 1960s and finishing in

Bangkok in 1992. His writing on village life, Buddhism, religious syncretism and social change has been influential within Southeast Asian studies. Besides empirical research, he was also interested in anthropological theories and their development, and in historical exploration of the past lives and religious beliefs of the people of Thailand and Southeast Asia.

Judy Ledgerwood is a cultural anthropologist whose research interests include gender, refugee and diaspora communities, violence and memory, and the transnational movements of people and ideas. Her recent research focuses on Cambodian Buddhism and cultural identity. Her doctoral dissertation at Cornell University was on changing Khmer conceptions of gender in refugee communities in the United States. She taught and conducted research in Cambodia in the early 1990s and continues to visit there regularly. She was a visiting professor at the Royal University of Fine Arts in Phnom Penh in 1992, 2002–03, 2007 and 2010. She has taught at Northern Illinois University since 1996. Her most recent edited book is *At the edge of the forest* (Cornell SEAP, 2008, with Anne Hansen).

John A Marston is a professor at the Center for Asian and African Studies of El Colegio de México in Mexico City. His interest in Cambodia grew out of work in the 1980s in a refugee camp on the Thai–Cambodian border and in the Philippine Refugee Processing Center. He completed a doctorate in anthropology at the University of Washington in 1997 based on fieldwork in Cambodia in 1992–94. He is co-editor of the book *History, Buddhism, and new religious movements in Cambodia* (University of Hawaii Press). His articles have appeared in the *Journal of Southeast Asian Studies*, *Critical Asian Studies*, *Estudios de Asia y África*, *Contemporary Buddhism*, *Southeast Asian Affairs*, and in numerous edited volumes.

Eve Zucker is a Visiting Scholar at UC San Diego's Department of Anthropology and a CAORC Senior Fellow at the Center for Khmer Studies in Cambodia, where she is conducting research on the topics of morality, memory and social change. She holds a PhD in social anthropology from the London School of Economics and an MA in cultural anthropology from the University of Wisconsin at Madison. Her work experience includes a term as a research intern for the Cambodia Genocide Program at Yale University, and she has participated in various projects in Cambodian higher education. She has lived and worked in Cambodia on four occasions for a total of 43 months, 13 in the upland Khmer village in southwestern Cambodia, where she conducted doctoral research on memory and the remaking of moral order in the aftermath of violence.

Remembering May

David P Chandler

The other contributions to this volume draw on May Ebihara's admirable work as an anthropologist and pay tribute to her impact on the field of Cambodian studies. In these few lines I want to record my personal debts to her. I see now that the 20-odd years that we knew each other were filled with rare but joyful meetings, serious discussions and light-hearted 'catching up', often by mail, with the ups and downs of our lives and our careers. It was an enormous privilege for me to be her friend. Except at the very end, when she was so miserable, being her friend was also always fun.

May and I almost overlapped in Cambodia—I arrived in October 1960, a few months after she had left—and though we knew of each other's existence we didn't meet until 1982, when we attended a mammoth conference at Princeton dealing with Cambodia, organised by a pair of intrepid undergraduates. The conference attracted speakers from all over the world and from every shade of the political spectrum. It was the largest conference about Cambodia that had ever been put together. Predictably, it contained moments of grandeur, conflict and farce.

May and I shared a panel and took to each other at once. I remember a delightful train ride back to New York, when we chatted non-stop about Cambodia and the bizarre aspects of the conference. That afternoon, we fell happily into the habit of sharing high and low gossip that continued until shortly before her death. In fact, in the telephone calls that I made to the hospital from Australia in 2004, she was still eager to absorb and share the most recent 'news of the profession' and to take gossip on board with her customary worldliness and *joie de vivre*.

In the 1980s and for most of the 1990s, I lived in Australia, while May was living in New York. I made a point of calling on her and Marvin in their apartment whenever I passed through the city (and they lived, conveniently, almost next door to the apartment building where I usually stayed). These were joyful occasions. We also met each other many times at the annual meetings of the Association for Asian Studies, where the two of us chaired and acted as discussants on several lively panels dealing with Cambodia's culture, history and politics. May was in her element at the AAS, seeking out dozens of friends, 'checking out' the latest gossip and rounding up people with whom to go off to dinner to the 'latest place'. In the years I knew her, May was always young, always curious and almost always the life of the party, although she never raised her voice, never drank a drop of alcohol and never dominated the talk.

In 1996, she travelled to Melbourne to take part in a three-day conference marking my retirement. It was a special pleasure for Susan and me to entertain her and many of our mutual friends in our house when the conference was over and to introduce her to the joys of shopping (one of her many innocent addictions; jewellery was another) in Melbourne.

Looking back on those years, I feel that we got along so well and made friends so quickly, first of all, because we made each other laugh. We also shared a love for Cambodia, developed when we were young. This affection never faltered, even in the terrible 1970s, or in the years that we were unable to visit the country. I think we recognised each other as people who had undergone a similar experience at roughly the same time that had altered and given direction to our lives.

When Cambodia opened up again for Western scholars in 1989 May hurried back to the village called Svay, where she had begun her fieldwork 30 years before. Over the next seven years, she visited the village many times and embarked on an ambitious project there that sought to place what she had learned in 1959–60 and the villagers whom she had befriended at that time into the context of the late 1980s and early 1990s.

The people of Svay, stunned by events in their recent past but hospitable as ever, were delighted to see her and were only too happy to help with her research. As one of them told her, on the first day she was there, 'We knew you would come back'. She had made these friends for life and now many of those she had befriended were dead, several of them victims of the hardships of the DK regime. Her bonds with the survivors made her project easier in some ways, but also extremely poignant, because of her empathy for the losses that had taken place and the psychic damage that the villagers had suffered, May's extensive notes and interviews are now being assembled with a view to publication. In several luminous published articles in the 1990s that drew on this research she wrote movingly, in characteristically lucid prose, about what had happened to her friends and to Cambodian village culture in the maelstrom of what villagers called the 'Pol Pot time'. These elegant papers provided an invaluable 'before and after' perspective that was necessarily lacking from other people's anthropological research.

May's ashes are now housed in a stupa on the grounds of the *wat* in Svay.

For over 20 years, May Ebihara was a friend and a mentor for me and for many of our generation of scholars, including Charles Keyes, Gerry Hickey, Herbert Lewis and the late Tom Kirsch. She was also a role model and an inspiration to a small army of younger scholars, many of them women, who have reshaped, enlightened and enriched the field of Cambodian studies. Several of them have written papers for this collection.

In these few words I've tried to honour May Ebihara's life, her work on paper and her work with people, her love of Cambodia, her capacity for friendship and the love that so many people, myself included, bore for her. I want to pay tribute to her sadly missed wise counsel, stylishness and fun.

I'll close with a personal recollection. When Susan and I visited Svay in 1991 for a wedding we were overwhelmed by the hard-wired good humour and hospitality of its dignified, resilient people. We were moved by the strong affection that so many of them had for May. *Chĕtt l'â*, they told us. *Neang slaut.* A beautiful heart. A straight-forward young woman. Not a bad assessment. They knew exactly who she was and, in a connected thought, they had always known that she would come back.

She did, and now she's gone. She lingers, nonetheless, in Svay and wherever her friends remember her, her eyes twinkling with amusement, wearing just the right colours and just the right Cambodian jewellery. Her lightly worn wisdom, her crystalline lucidity, her impishness and her joie *de vivre* are embedded permanently in our hearts.

Introduction

John A Marston

May Ebihara was the first American anthropologist to do field work in Cambodia; her work has had a major impact on the scholars who followed her. She was present at a particularly moving panel in her honour at the Association for Asian Studies meetings in Washington DC in April 2002. At that time, with the encouragement of her friend, historian David Chandler, planning began for this volume—a collection of chapters in her honour by the panel participants and other scholars close to her. While the book was not completed at the time of her death in 2005, she knew about the project and had read drafts of some of the chapters.

We learn much about her life in the interview included in this book. She was born in Portland, Oregon, and spent part of her early childhood in the Second World War in an internment camp for Japanese–Americans. An early fascination with archaeology led her to study anthropology at Reed College in Portland, where she began to do social anthropology, focusing on Native Americans in particular. This led to graduate work at Columbia University, where she quickly became a consummate New Yorker and made the fortuitous decision to do field research in Cambodia in 1959–60. From 1969 until the time of her retirement, she was on the faculty of the City University of New York (CUNY)—at Lehman College and, from 1970, at the CUNY Graduate Center. When Cambodia began to opento Western scholars again, after years of war and the complexities of access during much of the socialist People's Republic of Kampuchea (PRK) period, she returned for a brief visit in 1989 and then made several research trips to her earlier field-work site, a rice-growing village in southern Kandal province called Svay.

May Ebihara's importance as a scholar combined with the personal impact she had on those surrounding her. The impetus behind this book certainly lies in its contributors' devotion to her as a person, as well as in their respect for her as a scholar. This is not an extraneous point; one could even go so far as to say it is very much in keeping with Southeast Asian cultural patterns. Anthropologists are especially aware, one hopes, of how what is categorised as private lies behind and informs what is categorised as public. Ebihara took a personal interest in the next generation of scholars, and her support at this personal and moral level was of enormous help to those she mentored, such as me. Quite apart from recognising her considerable accomplishments as a scholar, we came to love her for what she was as a person.

My own first actual contact with her was when I applied for a Social Science Research Council/Indochina Studies Program (ISP) grant in the mid-1980s, when I had some background in Khmer language, but had not yet done graduate work in anthropology. My proposal was rejected, but the committee expressed interest in the topic and suggested that a stronger proposal might be accepted the following year. Ebihara was on the committee and, more than anyone else, made herself available to guide me as I re-worked the project. This personal investment of hers led to further personal investment in me, leaving me with a sense of debt to her which would be impossible to quantify. Two of the contributors to this book were also members of that ISP committee and three of the others were recipients of ISP grants. Each of us came to establish a special relationship with her through the processes of the committee.

The idea of community looms large in this book—primarily, of course, with reference to the nature of rural communities in Cambodia and Thailand. It is perhaps no accident that the sense of scholarly community figured so prominently for those of us connected to Ebihara. Scholarship on Cambodia involves the study of overlapping communities that are joined by different fields of interest. For many of us studying Cambodia, our link to her early in our work and the support we received from her were important in our sense of being part of a community of Cambodian scholars. The people she introduced us to and the scholarship she directed us toward, often in the context of academic conferences, had something to do with this, but, most of all, it was simply the fact that we knew that she, understanding and sharing our passionate interest in this place called Cambodia, accepted us as part of this community of scholars. Among other things, this gave us a sense of being part of a lineage.

The community of scholars working on Cambodia has sometimes been a locus of fierce disputes, growing, perhaps, out of the fierce political divisions in Cambodia itself. Ebihara's role in this respect was to provide neutral ground—to be someone with whom almost everyone could communicate and, on occasion, to serve as peacemaker. This may have been because she was the most senior woman scholar around.

One aspect of her role as a focal point of community is that she was a clearing house of information about the community of scholars working on Cambodia. Perhaps the key word here is gossip—a word she herself delighted in using. A male anthropologist once said, using a standard anthropological definition to refer to his own academic department, that a community is defined as a group of people competing for the same resources. I prefer to think of a community as a group of people who can use each other's personal dramas as a common reference point. Ebihara once said that one of her key field techniques in Svay was sitting and gossiping with people in the village—a revealing comment in that it demonstrates how deeply tied to personal interaction her research was. Part of her role in the community of scholars working on Cambodia was the news we exchanged when we saw her, or, more typically, passed on to her during long telephone calls. Not all of the news exchanged was really gossip. Even though we might use the word to refer to other kinds of news, true gossip was a relatively small proportion of our communications; but it is fair to say that the exchange drew on a common fascination with the details of the lives and activities of the group of scholars working on Cambodia. As already noted, it is not extraneous that the world created was a personal one in addition to a scholarly one. For all of us, I think, this added to the sense of being part of that community. While for me it was primarily the community of Cambodia scholars that was involved, it is clear that, for other students and friends, her 'gossip' was a link to the even more complex and, to some eyes, glamorous community of anthropologists.

Her personal role was, in the end, deeply connected to her scholarly role. Different scholars of Cambodia have drawn in different ways on the wealth of information in her work. The importance for the next generation of English-speaking scholars of Cambodia was that it provided a *general* framework for looking at Cambodia. As she points out in her interview, village studies of the sort she undertook for her doctoral dissertation were already going out of fashion at that time. Nonetheless, they are especially helpful to subsequent scholars going into the field because they provide an holistic sense of patterns and relationships. I once told her, jokingly, that Svay had become for us the archetypal Cambodian village. Obviously, we should be careful with any kind of archetype, but I, for one, would argue that they are enormously helpful; Ebihara's village study has withstood the test of time as a painstakingly detailed picture of Cambodian village life in the 1950s which continues to illuminate our understanding of Cambodian villages as they exist today. If Chandler provided for our generation the most accessible frame for the broad sweep of Cambodian history, Ebihara's village study has provided a social frame for Cambodia through the lens of village life and we return to it as such again and again.

One thing about Ebihara that is difficult to articulate is her incredible talent for finding the right *tone* for writing about Cambodia. I have always loved her prose and thought that it has been too little commented on; its quality, I think, has to do with the precision of the tone. Her writing is beautiful, I have finally concluded, because of a dignity of restraint, which itself had a moral dimension, combined with a respect and love for Cambodians revealed in her joyous attention to the details of their lives. Those of us working on Cambodia respond intuitively to her work because we sense in this ineffusive, but attentive, prose a profound connection with her subject—a connection we want to believe is similar to our own, which confirms our reactions and guides us as we further interact with Cambodians. Just as in conversation she always knew *exactly* what to say, she had an uncanny knack of knowing what was appropriate to write. This accuracy of tone is there in her earliest work—her doctoral dissertation and writing about gender roles in Cambodia—and we find the same sure, appropriate tone when she writes about the Pol Pot period, the refugee exodus and the reconstruction of Cambodian villages. She was always wary of the way Cambodia was so often depicted in the popular media, after the Pol Pot regime, as a place associated with death and gruesome violence. No-one can deny the death and gruesome violence, and she herself contributed to the documentation of the Democratic Kampuchea (DK) period, but she always had the capacity to look with a clear head beyond the death and violence to the humanity of the Cambodian people—to their real human suffering and to their real warmth and humour. Ebihara's work resonates not just because of what it says explicitly, but because of what it is implicitly consonant with, and this contributes to its enduring quality.

Cambodianists who have begun their research even more recently would have difficulty imagining how difficult it was to go to Cambodia in the 1980s and the sense of breakthrough when it began to be possible. While a number of scholars were able to make short visits in the early years of the PRK, there was a period of several years when scholars from Soviet-bloc countries or who showed sympathy with the regime were the only ones going to Cambodia; access to rural areas was not easy for anyone. Ebihara was one of the first of the relatively senior scholars to go back once politics began to liberalise, and the fact that she was able to revisit Svay so early on impressed those of us with a long fascination with the country who were also seeking out ways to spend time there. Before the 1991–2 UN Advanced Mission in Cambodia (UNAMIC), Western visitors, after jumping through hoops to get into the country, still found it difficult to get permission to leave Phnom Penh. One of my most vivid memories of Ebihara is when, in 1990, during one of her first returns, she invited me and Toni Shapiro, both graduate students, to accompany her when she sponsored a *bon* (religious ceremony) in Svay. It is difficult to convey the excitement of that moment—an excitement which in those days arose in part just from the possibility of getting out of Phnom Penh and seeing rural areas. It also meant seeing for the first time the village I had read about. More than that, it was, of course, a chance to share an 'anthropological' experience with the anthropologist who had originally researched the place—to feel that in some small way an anthropological torch was being passed on. It is a tribute to her that she would always find the perfect gesture, in the *bon* itself and in including two younger anthropologists.

The research she started on Svay at this time, together with Judy Ledgerwood, has a special interest, primarily because of the important information it generated, but also because of the new sense of hope it gave us with regard to the possibility of continuity between Cambodia before Pol Pot and present-day Cambodia—first of all in village life itself, but also in the anthropological tradition looking at it.

I think it is fair to say that my generation of specialists on Cambodia is particularly fascinated with the living scholars whose experience of Cambodia predates the cataclysms of the 1970s—in part, no doubt, simply because there are so few of them. Among those who have been most visible to me are David Chandler, Michael Vickery, Serge Thion, Steve Heder and Laura Summers, all of whom are unforgettable people in their own way. (Of course scholars working in France would have had contact with a different and larger group.) Since I am an anthropologist, I suppose it is inevitable that Ebihara's name would loom particularly large on the list of scholars. She stands out as the scholar with the deepest connection to Cambodia at its village roots, and her body of work evokes both the cataclysms and the unities of those roots. It is my hope that this volume honours her not only as an important scholar but also as a great soul, whose ability to see the Cambodian past as linked to the Cambodian future has enriched us all.

Cambodia

The majority of the chapters in this volume are by Cambodianists writing about village society. These chapters are framed by three by senior scholars of Thailand whose work puts the rest of the book into a larger historical and geographical perspective. Publications on rural Cambodian society are still relatively infrequent; this book arguably represents the most extensive single body of writing on the topic since the 1980s.

In the 1980s, research on rural Cambodia was still quite limited. (Typical of writing about rural Cambodia at this time were the reports of NGO-based agronomist François Grunewald (1990), reports by the International Rice Research Institute (Cambodia 1989) and reports on Oxfam's activities by Chanthou Boua and Ben Kernan (1989). Ebihara's return to Cambodia and her subsequent village research with Ledgerwood was part of a general opening-up which was helpful to other anthropologists. In the period leading up to the 1993 elections, when Ebihara and Ledgerwood worked together, it was still difficult to get permission to spend the night in a village. Alex Hinton, for example, when doing his initial doctoral research on a controversial topic, struggled with permissions and the requirements that he be accompanied by bodyguards.[1] Such restrictions relaxed considerably after the UN-sponsored national elections. The pioneer research projects were often those of international organisations or NGOs. Some of them date from the 1980s, but activities expanded after the 1993 elections; some of this applied research was conducted by professional anthropologists and sociologists, such as William Collins, John Vijghens, Chou Meng Tarr, Fabien Luco and, later, Yunita T Winarto. The research reports generated by these projects, on such topics as domestic violence, sexuality, grassroots political organisation, conflict resolution and health care, remain a core body of data for scholars of village life. Eventually research of a more purely descriptive nature, aimed at a more academic audience, began to be undertaken, although most scholars ended up doing at least some applied work. Ang Choulean, based at the Royal University of Fine Arts and the Apsara Authority in Phnom Penh, worked with teams of young Cambodian scholars to document ritual practices. Foreign scholars, such as anthropologists Alexandra Kent, Ing-Britt Trankell and Jan Ovesen, psychiatrist Maurice Eisenbruch and development researcher Joakim Öjendal, directed their attention to rural Cambodia; a number of doctoral students, some with previous experience in the country or in refugee camps, came to do field work in Cambodian villages—Soizick Crochet and Eve Zucker, both of whom have contributed to this volume, Kobayashi Satoru, geographer Timothy Conway and religious studies specialist Erik Davis. Viviane Frings, a doctoral student in history, did research in Cambodia in the early 1990s before the UN Transitional Authority in Cambodia (UNTAC) was established. Although her access to the countryside was quite limited, she was able, on the basis of government documents, journalism and NGO reports, to write an English-language working paper and a French-language book about agricultural co-operatives in the PRK period (Frings 1993, 1997a). A new generation of Cambodian anthropologists emerged as well, most of whom did at least some work for NGOs or international organisations before pursuing advanced degrees in Western countries—as in the case of Kim Sedara, a contributor to this volume, and of scholars such as Chan Sambath or Chay Navuth.

A recent surge of work on Cambodian religion (Marston & Guthrie 2004; Harris 2005; Hansen 2007; Edwards 2007; Kent & Chandler 2008) has been partly historical and urban in orientation, but typically includes sections with a bearing on rural practice.

All this scholarly activity has resulted in a growing number of works on rural life, focused on health issues, religion and political organization in particular, although it has sometimes been hard to see the overall patterns. This volume, I believe, will provide a sense of the directions this emerging body of scholarship is taking.

The gap in village research in the 1970s and 1980s is, of course, the result of the war and the profound political upheavals the country was going through, which no student of Cambodia can totally ignore. Apart from research on the Angkorean period, most academic writing on Cambodia since 1979 has been about the Pol Pot period and is mostly by historians and political scientists, including important work by Chandler, Ben Kiernan, Steven Heder and Michael Vickery. Perhaps the main point to be emphasised in the context of a book like this is that much of the drama of what happened was played on a rural stage, where the rural population was organised into co-operatives and mobilised to fulfil impossible economic goals in the very violent enactment of a radical grassroots vision when the urban population evacuated to the countryside. Hinton's recent work has been important in approaching the events of the period using characteristically anthropological analyses of cultural and social organisation in a way that contrasts with the approaches of better known earlier studies. Some of my own writings have been in a similar vein. Hinton's chapter in this volume reminds us, dramatically, of the cataclysmic historical events which other chapters make implicit reference to. The chapters of Keyes, Zucker and Frieson also deal with the Pol Pot period and its impact. Keyes compares village contexts of Thailand and Cambodia, in order to ask why the revolutionary movements in both countries should have different results. Zucker, in examining the issue of trust, deals directly with the effect of trauma in the aftermath of Pol Pot in a way that echoes some of Ebihara's later work. Frieson discusses the ways that family relations were reconfigured during the period. The other chapters by Cambodianists deal with the country as it exists in the aftermath of Pol Pot—an aftermath shaped not only by the scars from the period but by the economic and political changes since then: in village organisation which varies from region to region and village to village, in religion, in reciprocal exchange and in gender relations.

Community: the Svay-Tepoztlán connection

A major theme running through this book and through Ebihara's work is the idea of community. While there was no original plan for the book to have a theme, the idea of community was salient enough in the original drafts of the chapters that we asked contributors to stress this as they made revisions. Zucker and Ledgerwood both eventually decided not to pursue their original topics, which enabled them to focus on topics more directly related to the emerging theme of the book.

By 'community' we are not as concerned with the term as it is used to refer to a clearly bound social unit as we are with its broader reference to manifestations of social connectedness at a local level. As a close reading of Ebihara shows, it is not always easy to say what the operative unit of community is in rural Cambodia. Is it the *phoum* (often translated as 'village'), a political entitytypically corresponding to the group of families clustered around the shrine of a locality spirit? Is it the cluster of persons linked to a given Buddhist temple? Or is it the *khŭm* (translated as 'commune' or 'subdistrict'), a political unit comprising several *phoum*, which might tend to be associated with a single major *wat*, but rarely corresponds exactly to a *wat* community? One would stress, however, that the fact that the unit of community is not easily defined does not in itself imply that it lacks a sense of cohesion.

The concept of community as a local grassroots phenomenon is not as current among anthropologists as it once was. Scholars nowadays might tend to approach the issues using concepts of identity, sociability, social capital or social cohesion instead, or they might use 'community' to refer to imagined networks at a national or global level. We choose the word for a number of reasons. First of all, it underlines the reference to the kind of 'community study' that Ebihara was consciously doing in her original field work. There has been other recent work on rural Cambodian life which uses the term, notably a 1999 Conference on the Meaning of Community in Cambodia (WGSOC 1999). And whereas, when Ebihara did her original field work, 'community' (if not the forms of community) may have been more or less a given, there has been—inevitably in the aftermath of war and radical social experiment—a greater self-consciousness about community in rural social organisation in the process of recreating it. In this context, the complexity of what is being recreated is better described in terms of community, than in terms of social capital, social cohesion, or sociability.

As Ledgerwood discusses in her chapter, there has been some low-key debate among Cambodianists over the degree to which present-day Cambodian rural communities are cohesive. The emphasis on a lack of cohesion in *When every household is an island* (Ovesen, Trankell & Öjendal 1996) and in the work of other scholars was critiqued in a chapter by Ebihara and Ledgerwood (2002). These issues were also discussed in the 1999 conference.

Ovesen, Trankell and Öjendal (1996:66–7) wrote:

The common picture is that the traditional social cohesion and self-help mechanisms in the villages that were destroyed under Pol Pot are now slowly returning to normal. There is an element of wishful thinking in this view, for it is questionable whether such a 'normal', traditional social cohesion on village level ever existed in the first place. It is less questionable, however, that the deterioration of social solidarity appears to be continuing still, and that it is reinforced by the liberalization of the economy and the consequent monetarization of most social relations beyond the nuclear family.

Ebihara and Ledgerwood (2002:272–91), replying to these ideas, wrote:

Emphasizing resentments and conflicts within a community can create a false picture of a collection of houses with no sense of social cohesion. On the other hand, overemphasizing the social bonds of kinsmen and friends could present another mistaken view of a community in perfect harmony. In fact, any community will be characterized by its own particular set of social relations that falls along a continuum between these extremes, although the notion of a culture of houses with no social ties would seem the more improbable situation.

The chapters in the present book tend to emphasise the degree to which both positions are valid in different contexts and, as Ebihara did herself, give final emphasis to the concrete empirical data over any theoretical model. Crochet, who elsewhere has supported the Ovesen, Trankell and Öjendal position, and Ledgerwood, both by chance in this volume, use the story of several different blind men examining an elephant to make the point that village life can be seen from many seemingly contradictory perspectives.

In our interview, Ebihara discussed the issue with me, referring to the well-known 'contradictory' ethnographies of Robert Redfield and Oscar Lewis, who did field work in the same Mexican village, Tepoztlán. Redfield, writing at the end of his career, and about the time that Ebihara did her field work, ruminated about the implications of the contrasting research, using the metaphor of different lenses:

Maybe one can conceive rather deliberately and explicitly both the 'this' and the 'that' and use these alternative and perhaps complementary mental constructions to help toward understanding of the one community before us. Like the green and red lenses with which certain photographs are viewed to enable the eye to see the colors of reality, so we might construct alternative lenses which, used together, would give us an improved view of the village before us (Redfield 1960:133).

He goes on to write about how the polarity between models of communal solidarity and individualism figures in the work of some of the foundational thinkers in anthropology: Maine, Morgan, Tönnies and Durkheim. Redfield, like these thinkers, saw the communal pole as more ancient and related to the sacred, whereas individualism was more modern and secular—an elaboration of the dichotomy we might now find harder to accept. Redfield's essay is surprisingly prescient in referring to these social systems as 'imagined'. And, in the end, he understands the degree to which the debate may occur within the mind of the anthropologist.

None of us can truly say that his way of work is necessarily the best way or that it either should or will prevail over all others. All advance in knowledge is a dialectic, a conversation. To hear the relative truth of what one is one's self saying one must listen to what the other worker says about what one's self has described otherwise. The point I have striven to make...is that, among the many and varied instruments for the understanding of little communities, is to be included a controlled conversation, a dialectic of opposites, carried on within one's self (Redfield 1960:148).

As Ebihara points out, community studies had already become less fashionable among anthropologists in the late 1950s, when she first worked in Svay.[2] Changes in the way anthropologists looked at peasant society had to do not only with changes in their discipline, but also with changes taking place in peasant society, where links to larger economic and political systems became increasingly salient. A growing scholarly concern with peasant movements, among historians and political scientists as well as among anthropologists, was related to developments in countries emerging from colonialism, most notably, of course, the war in Vietnam, which quickly extended to Cambodia.

As any linguist knows, the line between the descriptive and the prescriptive is a fine one, and it is probably no accident that anthropologists were allowed to study rural life in newly-independent countries around the time that there was thinking within those societies about what social organisation at the village level could and should be—about whether it should be imposed from above or, at least occasionally, arise from with the rural populations. The radical collectivisation of Cambodian rural society was, of course, one of the most disastrous of the social experiments. But ongoing discussion about what rural Cambodian society should be—by government, NGOs and international development organisations—continues to be part of the discourse of 'community' in the country and may colour the academic discourse more than we sometimes acknowledge.

Victor Turner, in his 1969 book, *The ritual process*, developed a concept that he called 'communitas'. He drew on the work of Martin Buber, which, in turn, made reference to the formation of Israeli *kvuzoth* and *kibbutzim*, although Turner was proposing something that went beyond that. 'Communitas', as Turner described it, was a periodic alternative to or escape from social structure.

Essentially, communitas is a relationship between concrete, historical, idiosyncratic individuals. These individuals are not segmentalized into roles and statuses but confront one another rather in the manner of Martin Buber's 'I and Thou.' Along with this direct, immediate, and total confrontation of human identities, there tends to go a model of society as a homogeneous, unstructured communitas, whose boundaries are ideally coterminous with those of the human species. Communitas is in this respect strikingly different from Durkheimian 'solidarity', the force of which depends upon an in-group/out-group contrast. To some extent, communitas is to solidarity as Henri Bergson's 'open morality' is to his 'closed morality'. But the spontaneity and immediacy of communitas—as opposed to the jural-political character of structure—can seldom be maintained for very long. Communitas itself soon develops a structure, in which free relationships between individuals become converted into norm-governed relationships between social personae (Turner 1969:132).

Turner, more than other scholars we have referred to, very much reflected the spirit of the time in which he was writing, and the wider implications of his work go beyond the kind of local-level community we are concerned with here. His work is worth mentioning, however, as a reminder that community is not necessarily a constant, but may have a cyclical character, or arise at certain times of need. He would have considered the dialectic he was describing as different fromRedfield's—not as the alternative lenses of cohesion and individuality (in part existing simultaneously in the mind of the ethnographer, in part a historical progression) but as a communal spirit which, at times, became an alternative to structure. Yet the two dialectics may shed some light on each other.

In the title of his 1978 book, *The remembered village*, MN Srinivas referred to the fact that the ethnography was reconstructed from memory after his field notes had been destroyed by fire; the phrase also suggests a condition of community which is no longer with us and which we imperfectly reconstruct in ways consistent with our present orientations. This is more like the way James Scott uses the phrase in *Weapons of the weak*:

> As we listen to the rich and poor of Sedaka attempting to make sense of the massive changes they have all experienced over the past decade, we find ourselves in the midst of an ideological struggle, however, small in scale…As in any history, assessing the present forcibly involves a reevaluation of what has gone before. Thus, the ideological struggle to define the present is a struggle to define the past as well. Nowhere is this more apparent than in the accounts given by poor villagers, who have had the least to be thankful for over the past decade and whose current prospects are bleak. They have collectively created a *remembered village* and a *remembered* economy that serve as an effective ideological backdrop against which to deplore the present (Scott 1985:178).[3]

The ultimate implication here, which grows logically out of poststructuralist thinking, is that notions of village-level solidarity represent hegemonic discourse, even in the working out of local-level personal relations. Note the fine distinction from Turner, for whom 'communitas' represented a periodic escape from social structure. Here we see the ritual affirmation of community as a way of masking the harsh realities of structure.

What is interesting, for the purposes of this discussion, is the degree to which, despite this, Scott seems to be looking back with fondness at the ritual blurring of class distinctions as it created 'imagined community', now left behind as more commodified relationships emerge. (As Charles Keyes has reminded me, the internalisation and routinisation of this sense of community can be described by what Bourdieu calls 'habitus'.) To the degree that he shows an historical progression from the communal to more individualised relations, Scott is in the tradition of Durkheim and Redfield.

Early theorists of peasant society, such as Redfield, recognised that a peasant community (in contrast to a degree to smaller-scale slash-and-burn societies) was deeply linked to the state and national culture. Ebihara discusses this with reference to Svay as well. Since the 1960s, as everywhere, the larger world has touched local Cambodian communities more and more. Reviewing the literature on Cambodian village society, Hughes (2001) has summarised the forms of external influence: the war, the free market, political reform, and media—forces that feature prominently in the chapters of this book. The possibility that rural Cambodians will leave their home communities has also increased.

More recent anthropological work on community goes in directions that depart significantly from the local-level concerns we are dealing with in this book. It heads towards the idea of the nation as 'imagined community', towards the idea of social capital (where the aspects of social cohesion being stressed are those linked to formations of civil society) and towards other forms of community extending beyond the local level—communities of ethnicity, cultural citizenship, religion, caste, and sexuality, as well as of social movements, sometimes linked by new forms of media. Marcus (1995), perhaps pushing the idea a little too far, writes of 'the collapse...of the easy distinction between system and lifeworld'. Since we have already referred to Redfield and Lewis's conflicting descriptions of Tepoztlán,we might also mention that a recent study of Tepoztlán, by a someone other than an anthropologist (Rabasa 2001), has in its title the phrase 'the impossibility of the local' and discusses, in the context of a 1995 movement against a development project there, how the internet helped make the local international and the international local. Identity is an issue in many of these studies, in a way that corresponds to the increasing importance of identity politics in social life.

While such studies of community as identity depart from the themes of this book, it is relevant to remember that there will also be identity with local community. Two points related to this stand out. The first is that local identity has sometimes been defined in terms of opposition to outsiders or urban population, which was a factor in the dynamic of the Pol Pot period. And while community identity is sometimes used *by* state authority, it can sometimes, as Chatterjee points out (1988:384), be mobilised *against* state authority. The other point that stands out is that, as rural populations migrate to urban areas, their identity with home communities can sometimes remain strong. Mills (1999), studying women's migration to urban areas in Thailand, discusses the persistence of their identity as people from the northeast and of their identification with rural northeastern gender roles. Keyes (2006), drawing on the theories of Lefebvre, goes beyond this to stress continued attachment to village communities per se.

In the end, one is tempted to say that those who write about community are those who value it in some sense, including those who find evidence of its existence as well as those, perhaps, who decry its absence. One might argue, simply, that the concept seems to have explanatory power in the case of Cambodia, but questions remain about why and how it has explanatory power in this particular place. The answers may lie in disciplinary expectations, in the motivation of those who are attracted at a particular moment of time to the situation of Cambodia, or perhaps in the persistent possibility of rural community in Cambodia, in spite of everything and in contrast to many other societies of the world. It is wise to continue analysing our motivations and the implications of the ways we see a place, with ultimate reference, as Ebihara would have emphasised, to the concrete empirical data.

The contributions to this volume approach the issue of community from various angles. First and foremost are those who consider community as revolving around religion, particularly the Buddhist temple as a centre of moral community (Keyes & Ledgerwood) and the importance of spirit practices. While Kirsch's discussion of historical progression may seem far removed from the issue of village community, his chapter is also concerned with the social solidarity in Brahmanism and Theravāda Buddhism. Others consider community in terms of the nature of trust in Cambodian society (Zucker), kinship networks (Crochet) and reciprocity (Kim). Finally, we can look at community solidarity in terms of gender relationships (Frieson). The sum total is a particularly rich conversation about the underlying bases of rural community and how they are changing.

The chapters

The book begins with a chapter written by Thomas Kirsch before his death and not published previously, 'Cosmological factors in the "collapse" of the Khmer and the "rise" of the Thai: speculations'. Treating the suggestive topic of social organisation as it relates to religion, it provides a broad historical frame for the rest of the book. Writing from an anthropological perspective, he uses the findings of modern research on hill tribes to speculate on pre-existing Southeast Asian social patterns and their importance at the time of original Indian influence. He argues brilliantly that, whereas, in India, the caste of rulers was kept separate from the priestly caste, they merged into one caste in Southeast Asia because of pre-existing social patterns. He goes on to discuss the shift from Angkorean political systems to the Theravāda Buddhist systems associated with the emerging power of Thai civilisations, arguing that continuity in the institution of the monkhood provides for more stability of social order at times of royal succession.

Charles Keyes' 'Communism, peasants and Buddhism: the failure of 'peasant revolutions' in Thailand and Cambodia' is based on his long familiarity with Northeastern Thailand, where he conducted anthropological field work in the late 1950s. In charting the counterpoint of revolutionary movements in Thailand and Cambodia, he throws light on both. The chapter examines the process whereby Communist movements in Thailand came to fail, comparing it to what took place in Cambodia. He argues that revolutionary ideologies were ultimately imposed from elite classes. Their failure to recognise the Buddhism as the moral centre of village life meant that they were bound to fail in Thailand and to have disastrous results in Cambodia.

Whereas Keyes discusses the processes leading to Communist revolution, Alex Hinton analyses in close experiential terms what took place during the Pol Pot period. While in its theme and use of anthropology Hinton's chapter is somewhat different from other chapters, its exploration of the nature of terror under Pol Pot is important, as one cannot really understand contemporary Cambodian society without recognising the impact of the Pol Pot period and how it was intertwined with Khmer culture. As Hinton shows us, the period and its terror can be described using various reference points. First of all, he discusses the way that experience of terror is deeply embedded in the experience of modernisation. Next he discusses it in more sociological terms, as the experience of the disciplinary practices of the Khmer Rouge. He goes on to explore what he calls the 'semiotic' dimension of terror—the way a whole cultural/symbolic system developed in relation to it. Finally he discusses the implications of what it meant simply in experiential terms—the ways Cambodians describe what it meant, physically and emotionally, to experience terror.

Eve Zucker bases her chapter on her recent doctoral research and provides one of the most original approaches to the issue of Cambodian community. She examines the meaning of distrust and trust in the context of a remote village. She is investigating the effect of war on the capacity of villagers to trust each other and discusses some of the specific policies of the DK period which would have led to distrust.Her chapter, however, goes beyond that to examine the larger underlying patterns that shape an individual's disposition to trust or distrust (for example, the impact of blackmarket practices and of AIDS) in the context of the specific time and place of her field work.

Judy Ledgerwood's chapter has the distinction of being based on field work in the community in which Ebihara did her research. Ledgerwood takes as her point of departure an article by Kobayashi Satoru, which examines the phenomenon of overlapping *wat* communities and suggests that it can be a focus of competing discourses which villagers use to manoeuvre for advantage. She provides a detailed ethnographic account of overlapping communities in the area of Ebihara's research, exploring the implications of the phenomenon in terms of villagers' sense of community. To a degree, she supports Kobayashi's findings, although she shows that, in this particular case, the phenomenon does not result in serious social conflicts.

In 'Catching facts or sketching the elephant? Village monographs on Cambodia, yesterday, today, tomorrow', Soizik Crochet, in a study reminiscent of Ebihara's work, provides a meticulously detailed study of kinship and residency in a village in Kampong Thom province, comparing her findings with those of Ebihara and other scholars and discussing the differences she finds in geographical terms and in their implications about social change in the period since the war. She considers, for example, the effects of the fact that in the village she studies there is now a significant social division between a core group of families who lived there before 1975 and groups of families who moved into the area during or after the social upheavals of the 1970s, and concludes that links to relatives are in practice stronger than links to community per se.

Kim Sedara's chapter is based on village-level field work in Siem Reap province. He examines the issue of village reciprocity. Drawing on a theoretical distinction between generalised and balanced reciprocity, he examines specific cases of reciprocity as they occur within households, with the village, and between people of different villages, to determine the degree to which traditional reciprocity may be shifting toward monetary exchanges. While he does find increased use of hired labour, he concludes that norms of reciprocity are still intact in many contexts.

Ebihara's work on the role of Cambodian women is reflected in the chapter by Kate Frieson. She uses current survey data to show how rural Cambodian women have become more vulnerable since Ebihara did her original field work. Starting with some of the Ebihara's basic findings—the relatively equality of village impoverishment, the autonomy of the family unit and the relative balance of relations between men and women—Frieson shows how a basic social reconfiguration occurred during the Pol Pot and PRK periods, which, among many other things, shifted gender relations. She discusses the way deaths caused by the war and the violence of the Pol Pot period created gender imbalances and how many households headed by women have proved to be in weaker positions than those where a man was present.

Jane Hanks, now in her 90s, has the distinction of representing the generation of scholars who preceded Ebihara. As a path-breaking anthropologist of Thailand, she was known and deeply admired by Ebihara for many years. Her contribution, 'Females and fertility', can be compared to her classic piece, 'Reflections on the ontology of rice'. It too has the form of a brief essay, almost a prose poem, rather than an academic chapter and it also manages to suggest, very succinctly, ideas that resonate with scholars of the region—in this case about the meaning of femininity in Thai society and culture.

This volume represents, first of all, a group of friends gathered together to honour one person. It is more than that, however, in the degree to which it offers an approach to the study of rural society in mainland Southeast Asia—primarily of Cambodia, but also of Thailand. It shows rural society in a complex process of change, a change that touches in particular on the institutions of 'community'.

Notes

1   I do not go into the work of anthropologists that was not village-based, such as that of Toni Shapiro and me, based largely in Phnom Penh, or of Lindsay French in refugee camps. There is also a body of work on Cambodian refugees in countries of resettlement. Derks' (2008) book about urban women workers, based on doctoral work in development studies, is a major contribution to the field . Ollier and Winter's 2006 edited volume, taking a cultural studies perspective, is also primarily urban in focus.

2   At around this time Geertz (1961) discussed the reasons why village studies on peasant societies were being called into question and went on to predict that it was unlikely that they would be abandoned as a method of research.

3   Hughes and Öjendal's reference to Scott's use of the phrase, in their introduction to an issue of the *Journal of Southeast Asian Studies* devoted to Cambodia, influences my usage here (Hughes and Öjendal 2006).

Chapter one

Cosmological factors in the 'collapse' of the Khmer and the 'rise' of the Thai: speculations

A Thomas Kirsch

Anthropologists and historians of Southeast Asia share an interest in a variety of puzzles manifested in the historical record of the region. Wolters is one of those Southeast Asian historians who have encouraged an interdisciplinary exchange of ideas on these puzzles. This paper is offered in that vein; that is, although my topic is historical, my perspective is intended to be anthropological.

The specific puzzle of Southeast Asian history that I want to address is one that has recurrently intrigued students of the region—the 'collapse' of the Khmer regime in mainland Southeast Asia in roughly the 14th century and the 'rise' of the Thai to prominence as actors on the Southeast Asian stage at about the same time. Each of these puzzles could be approached singularly, as a distinct and separate problem. I want to juxtapose them, not only because they can be linked historically, but also because I believe this juxtaposition can shed light on factors operative in the Khmer collapse,on the one hand, and the Thai rise, on the other. To some extent, my effort is a search for an anthropological context in which to locate the two phenomena—to determine what it was that collapsed and what it was that rose. The context I want to use here is evoked by Lauriston Sharp's 1962 Presidential Address to the Association for Asian Studies (AAS), in which he sought to synthesise the Southeast Asian region in terms of cultural 'continuities' crosscut, as it were, by a number of 'discontinuities', which Sharp called cultural 'faultlines' (Sharp 1962:3). Although this is not Sharp's terminology, I would view these various discontinuities, or faultlines, as highlighting important structural transformations that might be called 'evolutionary' (see Bellah 1964).

Viewing the Southeast Asian region in this broadly evolutionary framework underlines the significance of one of the important faultlines of Southeast Asian history, the appearance in the late first millennium BC or early first millennium AD of relatively complex social forms throughout much of Southeast Asia, shaped by cultural elements derived from South Asia, in what Coedès (1968) refers to as the 'Indianised' states of Southeast Asia. Wolters is one of the historians of the region who has helped us to understand more clearly what was involved in the Southeast Asian adoption of Indian cultural elements and the effects this had on Southeast Asian peoples. It is certainly clear that Indianisation must be viewed not as an event, but as a complex process, a process refreshed and invigorated, perhaps, by continuing contacts between South and Southeast Asia. It must also be viewed as a process that had its own distinctive Southeast Asian dimensions—a kind of logic of its own, informed and shaped by indigenous cultural values and social forms. It is these underlying values that I take as representing the continuities of Southeast Asia's distinctive history.

Indianisation was not the only process of cultural transfer and transformation occurring in early Southeast Asia. A process of Sinicisation was also occurring in Vietnam in roughly the same era. There were, of course, many important differences between the situation in which Sinicisation was taking place and that in which Indianisation was taking place. Not the least of these differences was the deliberate policy applied by the Chinese on the Vietnamese for cultural assimilation and political subordination. It seems clear that there was no comparable pressure from South Asia to set up overseas colonies or to proselytise South Asian culture. That is, the Indianisation process seems to have had a voluntaristic dimension in contrast to Sinicisation. One also gets the impression that Indianisation, compared with Sinicisation, was relatively swift and easy, however these judgments might be translated in concrete terms. If this impression is correct, it suggests something further about those peoples who were responsive to the Indianisation process. At least, it suggests to me the likelihood that these Southeast Asian peoples had already developed the technological and material base which could have supported more complex social forms than seem to have existed prior to their encounter with Indian culture. That is, these Southeast Asian peoples may have already developed a subsistence base capable of sustaining the types of complex society we find subsequent to the initiation of the Indianisation process. This speculation is given some support by recent archaeological research in Southeast Asia (Solheim 1969; Bayard 1980; White, Pisit & Goodenough 1982) which tends to confirm a suspicion long held by some scholars (Sauer 1952; Linton 1955) that the region was one in which agriculture was 'independently' invented. Viewed in this way, we can see that the primary contribution of the Indianisation process to Southeast Asia was not technical or economic, but cultural. Indianisation provided Southeast Asians the cultural (symbolic, ideological) resources to establish, maintain and elaborate the more complex social forms their subsistence base could support—societies with non-productive religious, political, administrative and literary elites. Thus, adoption of Indian cultural elements either allowed for the structural transformation of relatively 'simple' societies or allowed for the substantial elaboration of societies that were already moderately 'complex', though significantly less complex than subsequent societies.

The apparent ease and rapidity with which the Indianisation process took place suggests something else. That is, there may have been some kind of fortuitous fit or isomorphism between various aspects of pre-Indianised Southeast Asian societies and the Indian cultural elements that came to be adopted. Coedès, among others, has speculated about what the pre-Indianised societies of Southeast Asia might have looked like. For example, one could examine the ethnographic features of Southeast Asian people who were marginal to or unaffected by the Indianisation process and apply inferences based on these peoples to pre-Indianised peoples (Coedès 1966). Another source of conjecture about pre-Indianised people might be to investigate how Indian-derived elements were modified and given a distinctively Southeast Asian cast in the Indianisation process (Benda 1962). Both procedures are fraught with theoretical and methodological difficulties, but the exercise might prove useful.

The ethnographic example I want to use to speculate about pre-Indianised Southeast Asian culture and society is especially problematic, for the peoples involved were most certainly not represented in Southeast Asia in the early eras of our interest. Still, I believe the case is suggestive and there may be some useful parallels between its situation and that of pre-Indianised Southeast Asia (Bayard 1980). The case I refer to is that of the Kachin of upland Burma, as analysed with insight by Leach (1954), which I have extended to other upland peoples (Kirsch 1973).

Among Leach's more notable contributions in his analysis of the Kachin was his recognition of an 'oscillatory' process that helped account for a range of social and cultural diversity manifested by the Kachin. Leach argued that, over generations, the Kachin social order developed from a 'democratic' form, consisting of a large number of relatively shallow lineage segments of roughly equal rank, to an 'autocratic' form, consisting of a small number of large, ranked clans led by powerful 'chiefs'. While the democratic form was relatively egalitarian and internally undifferentiated, the autocratic form included a complex social hierarchy which included powerful chiefs who controlled domains of varying size and extent, 'aristocratic' lineage, a mass of 'commoner' lineages, as well as 'slaves'. In addition to these various 'classes', there were also a number of (part-time) specialists, such as shamans, sacrificial specialists, myth tellers and blacksmiths.

Leach identified two features of importance in the oscillatory process. One was a motivational factor, a 'wish for power' which he saw as general in human affairs. The other was the existence of a number of 'inconsistencies' in the Kachin social–cultural order, particularly those located in the Kachin system of kinship and marriage. Individual Kachin, in their quest for 'power', manipulated these inconsistencies to enhance their position (and that of their kin) vis-a-vis other contenders for 'power'. Leach argued that both democratic and autocratic forms of Kachin society were inherently unstable because of these inconsistencies. One of the expedients attempted by powerful chiefs was to sidestep the inconsistencies by forming marriage alliances with lowland Shan princes. But this effort violated the norms of Kachin society on which the chief's position was based. The chief's former supporters withdrew their allegiance and reinstituted a more democratic regime, starting the oscillatory process anew. Thus, Kachin chiefs were not successful in their efforts to establish an absolute monopoly of political power because to do so undermined their pre-eminent position based on Kachin values.

I noted (Kirsch 1973) that the specific justification for an autocratic chief's high position, in Leach's analysis, was the claim that he had a special relationship with the spirits deemed to control the fertility of his domain and his exclusive right to sacrifice to these spirits. Thus, in my effort to extend Leach's analysis to other upland people, I shifted my focus from the political to the ritual arena, examining in particular a system of ritual feasting found widely among the hill people. I found considerable evidence to support the view that the oscillatory process identified by Leach was widespread in upland Southeast Asia and that the feasting system helped account for that process. Rather than viewing these upland peoples as seeking to gain power, I saw them as seeking to manifest and display their ritual efficacy in a variety of ways—what Wolters in other contexts calls 'prowess'. Those who were successful in this effort had attributed to them innate qualities of spiritual excellence—what we might call charisma—and a special relationship to the supramundane world, capacities deemed essential for insuring the prosperity and fertility of their lands. Although those who were chiefs or members of aristocratic lineages used a rhetoric of purity of kinship and descent to support their claims to pre-eminence, such claims had to be continuously validated by effective ritual performances with practical effects. At any rate, the oscillatory process amongst these upland people was not simply one of increasing political differentiation, or the development of classes; it was also one of increasing spiritual differentiation as well, a view of persons and groups as having qualitatively different moral characteristics. Both the political and the spiritual differentiation were unstable because high-ranking chiefs were unable to institutionalise their absolute monopoly of ritual authority. The efforts of chiefs to do so alienated their closest kin and allies, as well as the broad mass of supporters who would be denied the opportunity to seek ritual excellence on their own. Ultimately the resources used by the chief to validate his position were acquired from his followers who downgraded their own productivity when taking a stance of dependency toward him.

There are many important differences between the situation of these upland peoples and the probable features of the pre-Indianised peoples of Southeast Asia. For one, an important factor in understanding the motivational system of the upland peoples is their involvement in swidden cultivation. I speculate that the pre-Indianised peoples had probably developed some form of irrigated rice cultivation (Van Liere 1982). For another, the upland peoples have unilineal kinship systems, whereas it seems most likely the pre-Indianised peoples had bilateral or'cognatic kinship systems. (Leach's analysis of the Kachin emphasises their system of kinship and marriage.) Despite these fundamental differences, I believe there are some aspects of the upland peoples that can be applied to the pre-Indianised peoples. For example, contrasting the situation of the upland peoples with that of those who were successfully Indianised highlights an important aspect of the Indianisation process. In particular, Indianised culture allowed for a radical differentiation between a category of elite and a category of masses, which had proven impossible in the context of the upland peoples, as evidenced in the oscillatory process. Such a differentiation is a major cultural–social breakthrough, although precisely how it was achieved is not completely clear. Be that as it may, one can speculate that this differentiation may have been facilitated by the existence of some form of irrigated rice cultivation, once the cultural categories and conceptions of Indianised culture were available. At any rate, this differentiation between elite and mass, once established, allowed for an expansion and elaboration of Southeast Asian societies such as had not occurred prior to the Indianisation process. One might say that this differentiation took the horizontal dimension of upland oscillation and made it vertical. That is, the masses for the most part lived in farming villages which were relatively egalitarian. The elite order was composed of more finely graded levels of spiritual and social difference, concentrated in court centres and in or near temple complexes. To push my ethnographic analogy further, I argue that, especially early on in the Indianisation process, the 'kings' of Indianised societies were fundamentally similar to upland 'autocratic chiefs'. Indianised cultural categories magnified, elaborated and, eventually, altered their position; yet, in many respects, the qualities, attributes and motivations of the Indianised elite display many of the same features as those of the uplanders. That is, an indigenous Southeast Asian configuration of assumptions and values, emphasising achievement and conflating ritual and social status, was used to filter and interpret Indian culture, making it something quite different from what it was in the South Asian context.

One of the most notable differences between Southeast Asian Indianised society and the classic situation of South Asia is the apparent reversal of the social–religious hierarchy. In classic South Asian Brahmanism, the Brahman takes moral and social precedence over the warrior–king. But in Southeast Asian Indianised society, it was the king who had moral and social precedence over the Brahman. This apparent reversal actually parallels the structure of upland peoples set out in my ethnographic example. Just as the upland 'autocratic chief' is the primary point of articulation between the human world and that of the spirits, and the ritual specialist is simply the chief's functionary, the Indianised king was the point of articulation between the cosmos and the social order, and the Brahman, in large measure, his functionary. Similarly, the configuration of values of the upland peoples emphasises achievement at the expense of ascription, whereas the South Asian caste order emphasises ascription as opposed to achievement. When categories of caste were introduced into the Southeast Asian Indianised social order, they apparently lost most of their ascriptive qualities, becoming something more akin to a functional division of labour (Mabbett 1977). Thus, I propose that, when Southeast Asians encountered caste, they adapted it to a pre-existing indigenous configuration of values emphasising 'achievement' and to a pre-existing hierarchy of social categories and distinctions. Thus, indigenous 'chiefs' were identified as 'kings' with charismatic powers, shamans and other indigenous ritual specialists as Brahmans, indigenous 'aristocrats' as 'warrior–leaders', 'commoners' as 'farmers', etc. This pattern accorded more closely to Southeast Asian social–cultural realities than did that of classic South Asian culture.

Upland peoples manifest a configuration of values emphasising personal achievement linked to notions of innate spiritual excellence and a special relationship to the spiritual order. Even aristocratic chiefs who emphasised their status by birth had to validate their position by continuing effective performance. These performances were not simply symbolic. They required that the chief manipulate the complex upland system of marriage alliances, manifest their personal fecundity and sexual prowess, organise the distribution of the surplus production of their supporters through such devices as the feasting mechanism and through use of wealth invested in bride prices, and fend off the efforts of others to wrest a position of pre-eminence away from them. In some areas, success in headhunting and feud were also factors. In fact, these chiefs might be seen as extremely efficient and effective managers of a complex set of material and symbolic values, constantly seeking the main chance and continuously engaged in maintaining their superior status. Observers of such effective chiefs and their aristocratic followers were struck with their demeanour, commanding personalities and charisma.

Indianised kings display a similar configuration of values, albeit in a larger and more complex milieu. Kings manipulated a marriage system no less intricate, though certainly different from, that of upland peoples. Through strategic marriages they established links with powerful families in various geographic locales who might serve as their supporters in a quest for hegemony (Kirsch 1976; Ledgerwood 1995). The king's harem thus served not only as a vehicle for manifesting his personal fecundity but also as a means of mobilising his supporters and integrating his kingdom. To insure the operation of his kingdom, a king had to have sufficient legitimacy amongst the masses to gain a substantial portion of their surplus production to support a widening staff of non-productive ritual specialists, scribes, administrators and elite followers. In addition, the most successful kings, such as Suryvarman II and Jayavarman VII who were famous for their building efforts, were able to mobilise mass populations to subsidise and/or construct the great monumental architecture characteristic of these Indianised societies, not to mention the routine public works necessary to maintain the social order. Wolters (1982) suggests that the king served as an exemplar of ascetic practice for his close followers, thereby earning their devotion. If this was the case, this asceticism most likely involved an active mastery and control of the self rather than quietistic passivity. For, after all, the king was also expected to sleep each night with the Naga princess in a tower, with 'Siva continuously descending'.

The effectiveness of the Indianised king was under continuous test. Chinese observers, filtering their observations of Indianised kingdoms through a set of Chinese expectations, saw numerous usurpers gaining political control. But this situation suggests that political–religious pre-eminence was not a function of purity of birth or dynastic succession, but of other factors as well (Kirsch 1976). On the one hand, there were external enemies seeking to gain pre-eminence through raiding, warfare and the subordination of their rivals. On the other hand, there were continuous internal threats in the form of rival contenders who might be close kin seeking paramountcy. The Indianised king, no less than the upland chief, could not rest on his high birth, his powerful affinal connections or his past achievements. Like the fastest gun in the West, there were always potential rivals, for the king's position was ultimately based on personal qualities, not on stable institutional arrangements. The king was under constant pressure to perform effectively, thereby manifesting both his charismatic qualities and his qualification for leadership. And, as in the upland, such effective performance included symbolic-ritual manipulation and concrete material control.

Wolters views the map of early Southeast Asia as a:

patchwork of often overlapping *mandalas*, or 'circles of kings'. In each of these *mandalas*, one king, identified with divine and 'universal' authority, claimed personal hegemony over the other rulers in his *mandala* who in theory were his obedient allies and vassals (Wolters 1982:16-17).

No doubt there were certain relatively stable centres of population and political–religious authority throughout the region, but Wolters' image evokes the person-centric nature of these early polities, as does Tambiah's notion of the Southeast Asian 'galactic polity' (Tambiah 1976:102ff). The region was one of constantly expanding–contracting, pulsating—shifting fluidity, a situation closely parallel to that displayed in the kaleidoscope of upland domains. Yet, this actual fluidity in the microcosmic world of men was made meaningful, as Wolters suggests, by linking it with a sense of a universal macrocosmic order that was reflected in Indian religious ideas.

One important element in the complex of Indian cultural elements adopted by Southeast Asian peoples was the Indian pantheon of deities. In my speculation that pre-Indianised leaders were similar to upland chiefs, the encounter with Indianised culture allowed them to identify with figures in that pantheon the local spirits they had special relationships with. Such an identification would, thereby, link the political leader and locality spirits with more abstract, universal spiritual elements—enduring facets of order, such as birth, death, destruction, and regeneration, personified in the pantheon. The pantheon itself was ideally suited to articulate with and encompass any pre-existing indigenous animistic spiritual entities and cosmology. At the top of the pantheon were major figures such as Siva and Vishnu who could be identified with the highest levels of political–religious authority. The numerous avatars of these high deities and their respective consorts—Pavarti, Laksami, Kali, Krishna, Rama, Sita, etc.—could accommodate and incorporate lower-order levels of political–religious power. It was in the person of the king, identified with high-level deities, that the microcosm of the world of men and the macrocosmic world of the gods were fused together. Siva was both continuously descending and immediately present in the king himself. Thus, statues of deities were carved with the faces of kings and their close relatives. Kings were of the same stuff as divinities.

The pantheon of deities, then, might be seen as the cosmological skeleton on which the social order was hung. One of the puzzles of Indianised society has been the purported tolerance of kings; that is, although the king might be personally identified with some specific deity, such as Siva, Vishna, Lokesvara, he encouraged and supported the worship of other deities. The puzzlement about such support might be lessened if it were recognised that Indianised religion involved a classic cult system, based on the entire pantheon of deities. All deities of the pantheon were essential ingredients in the cosmological order. To identify oneself personally with one deity—say, Siva—was not to deny the divinity of any other deity. Such identification might speak to the relative hierarchical ordering of deities, but was not a repudiation of any. Indeed, as the reign of Jayavarman VII attests, even Buddhist figures could be incorporated in the pantheon and cult system with no difficulty. Thus, one should distinguish between several aspects of Indianised religiosity. The entire pantheon of deities represents the religion of the social order. Yet, there might also be 'personal' religiosity, a personal identification or patronage of a particular figure in that pantheon. And, in addition, subsequent to the reign of Jayavarman II, there was the *devaraja* cult, which was simultaneously the 'personal' cult of king and, thereby, the cult of the polity that culminated in the person of the king.

Coedès (1966) has argued that Indianised culture had its greatest impact at the level of elite society, while the peasant masses apparently went their merry pre-Indianised animistic way. This view seems problematic for several reasons. Since Durkheim's day, at least, it has been recognised that, if a society is to cohere, there must be some system of widely-shared, collective representations, common symbols, values, conceptions and ideas. Aside from the theoretical problem, there is an empirical one. The notion that fundamental discrepancies between the religiosity of the elite and the masses persisted for something like 14 centuries seems, on the face of it, difficult to maintain. During this extended period, the masses gave their surplus production, their service and their lives to sustain the elite figures of their society. I would argue that Indianised religiosity pervaded all levels of Indianised society and was a fundamental part of its fabric. If so, how were the masses articulated with that religiosity? Some clues from the later stages of Angkor are suggestive. When Jayavarman VII conducted his great building campaigns, such as the temple complexes at Ta Phrom and Prah Khan, they were to be serviced by large numbers of retainers, including the residents of numerous villages (Coedès 1963). Substantial numbers of people located in villages were also assigned to support Jayavarman VII's 'health services', under the protection of a deity of healing. Thus, the masses were tied to the service of the pantheon through their identification with temples dedicated to various deities. While the villagers' understanding of the pantheon may certainly have been less sophisticated than that of a Brahman, priest, or temple administrator, it hardly seems credible to supposed they mistook the deities of the pantheon for their pre-Indianised locality spirits. Thus, mass religiosity was mobilised to sustain and support the pantheon of deities that provided the religious foundation for the social order. But I suspect mass religiosity went further than that. Mass religiosity was also harnessed to carry out the specific projects of specific kings. Thus, the masses' articulation with Indianised religion was twofold. On the one hand, they provided routine support of various figures of the pantheon through their temple service. But they also sustained and supported the activities of especially charismatic kings who embarked on expansive wars, provided public services such as roads and hospitals, dispensed justice (perhaps protecting the masses from the exorbitant demands of local elite) and built the major temple complexes that are their legacy. Rather than seeing these complexes as symptoms of royal megalomania and oppressive demands on a reluctant peasantry, they might be seen as the products of an enthusiastic identification with and devotion to Indianised religion by the masses in general, who saw the person of the king as the exemplar of the pantheon. That is, the masses viewed the successes and accomplishments of charismatic kings as something in which they had a stake. It is in this context that we can locate Du Bois' observation:

> In Southeast Asia...the wealth and sexual potency of the rulers, the splendour of the court and the temples were projected and sublimated expressions of cultural well-being. The lords seem to have been less the masters of serfs and more an expression of the peasantry's greatness (Du Bois 1959).

Viewed broadly, the accomplishments of Indianised cultures can be seen as symptoms of cultural wellbeing. Yet the record also indicates chronic tensions and instabilities as well, including, for one thing, apparent persistent warfare to establish hegemony by contending leaders. For another, the pulsating, expanding–contracting flux that seems to be characteristic of Indianised polities might be seen as symptom of intrinsic strain. In addition, the persistent jockeying for pre-eminence, manifested in what the Chinese observers viewed as 'usurpation'. And the apparent frequent change of capital cities further suggests a chronic instability. What was the source of these strains? I argue they were intrinsic to the very structure of the Indianised cultural–social order itself.

Among upland peoples the oscillatory process was the result of intrinsic social–cultural contradictions which manifested themselves most clearly when an autocratic chief sought to monopolise ritual power absolutely, denying others opportunities for ritual achievement. That is, the chief attempted to impose an artificial closure to the cosmological–social order. The situation of Indianised society suggests a parallel problem in the cosmological sphere.

The Indianised pantheon provided the cosmological framework on which social hierarchy could be arranged. But that pantheon lacked a built-in closure. In particular, the top-most ranks, Siva, Vishnu, Brahma, Lokesvara, were each potential candidates for the highest level of the pantheon. In fact, Siva was commonly taken *de facto* to be the pre-eminent figure, and most kings seem to have identified themselves with him. But Vishnu and Lokesvara also had their supporters as the pre-eminent deity. In addition, the fluidity of the pantheon allowed for more than one person to claim a special relationship or identification with Siva. The only test of the authenticity of any such claim was one's prowess, manifested by success. The Southeast Asian configuration of values, emphasising continuous achievement linked to sacred qualities could not be resolved by the structure of the cosmological system itself.

It is in such a framework that we might want to look at Jayavarman II's innovation in establishing the *devaraja* cult in 802 AD He did so with the explicit intent that there be but one *devaraja* in the kingdom. This intent could be read as Jayavarman's declaration of independence from the suzerainty of the Javanese king who had previously held sway. It can also be seen, however, as pointing to a fundamental problem in Indianised culture, the absence of cosmological closure, which precipitated the continuous questing for macrocosmic–microcosmic hegemony. Thus, Jayavarman's effort can be seen in a more literal sense—that there be one *devaraja* and, by implication, that there be one king. Jayavarman tried to achieve cosmological closure by establishing the *devaraja* cult and vesting exclusive control of its rituals in the matriline of the Brahman Sivakaivalya. While Jayavarman was successful in establishing the cult and vesting control of its rituals in one family line, if his intent was to find a means of stopping the continuous struggle for pre-eminence, he failed. The priests of the *devaraja* cult proved ready to perform the ritual consecrating a *devaraja* king for many contenders for pre-eminence. When a powerful king, such as Suryvarman II or Jayavarman VII, was in the ascendancy, the internal problems induced by this situation may have been muted. But the constant struggle for pre-eminence and/or the death of a powerful king not only left a hole in the social—political domain, but also left a hole in the cosmological order. That cosmology implied a degree of permanence and duration that the actual fluidity seemed to defy. And, if my speculation about the close identification of the masses with charismatic kings is correct, this instability might be experienced society–wide. Thus, while, on the one hand, the structure of Indianised culture was one of its strong points in establishing and elaborating new and complex social forms in Southeast Asia, on the other hand, it contributed to instabilities, tensions and weaknesses as well.

By contrast, the Thai, who were emerging as significant actors on the Southeast Asian scene from the 13th century on, held to a cosmological system informed by Theravāda Buddhism. While one could see the configuration of values associated with the Thai social order as being consistent with the achievement values of uplanders and Indianised peoples, the articulation of those values with cosmological elements was different in at least one important respect. Whereas Thai political pre-eminence manifested achievement values and was linked to notions of moral superiority, the Buddhist order of monks was located above the level of political–moral achievement. Thus, while various Thai leaders could jockey for a position of pre-eminence in a network of kings and strive for identification as a *chakravartin* or universal monarch, any particular rise or decline of either a specific ruler or a specific locale as a centre of power did not threaten an immediate cosmological consequence. The Buddhist order of monks provided a buffer between the cosmological dimension of Theravāda Buddhist culture and the microcosmic dimensions of the world of everyday experience. In addition, there was an important redefinition of religious interests involved in Theravāda Buddhist culture that might have had considerable significance.

I suggested above that in the Indianised social–cultural order the masses were linked to the cosmological order both through their identification with various elements of the pantheon of deities generally and through their close identification with the person of the king whose charismatic qualities attracted their devotion. Their service to the polity was through their service to the king, which was, in a sense, a matter of worship. The ultimate fate of the masses was linked then to the fate of the pantheon in general and to the fate of the pre-eminent king. In Theravāda Buddhist culture, the ultimate devotion of the masses was through a personal identification with the institution of the Sangha. The fate of the Sangha, as a high-level religious value, as a valued institution and as a concrete social organisation, was not tied to the success or failure of any particular king.

Thus, I argue that, in the case of Indianised societies, the articulation between cosmos and the social order was direct through the person of the king and unmediated by any enduring countervailing institution. In the case of the Thai, the link between cosmos and social order was indirect, in that the institution of the Sangha provided a buffer between the cosmological order and the social order. In the former case, the situation encouraged chronic tensions and strains which limited the ability of the Indianised system to withstand a confrontation with the Theravāda Buddhist Thai. The situation of the Thai, while it may have had its own share of chronic instabilities, did not, at least, pose the threat of the cosmos coming crashing down on the heads of its adherents. Thus, the articulation of Buddhist culture and society with cosmological factors gave the Thai an advantaged position in their struggle with the Angkorian Khmer, facilitating their eventual triumph.

Certainly no single factor can account for such complex phenomena as the collapse of the Khmer and the rise of the Thai. The cosmological factor may be only one in an array of involute and interacting factors. Still a consideration of the cosmological factor highlights what it was that collapsed and what it was that rose. The Khmer as an ethnic group did not collapse. Nor was the collapse the downfall of a particular regime. Nor did the collapse involve a regional shift in the centre of power in Southeast Asia as such. What collapsed was a cultural–social system—a way of organising a social order, incorporating a distinctive configuration of values and a particular way of life made meaningful through Indianised cultural elements, a system that had been viable for some 1,400 years. Similarly, the rise of the Thai was not simply the rise of an ethnic group, the supremacy of a particular regime or a shift in power centres. It marked the ascendancy of a different cultural–social system with its own distinctive configuration of values and way of life made meaningful through Theravāda Buddhist cultural and social forms. This system has proven viable for some 500 years.

While there are numerous and substantial similarities in content between the two systems, I maintain the ascendancy of the Theravāda Buddhist system marks another discontinuity in Southeast Asian history that can be seen in evolutionary terms. Be that as it may, I argue that the early successes of the Indianised system, as well as its eventual downfall, must be seen as a result of the internal structure of the system itself, and that the same holds true of the Theravāda Buddhist system.

Chapter Two

Communism, peasants and Buddhism: the failure of peasant revolutions in Thailand and Cambodia

Charles Keyes

On 13 May 1989 I had the privilege to be with May Ebihara when she made her first return to the village in Cambodia where she had carried out field work in 1959–60. As we approached the village across fields after leaving our vehicle, I was struck by its similarity with villages in northeastern Thailand where I have carried out research. In both places, villagers build their houses close together and their rice fields are outside the settled area, where the villagers plant fruit and other trees. It was from one of these trees that May was greeted on her first return to Svay since 1960.

> I came out under a tree and was astonished to hear a tiny voice coming from the tree saying, 'Oh, *nieng*, you've come back!' Startled, I looked up to see not a tree spirit but a little old lady perched in the branches (what she was doing there, I have no idea). But indeed, I had finally returned to Sobay [Svay] after almost three decades. (Ebihara 1990b:68)

That Svay, the village in Kandal province in which May Ebihara had carried out her research,[1] was still in existence after the upheavals stemming from the intense warfare in Cambodia in the 1970s, and particularly after the violent efforts of Pol Pot and the Khmer Rouge to create a totally new social order in Democratic Kampuchea (DK), was a stunning discovery for May. In the 1990s, she returned to Svay several times to document, through interviews, the memories of surviving villagers of the Khmer Rouge period and of the subsequent resurrection of their village.

The stories she gathered from villagers in Svay about their experiences during 'the time of Pol Pot', constituted dramatic refutation of the Khmer Rouge leaders' claims that their revolution had been for Cambodia's poor peasants such as the inhabitants of Svay. As May has written, the villagers spoke of 'desperate hunger and exhaustion, endemic illness, and ineffectual DK medicines that villagers say "looked like shit".' Their 'accounts testify to the manifold ways in which DK controlled, constrained and weakened bodies' (Ebihara 2002:100). Evidence from Svay suggests that the Communist Party of Kampuchea (CPK) under Pol Pot not only failed to institute a revolution that would have benefited the rural people of the country but also, in the short period in which they held power, had implemented policies that caused intense suffering for these very people.

There is much about the history of people in Cambodia prior to and during the rule of the Khmer Rouge that is unique to that country. At the same time, the revolution that the Khmer Rouge sought to institute was rooted in an ideology shared by Communist parties in other societies. During the DK era, the Communist Party of Thailand (CPT) was closely associated with the CPK ideologically and co-operated tactically with the CPK in the border areas between Thailand and Cambodia. Although the CPT failed to seize power, primarily because the Thai state was much stronger than the Cambodian state had been in the early 1970s, its failure, I maintain, was also due to the fact that its policies, like those of the CPK, were discordant with the values of the rural people it sought to recruit and whose lives the party said it was eager to improve.

Peasant revolutions?

I will focus my attention here on why the Communist Party of Thailand (CPT) failed in its effort to mobilise the rural people of northeastern Thailand where approximately 40% of the rural population of Thailand then lived and still live. It was in northeastern region of Thailand that the CPT made its most concerted efforts to recruit rural people for an attempted revolution in the period from the mid-1960s through 1980. A couple of years after Ebihara conducted her field work in Svay, I began field work in the village of Ban Nông Tün in the province of Mahasarakham, in the central part of northeastern Thailand. I studied this village again in the early 1980s and in 2004–05.[2] In this chapter I will draw on my own work, comparing it to Ebihara's to reflect on the failure of Communist-led peasant revolutions in both countries. It is my argument that the CPT, like the CPK, 'misrecognised' the characteristics of the society and culture of the 'peasants'.[3] I maintain that this misrecognition was about the economy of rural society in the two countries. The Communist analysis of the conditions in rural northeastern Thailand and rural Cambodia focused on the exploitation experienced by rural people. In contrast to this political economic analysis, I maintain that rural northeastern Thai, like rural Khmer, understand their economic situation in moral terms derived fundamentally from Theravāda Buddhism.[4] In sum, I argue that the misrecognition of rural society that lies at the root of the failure of Communist-led revolutions in northeastern Thailand, as in Cambodia, stems from a failure of Communist parties to take into account the moral economy of rural people.[5]

During the period from the early 1960s through the 1970s the Communist Party of Thailand succeeded in recruiting thousands of villagers in northeastern Thailand, as well as from other parts of the country, drawing on the grievances of these villagers toward the government—grievances that intensified as the government intruded more and more into village life in the course of promoting development projects. Between the late 1960s and mid 1970s, it appeared to many observers that the Communist parties of Cambodia and Thailand, like those of China and Vietnam, were proving successful in mobilising rural villagers in support of revolutions, 'massive movements to transform the social structure as a whole' (Wolf 1969:301).

Wolf's book, *Peasant wars of the twentieth century*, was one of many studies made in the two decades following the accession to power of the Communist Party of China in 1949 and the French defeat by the Communist-led Viet Minh in Vietnam in 1954 which examined the role of Communist parties in mobilising rural people (then almost always termed 'peasants') overcoming what Marx, referring to France, had observed was their inability 'of enforcing their class interests in their own name' (Marx 1958 [1859] I:334; Shanin 1966). Wolf, however, concluded his own study with this assessment of the impact revolutionary movements:

> The peasant's role is…essentially tragic: his efforts to undo a grievous present only usher in a vaster more uncertain future. Yet if it is tragic, it is also full of hope. For the first time in millennia, human kind is moving toward a solution of the age-old problem of hunger and disease, and everywhere ancient monopolies of power and received wisdom are yielding to human effort to widen participation and knowledge. In such efforts—however uncertain, however beset with difficulties, however ill-understood—there lies the prospect for increased life, for increased humanity (Wolf 1969:301–2).[6]

The rural people of Cambodia, such as those who lived in Svay, were swept up in one of the great tragedies of the late 20th century. The rural people of northeastern Thailand were more fortunate, but many of them also suffered during the Communist-led insurrection from 1965–80.[7] Although northeastern Thai villagers never experienced the traumatic upheavals that villagers in Cambodia did, they, like most Cambodian villagers, found that the visions for a revolutionary transformation of their society led to tragedy and not to an order in which they would experience marked improvements in their lives.

Research on the eve of radical change in rural Cambodia and Thailand

In the late 1950s and early 1960s, Ebihara and I both carried out research in rural communities whose inhabitants were typical of those in the category labeled 'peasants' in policies of the Communist parties of Cambodia and Thailand.[8] Ebihara carried out her first field work in Svay in 1959–60; I conducted mine in Ban Nông Tün a few years later in 1962–64. Both of us had undertaken our graduate training in anthropology—Ebihara at Columbia University and me at Cornell University—at a time when anthropologists had begun to shift their focus away from relatively isolated 'tribal' communities to what were then termed, following Robert Redfield, 'peasant' communities 'connected with or forming part of a civilization or national state' (Redfield 1956:10). Both of us had been influenced by what was known as the 'Bang Chan project'.[9] This pioneering project, undertaken primarily over a decade between the late 1940s and the late 1950s, entailed multidisciplinary research involving American and Thai researchers in the village of Bang Chan near Bangkok.[10] We were interested, following Lauriston Sharp, Lucien and Jane Hanks, and others who carried out the study in Bang Chan, in the sociocultural and socioeconomic conditions in villages on the eve of what was then assumed to be a fundamental transformation being brought about by the increased integration of Thailand and Cambodia in a global economy.[11]

Whereas Ebihara chose, as she once told me, to go to the neighbouring country of Cambodia to provide a comparative perspective on rural mainland Southeast Asia to that gained in the Bang Chan study, I chose to go to the northeastern region of Thailand, which was known to be much more rural at the time than Bang Chan. I was also interested in this region because of its ethno-regional distinctiveness. The majority of the people of northeastern Thailand are culturally and linguistically more closely related to the Lao of Laos than to the dominant people of central Thailand. People in Ban Nông Tün, like people elsewhere in the region, identified ethnically as Lao, but also recognised that their citizenship made them Thai (Keyes 1966b).

The fundamental social unit in both communities was the household, which was based on partnership between husband and wife in working land that they themselves owned, not land that belonged to a landlord. In both Ban Nông Tün and Svay, communal life centred on Buddhist temple-monasteries, called *wat* in Khmer, Lao and Thai.[12] Neither village was, however, an isolated community. Both had schools established by the governments of Cambodia and Thailand that offered several years (three in Svay, four in Ban Nông Tün) of primary education based on government-determined curricula. Village headmen in Cambodia and Thailand were linked to a centrally-administered government provincial bureaucracy, although this linkage had only limited significance for most villagers.

In the early 1960s Ban Nông Tün was like Svay in 1959–60, in that it was a village in which most everything the villagers consumed—rice, other foods, clothing, utensils and housing—was produced by them, rather than purchased. In both communities, households needed some cash income, however, 'to purchase,' in Ebihara's words, 'certain foods and essential household goods not produced at home, to pay taxes or debts, or to use for ceremonial purposes, such as giving offerings to the Buddhist temple or sponsoring weddings, funerals and other domestic rituals' (Ebihara 1990a:18). This observation was equally true of Ban Nông Tün. To generate cash income, villagers in both communities produced some crops for sale and some, mainly men, sought wage labour outside the village. In both communities a few men had gone to the capital cities of Phnom Penh and Bangkok to find temporary work.

Ebihara's (1990a:20) assessment that villagers in Svay 'spoke of themselves as 'poor country folk' in contrast to urbanites and those with non-agricultural occupations such as school teachers' was equally applicable to Ban Nông Tün. The relative poverty of villagers in both places was primarily a consequence of living in a difficult environment—oscillation of flood and drought, poor soils, and lack of water in the dry season—and of lack of the education and networks of connections that would have made it possible for them to seek higher-paying jobs outside of the rural economy. In neither case could village poverty, as Communist policymakers would later assert, be traced to exploitative landlords, local or absentee, or to crushing indebtedness. Although such conditions did exist in a few parts of rural Cambodia and rural Thailand at the time, most villagers in both countries had sufficient land and access to local resources such as forests to produce their basic necessities. Moreover, a village like Svay or Ban Nông Tün, to use Ebihara's words , 'constituted a social unit, an aggregate of known and trusted kinsmen, friends and neighbors…[T]he village was a focus for identity, contrasting "our village" to "others"' (Ebihara 1990b:19).[13]

Crises of power in rural Thailand and Cambodia

In the 1960s and 1970s villagers in Cambodia and rural Thailand began to experience crises of power that were rooted initially in the increasing grievances of villagers toward their governments. These crises were even more a consequence of political violence that became especially intense in Cambodia after 1970 because of American bombing in eastern Cambodia and the expanding Khmer Rouge insurgency. In Thailand, the Communist-led insurgency also intensified from the mid-1960s. Although the political and military conflicts experienced by villagers in Ban Nông Tün and elsewhere in rural Thailand between the mid-1960s and mid-1980s pale by comparison with those experienced by villagers in Cambodia, they did also threaten the way of life villagers in northeastern Thailand had known until then.

Although the circumstances leading up to the takeover of the Cambodian government by the CPK (also known as Ângkar and the Khmer Rouge) have already been well described (Chandler 1990; 1991; Kiernan & Boua 1982; Thion 1983; 1990; Vickery 1984; Heder 2004), relatively little has been written from the perspective of rural people during the tumultuous period from the mid-1960s through 1975. Ebihara has suggested, on the basis of other sources, that villagers were increasingly alienated from the government during this period because of widespread corruption and the government's inability to protect villagers from 'the spillover from the raging conflict in neighboring Vietnam' (Ebihara 1990b:21). Rural discontent increased markedly after General Lon Nol led a coup in March 1970 that ousted Prince Norodom Sihanouk as head of government. There can be little question that Prince Sihanouk's ouster, from the perspective of the rural people of Cambodia, created a crisis of power, because the only authority with legitimacy in their eyes had been removed. A week after the coup, rural people began demonstrating in increasing numbers against the new government. Kiernan has argued that 'while the Prince was a popular figure, other factors were also important in motivating the peasant demonstrations, in particular the existence of a strong revolutionary movement in the main sites of the unrest' (Kiernan & Boua 1982:206; Kiernan 1979). The Khmer Rouge capitalised on this crisis, especially after Prince Sihanouk became affiliated with them.

A crisis of authority in Thailand also began in the 1960s, following the death in 1963 of Field Marshal Sarit Thanarat, the country's military dictator. Sarit had launched Thailand's 'development era' (*samai phatthana*) when his government promulgated Thailand's first national economic development plan in 1962. Sarit struck an alliance with the Thai monarchy and was able to draw on popular support for the Thai king in promoting policies to transform the Thai economy. He also enjoyed considerable popular support among northeastern Thai, having been born in the northeast to a local woman and a Thai military officer, and because he had identified himself as a northeasterner throughout his rule.[14]

In conjunction with the first national economic development plan, Sarit ordered that the National Economic Development Board also draw up a specific plan for the development of the northeastern region. The unique focus on the northeast—no development plan was prepared at this initial stage for any other region—was primarily a consequence of the recognition that it was not only by far the poorest part of Thailand, but also deemed to pose a security problem (*panha kanmankhong*). The government feared that cultural and linguistic linkages between the Thai–Lao of northeastern Thailand and the Lao of Laos could be used to foster separatism or facilitate the spread of communism

(Keyes 1964). These linkages made job opportunities in Vientiane, created by the American presence in Laos, attractive for some northeasterners. About a dozen or so villagers from Ban Nông Tün had worked or were working in Vientiane when we were carrying out our first field work in the early 1960s. A few villagers also listened to radio programs from Laos, but they much preferred the traditional northeastern Thai and Lao musical productions from a station in Khon Kaen in northeastern Thailand. Although all villagers were aware of their kinship with the Lao, we still found that they identified strongly as citizens of Thailand (Keyes 1966b). The 'northeastern problem' became one that was much more a consequence of the actions of Thai government agencies in the region than of any irredentist appeal.

Sarit's successors, Field Marshal Thanom Kittikachorn and Field Marshal Prapas Charusathien, who ruled as military dictators from 1963 to 1973, initially retained close ties with the monarchy, but they lacked the connections to the rural people that Sarit had had. Moreover, as they moved to implement the government's development agenda through a bureaucracy accustomed to the feudal (*sakdi na*) practice of giving orders to villagers rather than consulting them and through technocrats who disdained local knowledge, tensions between villagers and the government increased markedly.[15]

Although during this period the government built roads and extended electricity to villages, which northeastern villagers saw as contributing to positive improvements in their lives, the rampant corruption of the early development period led villagers to view their relations with the government in negative ways. Police at numerous checkpoints on roads to Bangkok demanded payments from villagers transporting products such as pigs to the urban market. Villagers had to give local officials 'tea money' to get permits for many activities, including temple fairs. Because few villagers had full title to their land—primarily because of the slow work of Land Department in the Ministry of Agriculture in carrying out cadastral surveys—some lost their land when government agencies took it for development projects. Police and local officials were often persuaded to 'look the other way' when powerful dacoits robbed and even killed villagers. An incident in Ban Nông Tün exemplifies why many northeastern villagers in the 1960s and 1970s had strong grievances toward the government.

When I made a return visit to Ban Nông Tün in 1967, I learned that my closest friend, with whom Jane and I had lived in 1963–64, had been robbed and nearly killed by a group of bandits who had protectors in the provincial police and the court system. Our friend's efforts to get justice led to his paying nearly as much in bribes as he had lost in the robbery. In an article I wrote about him and published anonymously in Thai in 1968, I ended by noting that 'people in similar predicaments elsewhere in the region have been offered help by those who say that they can rid Thailand of bandits and corrupt officials. Could we blame them for listening?'[16] Incidents such as this were common and led to a significant increase in disaffection with government institutions.

The causes of such disaffection were thought by many urban intellectuals to have ended on 14 October 1973, when a student-led movement gained the support of the King who demanded that the military dictators go into exile. *Sipsi Tula* (14 October), the term Thai use for the dramatic events culminating in the departure of Thanom and Prapas and their son/son-in-law, Narong Kittikachorn, did not, however, usher in a new order, especially for rural people in Thailand.

In the year after *sipsi Tula* the political situation appeared hopeful. A caretaker government appointed by the King and headed by Sanya Thammasak, a respected judge and former rector of Thammasat University, convened a national convention which was charged with electing a national assembly that would draft a new constitution. This convention included 658 village and commune headmen, constituting the largest bloc (27%) among the 2,436 members of the convention (Morell & Samudavanija 1981:102–3). Officials, particularly those associated with the Ministry of Interior, were able, however, to impose their will on many of these rural representatives when it came to the choosing of members of the National Assembly. As Morell and Samudavanija observe, there 'was a sharp decline in participation in the national legislature by local leaders and farmers' while 'representation of the old guard elements increased from 48 to 69 percent' (Morell & Samudavanija 1981:103). Even so, this legislature produced the most liberal constitution Thailand would know for 25 years.

The Constitution laid the foundation for a system of government to be controlled by an elected parliament rather than by the military. In January 1975 there was a democratic election of members of parliament, but the government, formed by a coalition led by the Democrat Party, was almost immediately undermined by conditions outside parliamentary control. Most significantly, many in the security forces (police, military, and border patrol police) were not willing to see their own powers curtailed by parliament. Some members of these forces fostered the creation of right-wing movements and, even more frightening, death squads who targeted left-wing politicians, labour leaders and leaders of rural protest groups. These counter-revolutionary elements capitalised on the negative reaction of many middle-class Thai to the Communist victories in Vietnam, Laos and Cambodia. The Khmer Rouge evacuation of Phnom Penh in April 1975 was particularly disturbing to many urban Thai who feared that the CPT might one day succeed in imposing a similar action in Bangkok.

Even before *sipsi Tula* some members of the Bangkok-based student organisations undertook to establish links with rural people by going to the countryside to 'teach democracy'. Most of these efforts were not at all successful, as I learned first-hand when, in 1972, I visited Ban Nông Tün and found villagers puzzled by a group of students who had spent several days in the village. Villagers said they stayed at the Buddhist temple-monastery and spent most of their time singing songs of protest comparable to those sung by anti-Vietnam War protestors in the United States. Even though these 'songs for life' (*phleng phüa chiwit*) often spoke of the plight of the poor, they did not appeal to villagers who considered them the music of the urban young rather than music with roots in the popular culture of rural people (unpublished field notes, 12 September 1972).[17]

In this politically turbulent period some rural people, emboldened by *sipsi Tula*, began to organise protests against the government, mainly over abuses of authority by government officials and dispossession of their land in the wake of government-sponsored development projects or through government recognition of claims to land made by companies and large landowners (Turton 1978:121–3). In November 1974 the Farmers Federation of Thailand (*sahaphan chao rai chao na haeng Prathet Thai*) was founded, becoming the first formal organisation in Thailand whose purpose was to promote the interests of rural people (Turton 1978:122). Although the government would subsequently claim that the Federation was a Communist front, and although some Party cadres may have contributed to its development, most who joined did so because they had legitimate grievances against the government.

These efforts by villagers to seek redress for their grievances through legitimate means soon proved either futile or, in some cases, fatal. Most villagers still found their political reality to be predicated on their relationship to civil servants, whose demeaning attitudes toward them had not changed. The officials that villagers dealt with were accountable only to their bureaucratic superiors and not to the citizenry or to their elected representatives. In 1975 several leaders of farmer groups were assassinated by death squads backed by the military or police. 'The police were said to have put about forged letters purporting to show that the killings were the result of internal dissension. No arrests of suspects were made except in [one] case' (Turton 1978:123).

The vision that many Thai shared of a more open democratic society was shattered in October 1976 when elements in the police and military, backed by right-wing groups, overthrew the democratically-elected government and brutally suppressed student activists in Bangkok. The new government instituted a broadly-defined law that allowed almost anyone critical of the government to be accused of 'endangering society' (*phai sangkhom*) and imprisoned without due process. This law was frequently used against rural people. In response to these developments, the CPT began attracting to its ranks new recruits from among villagers as well as from Bangkok students.

The failure of Thailand's Communist-led insurgency

Although there had been supporters of communism in Thailand in the 1930s, especially among some overseas Chinese in Bangkok and among Vietnamese refugees who had settled in northeastern Thailand after the French crushed the Nghe-Tinh soviets in 1931, the CPT itself dates its founding to 1 December 1942 (de Beer 1978:144–5). The Party had briefly been legalised after the Second World War, but when Phibun Songgram returned as Prime Minister in 1947, his government moved to repress all leftist movements. During this period, a number of left-wing Lao-speaking northeastern leaders who had emerged from the anti-Japanese Free Thai during the war were assassinated (Keyes 1967).

Despite or perhaps because of this repression, the CPT continued to attract new followers. At its third congress in 1961, the Party, according to the its official history, 'gained a firmer and more profound understanding of the revolutionary path of using the countryside to encircle the towns and of the role of the peasantry in national-democratic revolution' (CPT 1978:164). The rural areas that became the base for the Party were located primarily in northeastern Thailand. The CPT initiated armed struggle against the government in northeastern Thailand in 1965. During the late 1960s, the Party recruited a small but steady number of villagers, primarily in the provinces near the Mekong River, to become active combatants in the insurgency. They also gained the tacit or active support of many more villagers who provided food, other supplies and safe havens.

> The 'forest fighters'[18] as the guerillas call themselves, are not ideologically committed, but they have been persuaded by the few who are—the communist cadres who have been working among the villagers for years—that under the present conditions they face only hardship and suffering. They hear that the government is corrupt, oppresses the people and is interested only in Bangkok (Girling 1981:259).

The attraction of the Communist-led insurgency dramatically increased after the suppression of student protests and seizure of the government on 6 October 1976. An estimated 2,000–3,000 students, including most of the leaders of the *sipsi Tula* movement who were not killed or arrested in the crackdown at Thammasat University, fled to the jungle to join the insurgency (Morell & Samudavanija 1981:293). By the late 1970s it was estimated that 'communist military strength in Thailand…stands at something like 12,000 to 14,000 armed guerillas in all regions' (Girling 1981:257). A map first published in the *Far*

Eastern Economic Review in September 1977 showed that the insurgency was present in all but two provinces in the northeast, all but two provinces in the south, half the provinces in the north and nearly half of the provinces in central Thailand (Girling 1981:261).

According to the map, Mahasarakham province was one of two provinces in the northeast in which there was no known Communist infiltration. However, as I discovered when I made return visits to the village beginning in 1979, villagers were very much aware of the insurgency. One articulate villager talked of the grievances toward the government which led some villagers to turn to the Communist-led insurrection: 'He said that villagers have no faith in the government (*mai waicai ratthaban*) because of the continual experiences of corrupt practices that they have when dealing with government officials'. However, he immediately added that villagers (including himself) were not attracted to the Communists because they 'do not see anything good in the Communist systems found in neighboring countries' (unpublished field notes, 31 July 1980). To my knowledge only one person from Ban Nông Tün—a young man from one of the poorest families, who had been my assistant in carrying out surveys in 1963—had joined the insurgency in the mid-1970s. I later learned he had been killed in a fight with government forces in another province, to which he had moved.

Although the Mao-inspired strategy of encircling the cities from the countryside appeared to be succeeding to an extent in the late 1970s, by the early 1980s the Party had collapsed. This dramatic change can be attributed to several causes, which a comparison with the Khmer Rouge can help explain.

Like the CPK, the CPT also adopted Maoism, as well as Marxist–Leninism, as the foundation for its ideology, which in the history of the CPT is characterised as 'the correct path for the liberation of all semi-colonial, semi-feudal countries' (CPT 1978:161). The CPT, again like the Khmer Rouge, rejected the 'revisionism' associated with the reforms begun by Khrushchev in 1956 (CPT 1978:163). By aligning itself with the Communist Party of China in the Sino–Soviet rift, the CPT, in the late 1970s, lost the support of the Vietnamese and Lao Communist parties, which made logistical support of the insurgency by China more difficult. This difficulty intensified when the Vietnamese military drove the Khmer Rouge, the only remaining ally of the CPT in Southeast Asia, from power in early 1979.

The rigid Maoism of the CPT leadership[19] also alienated many of the students who had joined the insurgency after 6 October 1976. None of the CPT leaders had much charisma. At least two of the student leaders of the *sipsi Tula* movement, Thirayut Boonmee and Seksan Prasertkul, who joined the Party in the mid-1970s, might well have evolved into significant leaders if they had been encouraged by the CPT leadership and if conditions had been more conducive (see Wedel & Wedel 1987). Both had gained a charismatic aura in their roles in the student movement and also sought to adapt Marxist–Leninism to Thai intellectual conditions, as well as to socioeconomic conditions. As Seksan wrote in 1975: 'The theory of revolution is not ready-made theory...This applies to revolutionaries in Thailand: they may learn the revolutionary ways of other countries, but they must keep in mind that every struggle and every situation has its own unique character' (quoted in Wedel & Wedel 1987:147).[20]

Although Seksan and Thirayut and other students who joined the insurgency initially attempted to accept the discipline of the Party and not question the Party's line in order to contribute to the overthrow of the right-wing regime that took power in Bangkok after October 1976, they eventually found themselves in conflict with the leaders of the CPT. This conflict was dramatised in a film released in 2002 about Seksan and his wife, Chiranan Pitpreecha, and their time with the CPT. 'The Moonhunter', as the film was named in English, or 'Sipsi Tula: Songkhram Prachachon' [14 October—Peoples' War] in Thai, culminates with the break with the CPT in the early 1980s made by Seksan and his wife, and other student leaders, such as Thirayut. This break was not only over ideology, but also because of the strong negative reaction that many had to the excesses of the Khmer Rouge, which they began to learn about after it was ousted in early January 1979 (Wedel & Wedel 1987:196).[21]

Seksan, Thirayut, and the other former students as well as most other supporters of the CPT left the insurgency to take advantage of an amnesty promulgated by the Thai government in 1980. By then the political situation in Bangkok had changed dramatically. Early in that year General Prem Tinsulanonda, commander-in-chief of the armed forces, became Prime Minister. Although a southern Thai by origin, General Prem had had much experience leading troops against the insurgency in the northeast. He and his allies in the military clearly saw the need to take into account the real problems of social injustice and inequalities that existed in the countryside, if they were to defeat the Communist-led insurgency.

In an extraordinary assessment that in many ways echoed that of the CPT, General Chaovalit, one of General Prem's close allies and a subsequent Prime Minister, said in a speech to Thai students in the United States:

> The conditions in rural society in Thailand is [sic] very distressing and I think all of you know it very well. You might have even seen the people delighted to receive only ten or twenty baht. What is even worse are all the 'influences' which are deep rooted in the rural society. You may have seen them; if they are not happy with someone, that one may die, he may get killed...If someone has no

money, then he may get it from them at an exorbitant interest rate and after three or four years he has lost all his land. This is the real condition of oppression and exploitation in the rural areas (quoted in translation in Suchit 1987:69).

This perspective provided the rationale for the Prime Ministerial Order No. 66/2523, 'Policy of Struggle to Win Over Communism', issued in April 1980. The proclamation laid the foundation for a new political order.

The order was predicated on promoting policies 'to eliminate the revolutionary situation' over combating the insurgency with force. Toward this end, the first two elements in the implementation of the policy stressed the necessity to change the conditions in the countryside that were leading people to join or support the insurgency. A 'political offensive' was to be launched 'to instill in the people's mind a recognition that this land is theirs to protect and preserve and that it is partly they who are the owners, rulers and beneficiaries' . Even more important,

social injustice must be eliminated at every level, from local to national levels. Corruption and malfeasance in the bureaucracy musts be decisively prevented and suppressed. And all exploitation must be done away with the security of the people's life and property provided (quoted in translation in Suchit 1987:91).

Those who had joined the insurgency and had taken advantage of the amnesty were to be assisted 'to enable them to make a proper start to their new life in society' (quoted in translation in Suchit 1987:92). In practice, this meant not only that those who left the insurgency would not be prosecuted but also that many rural insurgents would be helped to resettle in areas where they could become farmers again.[22]

Although the vision on which Prime Ministerial Order No. 66/2523 was predicated is still to be fully realised in Thailand, the fact remains that after the early 1980s, the near-civil war in Thailand that had parallels to events in the late 1960s in Cambodia came to an end. Since the early 1980s, most rural-dwelling Thai have found it possible to work through elected politicians and, even more, through non-governmental organisations to seek redress for their grievances.[23] This change has also been markedly facilitated by the economic boom that began in Thailand in the 1980s, even though villagers have not benefited nearly as much as urban people have.

Village Buddhism and the failure of peasant revolutions

Michael Vickery, a leading scholar of Cambodian history and politics, wrote in 1984 that when the Khmer Rouge revolution occurred, 'it was based squarely on the poorer strata of the peasantry' (Vickery 1984:268). While this assessment is questionable, the fact is that, once they had established Democratic Kampuchea after April 1975, the Khmer Rouge moved to destroy the foundations of rural society. This was especially the case in those areas of Cambodia, such as the one in which Svay is located, which had not been in the 'liberated' zone before 1975. Ebihara has written of people from Svay that:

> Although the villagers had originally come from peasant backgrounds, the fact that they had not been in DK base areas before 1975 defined them as 'New People' who had not joined the revolution. Their experiences during DK thus paralleled those of countless other 'April 17 People': they were segregated by age and gender into different kinds of work teams; labor was exacted from them relentlessly; draconian discipline was used; family and kin ties were ruptured; malnutrition and illness were rampant; and deaths, including executions, were common place. The mortality rate was appalling: of the 139 West Svay villagers I had known in my early research who were still alive in 1975, 50 percent (70 persons) died during DK. Of the 32 families I had known, some perished completely and others were left with only one or a few survivors. (Ebihara 2002:94)

Even in areas where rural people had lived under Khmer Rouge control before 1975, the structures that had long sustained rural society—especially the household and the Buddhist temple-monastery—were eliminated.

There is no way of knowing whether the CPT, had it come to power, would have implemented similar draconian policies in the rural areas of Thailand. The CPT did share with the Khmer Rouge, however, a fundamental 'misrecognition' of the characteristics of the society and culture of the 'peasants' for whom they claimed they were creating a revolution.

Studies made by three men when they were students in France who later became leaders in the Khmer Rouge, Khieu Samphan, Hou Yuon and Hu Nim, focused on 'the exploitation of the peasant's labor by other social groups' (Kiernan & Boua 1982:32).[24] There are no equivalent analyses of conditions in the countryside in available CPT sources, but policy statements referring to rural people evoke similar assessments of the problems they face because of 'hooligan landlords', 'loansharks' and indebtedness.[25] These assessments were not based on the understanding rural people had of their own conditions; instead 'peasants' were seen as victims, not as people with their own understandings of the conditions they confronted. More fundamentally, those who shaped the policies of the Khmer Rouge and the CPT took no cognisance of or ignored the moral basis of rural society in Cambodia and Thailand.

Scott, in his analysis of the failure of uprisings of rural people in Southeast Asia who faced severe hardships in the wake of the Great Depression, stressed the necessity of examining the culture of rural people 'to discover how much their moral universe diverges from that of the elite' (Scott 1976:23–9). I would add, in regard to Cambodia and Thailand, that 'elites' must be understood to include the leadership of the Communist Party.[26] In both countries there was a failure to understand or a decision to reject the cultural foundations of rural society based on the traditions of Theravāda Buddhism.[27]

In an essay on the role of Buddhism in Svay as she observed it in her first field work, Ebihara wrote: 'The temple serves obviously as a moral-religious focal point, integrating the village(s) [that is, hamlets] within its congregation into a religious community through shared norms and common participation in rituals' (Ebihara 1966:187). The same conclusion was equally applicable to Ban Nông Tün, as well as to other villages in northeastern Thailand (Tambiah 1970; Kirsch 1977; Hayashi 2002), as the *wat*, the Buddhist temple-monastery, served as the cultural gyroscope for village life.

In the Buddhist practice of Ban Nông Tün, again as in Svay, and, indeed, throughout all rural communities in the Theravāda Buddhist countries of Thailand, Cambodia, Laos, Burma and Sri Lanka until modern influences began to make themselves felt, merit-making was understood primarily as entailing offering alms (*thawai than* (Pali, *dana*)) consisting of the 'requisites' of food, clothing, shelter and medicine for members of the Buddhist Sangha. Having a *wat* where monks resided and where ritual acts of alms-giving could be carried out, has always been essential for a Buddhist community to exist.

Monks in village *wat*s in Cambodia and Thailand almost always came from the ranks of village men. It was the tradition that some boys would enter the Sangha as novices, although the numbers who did so declined in Thailand and Cambodia after the introduction of government-sponsored compulsory public education. More importantly, most young men would enter the monkhood for a period of their choice, running from several months to several years. Older men who had retired from active life would also sometimes be ordained as monks.

The Khmer Rouge originally had strong positive connections to the Sangha; many of the founding members were ex-monks or ex-novices (Keyes 1994; Harris 1999:65). Prior to ceasing power in 1975, the Khmer Rouge often used village *wat*s to organise rallies at which monks were present. Khmer Rouge leaders were often conspicuous in showing respect to monks. Moreover, the Khmer Communists also appropriated from Buddhism some key terms for translation of Marxist–Leninist concepts (Hinton 2005:145, 195ff, 26–3; Ponchaud 1989:152). In what became a tragic turn, however, the Khmer Rouge made these Buddhist-derived ideas a justification for their radical ideology. In the new order that they sought to create, there was no place for *wat*s or the Sangha. Monks were forced to disrobe or were killed; *wat*s were converted into storage areas, prisons or even pigsties. In short, the Khmer Rouge moved to root out and destroy the traditions and institutions that were fundamental to the moral world of rural communities.

The CPT said little about the Sangha other than to criticise rightist monks (de Beer 1978:155).[28] Its commitment to doing 'away with the culture and education of the imperialists and feudalists' (de Beer 1978:152) and to eliminating superstitious practices (de Beer 1978:155) indicates that the CPT leaders considered the Buddhist traditions that were so important in the lives of villagers as impediments to the revolution. While some villagers joined with or supported the insurgency because of their grievances, their worldview was radically different to that of the leaders of the CPT.

In Cambodia since 1979 and in Thailand since the collapse of the CPT, villagers have found that the Buddhist tradition remains basic to their understanding of their relationship not only to rural society but also to the larger society in which they are located. Ebihara (1990b:43) observed that, in the post-Pol Pot period, 'family and kin, household production and consumption and Buddhism...remerged' among rural people in Cambodia. Others (Yang Sam 1987; Gyallay-Pap & Tranet 1990; Keyes 1994; Skidmore 1996; Marston & Guthrie 2004; Harris 1999; 2005) have also documented how a foundational step in the re-creation of Khmer society in the post-Pol Pot period was the restoration of Buddhism. Hun Sen and his associates initially adhered to a Vietnamese-style Communist approach to religion and imposed strict limits on the practice of religion, but they did allow for a limited restoration of the Buddhist Sangha by allowing only men over the age of 50 to be ordained.[29] In mid-1988 Hun Sen's government changed its policy towards religion and began to promote the resurrection of Buddhism actively by allowing the ordination of more men and providing government funds for the rebuilding of *wats*.

Ebihara observed in Svay that:

At both the village *vat* and the other one down the road, it was amazing and gratifying to watch the central temples (*vihear*) being rebuilt literally from the ground up, on what were mounts of dirt in 1990. In both instances, the temples have been constructed in classic style and are, in some ways, even more magnificently beautiful than the pre-war *vihear*. Each *vat* also has a contingent of resident monks, including some young novices. (Ebihara 2002:106).

While the trauma of the Pol Pot period has made it impossible for life to be exactly 'like it was before' (*dauch pi mŭn*) (Ebihara 2002:107), most villagers as well as urban people in Cambodia have found in their Buddhist traditions a basis for the restoration of moral communities.[30] Ebihara's own identity with villagers of Svay was accentuated when after her death in 2005, a part of her ashes were ritually enshrined in a *chaul bŏn*, merit-making ritual, at the *wat* in Svay.

In Thailand, since the 1980s, the Sangha has increasingly had a different relationship to urban and rural Thailand. In urban society, the *wat* no longer is at the centre of community. Many middle-class urban dwellers have become what I term 'post-Buddhists', in that, while they still claim to be Buddhists, they participate rarely in rituals. Other urbanites have turned to new Buddhist movements such as the evangelical Dhammakaya or fundamentalist Santi Asoke to confront the conditions of the world in which they now live. Only those involved in non-governmental organisations that look for inspiration to the modernist interpretation of Buddhism, especially as manifest in the thought of Buddhadasa Bhikkhu (1905–93), have any significant contact with rural people (Keyes 1999; 2002a). In rural communities, especially in northeastern Thailand, Buddhism has, however, had a different history to its history in urban areas since the collapse of the CPT.

The *wat* remains for villagers the focus of their membership in a moral community. If one travels anywhere in northeastern Thailand today, one is immediately struck by the fact that most village *wat*s have impressive new *wihan* (Khmer *vihear* (from Pali, *vihara*)) or image halls. These buildings have typically been built, as in Ban Nông Tün, by donations from villagers who have worked or are working in Bangkok or elsewhere. These new buildings reflect the strong identification that temporary and permanent migrants have with their home communities.

The Sangha in northeastern Thailand has been strongly influenced by the tradition of forest meditation that originated with Acan Man Bhuridatto Thera (1870–1949), a monk subsequently widely recognised as a Buddhist 'saint' (*arhat*) (Taylor 1993; Kamala 1997). Monks residing in the numerous forest monasteries (*wat pa*) in the northeast—only a few are found in other regions—are widely respected by villagers as exemplifying the Buddhist ideal of 'detachment' (*tat cai*, literally, to cut off one's heart) from the desires of the world while still living in the world.[31] In the late 20th century forest monasteries have proliferated as the forested areas of the northeast have significantly diminished. Forest monasticism has spawned a new Buddhist environmentalism that is village-based (Taylor 1991). In the late 1980s forest monks established a temporary residence in the forest of the village guardian spirit (*phi puta*) in Ban Nông Tün and, in the 1990s, another forest monk established a permanent forest monastery in what had formerly been the forested area where cremations had taken place but which had been abandoned for this purpose when a new crematorium was built in the grounds of the village *wat*. This forest monk has led villagers in a reforestation project around the monastery. Forest monks (*phra pa*) provide a marked contrast with the 'forest soldiers' (*thahan pa*), as Communist-led insurgents were known. While the latter 'misrecognised' of the basis of rural culture, the former are central to it.

Conclusion

Today those living in Svay and Ban Nông Tün face new problems because of the ever-increasing capitalist penetration of their communities and persistent negative encounters with representatives of their governments. They turn to a variety of means to deal with these problems, but they are not at all likely, given the history of Communist-led 'peasant revolutions' in their two countries, to join movements that seek 'to transform the social structure as a whole' (Wolf 1969:301). Villagers are not the passive victims of forces outside of their control. Rather, as they confront their problems and grievances, they still find fundamental meaning for acting in the world from moral communities centred on Buddhism.

The immediate post-Second World War period ushered in a new period of Communist-led peasant revolutions if which China and Vietnam are the most striking exemplars. The ideology that was fundamental to the leadership of Communist movements in Asia and elsewhere can be seen as arguably the most radical product of the Enlightenment. Those who followed this ideology were committed to the creation of a secular society in which religious practice and belief would eventually disappear as members of society reoriented their actions according to science and what were thought to be the laws of history. By the last decades of the 20th century, it was clear not only that the Communist vision of development and progress led by science had failed, but that efforts to implement it had increased the suffering of many in the societies led by Communist parties, as well as in those with strong insurgent Communist movements. The actions of the Communist parties in China, Cambodia and, to a somewhat lesser extent, in Vietnam and Laos, to suppress religious institutions not only intensified suffering but also contributed to a crisis of power which undermined their authority, particularly among rural people.

Today religious institutions and practices are resurgent, even in those countries still ruled by parties that call themselves Communist. Buddhism has played a role in this resurgence. Lue (Dai) people in southern Yunnan have devoted much energy and many resources, and have used resources coming from Thailand as well, to rebuild their Theravāda Buddhist monasteries and to restore the Buddhist Sangha (Peters 1990; Davis 2005). The great outpouring of people to receive the famous monk Thích Nhất Hạnh when, in 2005, he returned to Vietnam for the first time in nearly 40 years was indicative of the growing attraction of Buddhism in that country (Thích 2005). In Laos, Party leaders are today conspicuous participants in many Buddhist rituals (Evans 1998). The stories I have told about villagers in Ban Nông Tün and elsewhere in northeastern Thailand, in Svay and other parts of rural Cambodia demonstrate,

I maintain, why so many rural people in Thailand and Cambodia rejected the visions of new orders offered by Communist parties and continue to embrace moral communities grounded in their Theravāda Buddhist traditions.

The failure of Communist-led peasant revolutions should also be seen as raising questions about non-Communist secularists, who also misrecognise the continuing significance of religion as the basis of communal order for the majority of people. The need of humans to be assured that they live in a meaningful cosmos, that they have the means to confront what Geertz, following Weber, termed 'chaos—a tumult of events which lack not just interpretations but *interpretability*' (Geertz 1973:100), cannot be dispelled by evocations of a better order to come, brought about by the dispassionate actions of leaders following policies informed by science.[32] Connecting with communities such as those Ebihara and I have known in Cambodia and Thailand can, I believe, help provide an alternative to the misrecognition of the relationship between religion and social order that underlies not only the ideology of Communists but also of many secularists.

While villagers seek fundamental meaning in religion, they do not, like some of their leaders, seek to manipulate religion to promote this-worldly political ends. If faced with a crisis of authority, they may turn to those who advocate violence in the name of religious principles. They are not, however, the initiators of religious violence or violence against religion. In other words, a clear distinction needs to be made between the reasons why people such as villagers in Thailand and Cambodia find religion to provide a moral basis for communal life and the rationales that leaders use to manipulate religious institutions or to attack them. These are, I suggest, some lessons to draw from the rice fields.

Notes

1   I am indebted to David Chandler, Jane Keyes and John Marston for comments on previous versions of this chapter.

Although Ebihara uses 'Svay', the real name of the village in some of her writings (Ebihara 1968, 2002), she also has more often referred to it by the pseudonym 'Sobay'. In one early study (Ebihara 1966), she used another pseudonym, 'Kong'. In her most recent publication, Ebihara says that 'I am now using its real name because various colleagues in Cambodia studies are familiar with the village'.

2   I am grateful to the Ford Foundation's Foreign Area Fellowship program for support of the research in the early 1960s, to the United States Agency for International Development and the University of Washington for support of the work in the early 1980s, and to the University of Washington's Royalty Research Fund for support of the work in 2004–05.

3   The concept of 'misrecognition', as I use it in this chapter, is based on the work of Pierre Bourdieu (1977).

4   I am well aware that the moral basis of community in rural Thailand and Cambodia is not expressed only in a Buddhist idiom. Villagers often speak of their community using kin terms and practices centring on beliefs in spirits which also contribute to moral solidarity. Nonetheless, I maintain that Buddhism has provided the overarching framework for their sense of moral community.

5   I am led, in part, by James Scott's (1976) argument about the 'moral economy of the peasant', but, as I have argued elsewhere (Keyes 1983), I maintain it is necessary to recognise different types of 'moral economies' that are rooted in different religious traditions.

6   I have chosen to use Wolf to frame this initial discussion about peasant revolution, because his work was very influential on my thinking and on Ebihara's (as we discussed in several conversations) in the 1960s and 1970s.

7   For accounts and analyses of the CPT's efforts to recruit rural people and the history of the Communist-led insurgency in rural Thailand, see Caldwell (1973); Turton (1978); CPT (1978); de Beer (1978); Wedel (1981); Girling (1981:ch 7); Morell & Samudavanija (1981:ch 8 11); Wedel & Wedel (1987).

8   Ebihara's accounts of Svay, based on her research in 1959-60, are contained in her dissertation (Ebihara 1968) and in several articles (Ebihara 1966; 1974b; 1977; 1990a). She also drew on this research in linking the Svay of the earlier period with the Svay she encountered after her return (see especially Ebihara 1990b, 2002). My accounts of Ban Nông Tün are also found in my dissertation (Keyes 1966a), in several articles (Keyes 1966b; 1975; 1976) and in a report based on a restudy in 1980 (Keyes 1982).

9   Ebihara told me that she had originally considered working in Thailand after she had become familiar with the Bang Chan project, but then decided to go to Cambodia, since others were undertaking work in Thailand.

10 In their 'final' report on the Bang Chan project, Lauriston Sharp and Lucien Hanks (1978) provide references to the large body of work about Bang Chan. My knowledge of the research when I was a graduate student was derived, in part, from an earlier report (Sharp et al 1953), as well as from many other publications by members of the project and, in part, from learning about the project first-hand from Sharp.

11 Lauriston Sharp was my mentor in the study of Thailand during my graduate career at Cornell University. Ebihara developed a particularly strong connection with Jane Hanks from at least the time she was writing her dissertation.

12 Works on Cambodia and Laos usually follow French transliteration and spell the word *vat* or *vatt*.

13 Thai–Lao villagers also used the phrase 'our village' (*bān hao*) in the same way as Khmer villagers. David Chandler (personal communication) notes that the idea adopted by the leaders of Khmer and Thai Communist parties of the 'evil landlord' came from China and northern Vietnam. The characteristics of rural society in Cambodia and northeastern Thailand in the late 1950s and early 1960s, which Ebihara and I recorded, are supported by surveys carried out at the time (see Delvert (1961) for Cambodia and, for northeastern Thailand, Madge (1957), Long et al (1963), Suthep (1968) and Yatsushiro (1968)).

14 Jane Keyes and I were in Ban Nông Tün when Sarit died and villagers told us that they expected things to get worse in the northeast region because the new Prime Minister, Field Marshal Thanom Kittikachorn, was not a northeasterner, as Sarit had been.

15 Demaine (1986:112) observed that, two decades after the first development plan, 'the basic Thai view of "development" has not transcended the old patrimonial framework.' The term *sakdi nā* (which is usually glossed as 'feudal') became in the 1970s the term of choice for Thai left-wing intellectuals to characterise negative hierarchical relationships in Thai society. The term is particularly identified with the work of Jit Poumisak, *Chomnā sakdi nā Thai nai patcuban* [The real face of Thai feudalism today], first published in 1957, but not really known until it was republished in 1974 (Jit 1987). For an account of the feudal attitude of officials toward villagers, especially characteristic of officials in the Ministry of Interior, see Rubin (1973a; 1973b).

16 The article was published as 'Cotmāi cāk Īsān' [Letter from the northeast] in *Sangkhomsāt porithat* [Social Science Review], then practically the only outlet for critical reflection on politics in Thailand (Keyes 1968). The article prompted what was then known as the Communist Suppression Operations Command (later known as the Internal Security Operations Command) to send a team led by a police and army colonel to visit Mahasarakham and my friend in Bān Nông Tün was called to the provincial capital. Although 'he denied everything because otherwise he would have been a marked man' (unpublished field notes, 14 July 1980), all demands for bribes ended and the leader of the bandit group was sentenced to jail. By the time he was released over a decade later, he was not only blind, but also no longer had any patrons left in the police or justice system.

17   Another genre of popular music that emerged in this period—*pheng luk thung*, 'songs of the children of the rice fields'—with roots in traditional northeastern music would subsequently become a vehicle to express the hardships of life in rural areas, but usually with reference to romance rather than politics.

18   The Thai term for forest fighters, *tahan pa*, incorporates the term *pa*, which traditionally has been used in contrast to *ban* or *müang*, village or polity. The *pa* was historically considered to be the home of people who were wild and dangerous. Communist insurrectionaries, who were said to belong to the 'forest army' were, thus, relegated to being beyond civilisation.

19   In this connection, see the analysis of the Party published in Sweden in 1980, most probably by former student leaders. The analysis observes that the flexibility of 'middle-ranking cadres' who formulated 'local policies from the local situation' contrasted with 'the policies adopted by the top leadership' (TIC 1980:11).

20   It must be added, however, that Seksan and Thirayut, as well as other former students who came from Bangkok, lacked any first-hand understanding of conditions in the rural areas of Thailand. In this regard they were similar to the old leaders of the CPT and to the leaders of the Khmer Rouge. The CPT leaders came primarily from Sino-Thai urban dwellers. Although the CPK had been formed by former monks, many who came from rural areas, it was taken over by men who had been educated in France.

21   Chiranan's memoirs of her time in the jungle with the CPT, published in 2006, also document this break between the students and the Party. In conversation with me in June 2006, she told me that the students really never knew the CPT leaders, who were surrounded by an aura of mystery.

22   After they returned Seksan and Thirayut went to the United States for graduate study —something that would not have been possible in the post-9/11 world, as they would have been considered terrorists—and returned to Thailand to assume academic posts. Today, Thirayut is a well-known public intellectual and a prominent advocate for Thai civil society.

23   This conclusion has not, however, been true since 2001 for the rural people of the four southern provinces who are mainly Malay-speaking Muslims. The 'insurrection' in southern Thailand has very different characteristics to that led by the CPT.

24   Khieu Samphan's 1959 thesis, 'L'économie du Cambodge et ses problèmes d'industrialisation', has been published in an English translation by Laura Summers (Khieu Samphan 1979); a part of Hou Yuon's 1955 thesis, 'La paysannerie du Cambodge et ses projets de modernisation', has been published in English translation by Ben Kiernan (Hou Yuon 1982); a partial English translation, also by Ben Kiernan, of Hu Nim's 1965 thesis (for the University of Phnom Penh), 'Les services publics économiques du Cambodge', has also been published (Hu Nim 1982). Heder (2004:2) contends that these three men were actually 'nonentities in the movement at least through the late 1960s'. Nonetheless, their analyses were consistent with the Marxist–Leninism of the Vietnamese Communist Party that Heder maintains was the primary source for the ideology of the CPK.

25   See points 3 and 6 in the 'revised 10 points' that constituted the basic CPT program as published on 1 December 1976 and as given in translation in de Beer (1978:150–2).

26   Not all leaders of Marxist—Leninist parties had a tin ear for the culture of rural people. Paul Mus in his *Viêt-Nam: sociologie d'une guerre* (1952) showed how the Vietnamese Communist Party built their conception of socialism on the notion of *xã hội hoá*, 'to put in common', in which the first term, *xã*, means 'le village, la communauté villageoise traditionelle, avec ses connotations spirituelles et sociales' (Mus 1952:253; see also McAlister & Mus 1970:117).

27   Some specialists on Cambodia have been sceptical about whether Buddhism is the moral centre for village life in Cambodia. Vickery, after having reviewed Ebihara's analysis of the role of the Buddhist wat in Svay, concluded that 'at bottom, the mixture of Buddhist principles, old Hindu rites, and ancient folk beliefs which together constituted Cambodian religion, represented techniques for ameliorating one's material life, either now or in the future. If the religion was seen to fail in that respect, disaffection occurred' (Vickery 1984:12). I recognise that Khmer religion, like Thai religion, is syncretic (Kirsch 1977), and, as Marston has observed (personal communication 19 April 2006) that Buddhism is not the sole moral centre of Khmer communities, and, further, that Buddhism has often been manipulated by elites for their purposes. I still maintain, nevertheless, that research in rural communities in both countries, both in the past and the present, demonstrates clearly that the moral order conceived of by most villagers is predicated primarily on Buddhist concepts and practices.

28   The Khmer Rouge also did not launch an assault against institutionalised Buddhism until they assumed power.

29   In January 1988, when I made a trip to Cambodia as the head of delegation from the Social Science Research Council, I asked the representative of our sponsor, the Foreign Ministry, about restricting ordinations only to those over 50. He said that the restriction was temporary because the economy was inadequate to provide support for many monks. Later in 1988, the government changed its policy regarding ordinations.

30   I recognise this is a controversial contention, given the proliferation of heterodox cults in contemporary Cambodia (see several articles in Marston & Guthrie 2004) and the conversion of some Khmer to Christianity. Nonetheless, I am still persuaded on the basis of other work (for example, Harris 2005) that Buddhism remains for most Khmer the foundation of their moral world.

31   Hinton has recorded that the Khmer Rouge promoted the cultivation by cadres of the equivalent Khmer concept, *dăch chĕtt*, but not the attainment of Buddhist mindfulness, so that one would feel no emotion in taking the life of 'enemies' (Hinton 2005:262–3).

32   I have discussed at greater length elsewhere the Weberian approach to understanding religion and society on which I base my efforts to rethink the relationship between religion and modernity (Keyes 2002b; Keyes, Hardacre & Kendall 1994).

Chapter three

'Beyond suffering'—genocidal terror
under the Khmer Rouge: a view from
the work of May Ebihara

Alexander Hinton

I could feel my brain slowing down. It was hard to think about anything...
Food—that was our main obsession...But to some extent...I got used to being
hungry...What was worse than hunger was the terror, because we couldn't do
anything about it. The terror was always there, deep in our hearts. In the late
afternoon, wondering whether the soldiers would choose us as their victims. And
then feeling guilty when the soldiers took someone else. At night, blowing out our
tiny oil lanterns so the soldiers wouldn't notice the light and come investigate,
and then lying awake wondering whether we could see the dawn. Waking up the
next day and wondering whether it would be our last. (Haing 1987:289)

It was beyond suffering. (Ebihara 1993b:153)

'Plant a kapok tree' (*dăm daoem kor*). During Democratic Kampuchea (hereafter
DK), the genocidal period of Khmer Rouge rule (1975–79), this phrase floated
through Cambodian daily life in whispers and warnings. In Khmer, the term
for 'kapok tree', *kor*, is a homophone of the word *ko*, the third consonant in the
Khmer alphabet that has a secondary meaning of 'mute, muffled, and hollow'
(Headley et al 1977:113; Ponchaud 1977:89–90). A person who is mute is a
monŭss ko. The phrase 'plant a kapok tree' signified, therefore, that one had to
build a wall of silence in order to survive during this genocidal period, when
almost a quarter of the population perished from disease, starvation, overwork
or outright execution. Sometimes, the injunction was whispered between family
members and friends. In other situations, it might be invoked by a Khmer Rouge
cadre to advise someone how to act.

During DK, a large number of these tropes circulated, helping to create a
'semiotics of terror'. If the Khmer Rouge threatened 'To keep you is no gain;
to destroy you is no loss' and that 'Ângkar [the organisation] has the eyes of a
pineapple', the people whispered, 'Be careful—bodies disappear' or 'Ângkar
kills but never explains' (see Chandler 1991:260; Haing 1987:235; Locard
2004; Ponchaud 1978:65). Ultimately, one should 'See nothing, hear nothing,
know nothing and understanding nothing'. As such chilling phrases suggest,

life during DK approached the extremes of terror. Many Cambodians simply shut down, withdrawing inward in a sort of emotional constriction. Teeda Mam recalled how, 'Though talkative and friendly by nature, I had become wary and silent...I mentally reviewed everything before I spoke. It was best to play dumb. I tried never to stand out except by working extra hard'. The constant threat of death amplified such feelings. When people began to disappear mysteriously in her village, Teeda Mam explained how a

> black shroud of speechless horror enveloped me...Suspicion. Distrust. Gut-twisting terror. Each person clutched his thought more tightly to himself. Everyone worked harder. We dared not complain. Like walking dead men, we waited our turns in mute silence. Any person or event out of the ordinary filled us with panic (Criddle & Mam 1987:90–1, 151).

Fear, withdrawal, isolation and silence—such conditions are central to the experience of terror, an 'intense, overpowering fear' that is etymologically derived from the Indo-European root *tres-* 'to tremble' (*American* 1976:1329, 1546). This Indo-European root echoes Khmer idioms of terror, which are often expressed in terms of somatic symptoms and bodily metaphors of disequilibrium. How do we arrive at this state of 'trembling', that is at times paralysing and experienced at its extreme in genocide?

This paper represents an attempt to address such questions by examining DK terror through four frames, which I call 'modern terror', 'disciplinary terror', 'semiotic terror' and 'experiential terror'. These frames, which interrelate in various ways, are not posed as an all-encompassing framework by which to approach terror; they do, however, cast different types of light on some crucial dimensions of this murky phenomenon.

In this exercise, I draw heavily upon the work of May Ebihara, the first American anthropologist to have conducted ethnographic field work in a Cambodian village. Her research is crucial to any study of the Khmer Rouge period, since it provides a key reference point for understanding the background to socioeconomic changes implemented by the Khmer Rouge—changes that shaped the contours of DK terror. Moreover, after an initial visit in 1989, Ebihara returned to Svay, the Kandal village where she originally conducted research and, in the early 1990s, interviewed surviving villagers. Their accounts provide another vantage point onto the terror, the experience of which, villagers told her, was 'beyond suffering' (*huos vetonea)* (Ebihara 1993a:152). After discussing DK terror through these four frames, I conclude by returning to Ebihara's work to discuss some of the ways in which Cambodians have been affected by and responded to living in this time of terror.

The modernity of terror

While terror has been experienced in various ways through the ages, it has taken on particularly pernicious forms in the modern world. Modernity involves a proliferation of monetarised forms of exchange in the context of capitalism, the replacement of 'traditional' loyalties (to master, priest and king) with 'modern' ones (to secular authority) and a cultural shift from a predominantly religious worldview to an emphatically secular and materialist one; it is also characterised by the rise of secular forms of government, culminating in the nation-state (Hall et al 1995). The modern political state has assumed an unprecedented degree of centralised control and exercises enormous authority over its citizens through surveillance technology, its system of law and bureaucratic regulation, and its control over the means of force.

The nation-state offers advantages and does many positive things. However, it also has a brutal and even lethal potentiality, as illustrated by the genocidal violence and political terror that took place during the last century (Bauman 1989; Bodley 1999; Hinton 2002a; Scott 1998). Ironically, destruction has often been bound to an ideological dimension of modernity, the teleological myth of 'progress' and 'civilisation'. On the one hand, the human condition was portrayed as involving the inexorable march of progress from a state of savagery to civilisation. On the other hand, reason and science provided the means to facilitate this march through social engineering; human societies, like nature, could be mastered, reconstructed, and improved.

A given society's definition of these modern fetishes, however, involved a value-laden decision about what constituted an 'advance' and what the sought-after end should be. Many regimes, full of confidence that it knew the best way to achieve 'progress', implemented massive projects of social engineering. Like engineers, these regimes sought clarity, order and total control over the units they were manipulating.

The Khmer Rouge leadership embarked upon just such a course of social engineering, confident that the 'science' of Marxist–Leninism would enable them to revitalise Cambodia and create a communist utopia.[1] A 1977 speech that Pol Pot gave to commemorate the Party's 17th anniversary is illustrative in this regard, as it is suffused with high-modernist tropes of science and progress. Pol Pot declares that it was at the first Party Congress in 1960, when he and a small number of other committed revolutionaries were 'shut up in a room, without leaving' for three days and three nights, that the Party used 'scientific analysis' to establish the 'correct political line' (Pol Pot 1977:23–4). Pol Pot's subsequent explanation of how the Khmer Rouge 'analyzed and defined the real nature of Kampuchean society at that time', repeatedly invokes the expertise of the regime by emphasising how it used 'social science' and 'scientific analysis' to 'answer questions', to 'resolve' issues and find 'solutions', and reach correct analytical 'conclusions'.

Ultimately, the Party determined that Cambodian society was riven by two key 'contradictions'—a contradiction of a connection to foreign imperialism and an internal class contradiction between the oppressors and the oppressed. Because of its ability to use 'scientific analysis' to accurately diagnose and resolve these 'contradictions' through its 'correct line', the Party is portrayed as all-knowing, as constituting the 'correct and clear-sighted' leadership that 'sees' the truth. Such insight enables the Party to construct a blueprint that will 'resolve' Cambodia's problems by creating a new utopian society and 'guide' the people to this revitalising future in which they would escape oppression and became 'the true masters of their lands, the rice paddies, harvest, indeed, the fruits of their labor' (Pol Pot 1977).[2]

To achieve this goal, DK had to be reorganised in accordance with the political 'line' (*meakea*) that the Party Centre had ascertained by Marxist–Leninist science. This line called for a number of radical social, economic, and political transformations. To undermine the capitalist mode of production, the Khmer Rouge emptied the cities (bastions of capitalism and foreign influence), eliminated markets and the use of money, and collectivised economic production and consumption. Ideological mystification was to be combated through political education and a ban on the practice of Buddhism and other forms of worship. Ultimately, everyone had to work hard to 'build' a proper revolutionary consciousness. 'Private' leanings—toward family member or religion, and even signs of personal vanity—had to be replaced by a collective stand of renunciation and complete Party loyalty.

These changes are vividly detailed in a series of Ebihara's articles (1990a; 1993a; 1993b; 2002) contrasting life before and during DK. Her informants' accounts are of particular interest since the villagers had to flee Svay in the early 1970s, because of nearby fighting. Most moved to Phnom Penh and only returned to the Svay area when the Khmer Rouge rusticated urban populations. Where the village had once stood, they 'found a bombed-out landscape that was now largely wilderness' (Ebihara 1993a:152). The Khmer term they used for 'wilderness', *prei*, is symbolically loaded, implying that which is untamed, uncultivated or undomesticated (Chandler 1996). In this case, Ebihara (2002:95) notes, *prei* also signifies liminality, a transition from 'between the old society and the DK regime that inverted or destroyed most of the villagers' former ways of life and thrust them into a new revolutionary order'. Many DK killings also took place in the liminal space of the *prei*.

These changes tore apart the traditional foundations of village life. When villagers were eventually allowed to reinhabit Svay, they found it renamed 'New Village' and incorporated as a communal system in which property, production, and consumption—key to familial solidarity—were all collectivised. The long-term bases of family and village solidarity were undermined further in other ways. Meals were now eaten in communal mess halls. In many places, the Party oversaw marriage. Family members were commonly separated daily, and sometimes for weeks or months at a time, as they laboured on work teams segregated by age and gender. In keeping with their ban on Buddhism and other forms of worship, the Khmer Rouge blew up the Svay village temple and used the debris 'to fill the *vat*'s pond to cultivate plants' (Ebihara 2002:95). Village solidarity was further shattered by population dispersals. If villagers from 25 of the 32 households in the Svay hamlet were able to return at the beginning of DK, over half of the families were eventually relocated (Ebihara 1993a:153).

Little did the villagers know that these changes were centrally-mandated on the basis of the Party 'line', the basis of a Four-Year Plan that would enable Cambodia to make a 'super great leap forward' with unprecedented speed and success. Thus, Cambodia would move 'from a backward agriculture to a modern one in from five to ten years, and from an agricultural base to an industrial one in between fifteen to twenty years' (Chandler, Kiernan & Boua 1988:124).[3] Rice production was to double by the end of 1980, as the national average yield immediately rose to three tons per hectare—from a pre-revolutionary average of less than one ton per hectare. These goals would be attained by bringing new land under cultivation, double- and triple-cropping, building new irrigation networks, and working harder and longer hours.

Unfortunately, the Four-Year Plan ignored such issues as 'shortages of high quality seed, livestock and agricultural tools, as well as the absence of chemical fertilisers and pesticides—to say nothing about marketing mechanisms, transport, milling, cash incentives and the havoc of the recently concluded civil war (Chandler, Kiernan & Boua 1988:39),[4] including a number of demographic and ecological changes. Local realities were often brushed aside, as when centrally-planned irrigation projects were constructed without the advice of engineers or local peasants who knew the terrain. While some of these irrigation projects worked, many collapsed, broke down or never functioned properly—after thousands of Cambodians had performed backbreaking labour for long hours to build them, some perishing in the process.

Existing forms of irrigation were frequently replaced by symmetrical grids of paddy fields surrounded by dykes and canals. This type of simplified, checkerboard design, favoured by many high-modernist regimes for its 'rational' shape, legibility and ability to be monitored and controlled centrally, ignored local conditions to which the old agricultural system had been adapted by knowledgeable farmers.[5] When Ebihara returned to Svay in 1990, evidence of these agricultural schemes could still be seen:

> Walking in Svay's rice-fields, I saw evidence of DK's massive attempts to increase and rationalise agricultural production throughout the countryside... [DK] attempted to reconfigure the landscape with large dams and extensive irrigation systems...laid out in neat grids. South of Svay there are still traces of the enormous rectangular paddies that consolidated and smoothed over the small plots of varied shapes and sizes typical of former times (Ebihara 2002:96).

As Scott (1998) has suggested, high-modernist authoritarian regimes often run into trouble because their abstract schemes for 'progress' may be at odds with local-level realities and make unrealistic assumptions about what is possible. This is precisely what happened to the DK regime, as their unrealistic rice quotas failed to be met, their agricultural project often ended in collapse, and the large numbers of the overworked and underfed population began to fall ill and starve. Many local cadres were unable to meet the huge, inflexible production quotas established by the Party Centre as irrigation projects failed, infrastructure problems were encountered, paddy fields failed to produce 'three tons per hectare', and people were literally worked to death. Fearing the wrath of their superiors, such cadres often falsified their reports to act as if the quotas had been attained. Rice that should have been set aside for consumption was sent to Phnom Penh, where Pol Pot and his colleagues proudly reallocated it for other purposes, including export. In many regions, the result was starvation rations that led to decreased productivity, disease, illness and death.

When members of the Party Centre began to discover the truth about the production failures and horrendous living conditions, they suspected that subversive elements—not their unreasonable schemes—were to blame. For the Khmer Rouge, people, like livestock and animals, were units to be controlled and manipulated from above. If an area of Cambodia needed to be brought under cultivation, people would be sent there. If problems arose, it was necessary to look at the 'composition' of various 'elements' of the population, since blame could not be placed upon the 'enlightened' Party Centre and its political 'line'. Thus, a December 1976 political speech, thought to have been given by Pol Pot, states that:

> hidden enemies seek to deprive the people of food, while following our orders to an extent...They take our circular instructions and use them to mistreat the people and to deprive them, forcing them to work, whether they are sick or healthy.[6]

The existence of such 'hidden enemies', in turn, further confirmed the necessity of the political purges that were already underway.

It is tempting to say that the Khmer Rouge terror increased as the regime lost support among the people and searched for hidden enemies. There is certainly some truth in this suggestion. However, the Khmer Rouge had used terror to implement their plans during the civil war even in areas in which they had support (Quinn 1976). The use of terror to control the population may have been modeled on practices of other revolutionaries, particularly Lenin, Mao and Stalin. Upon taking power, socialist governments often find themselves in the position of implementing structural reforms (eliminating private property, undermining religion and establishing co-operatives) that are unpopular among a populace that has not yet absorbed its ideology. Terror provides an effective means, at least in the short term, of enforcing compliance under such circumstances.

More broadly, we might argue that control is key to the link between modernity and terror. Given an increased centralisation of power, the modern nation-state has an unprecedented ability to impose its will upon its subjects. Democratic institutions may provide an effective counterbalance to the negative potentialities of such control, though state terror has and continues to be perpetrated in the name of democracy (Mann 2005; Sluka 2000).

Disciplinary terror

One of the distinctive characteristics of the modern nation-state is the enormous control it exercises over its subjects. To varying degrees, people are registered, observed, tracked, constrained and coerced. In the modern world, the limits of 'democracy' and 'freedom' are coextensive with the parameters of bureaucracy and law. For high-modernist regimes, control over human bodies is crucial to the success of its projects of social engineering, since their projects are premised on a new order and arrangement of these 'units'. By 'disciplinary terror', I refer to ways in which the regulation and arrangement of human bodies contribute to terror, both through the conditions of life these arrangements produce and through the institutional spaces of terror that these arrangements establish (Foucault 1979). While there are broad continuities that emerge from shared links to 'modern' forms of knowledge, such disciplines are structured by local forms of knowledge.

For the Khmer Rouge, these arrangements of human bodies were linked to the concept of *kar chăt tăng*, a compound that can mean 'assignment' (as in duties), but often implied a broader conception of 'organisation' during DK. As noted above, this organisational dimension of the DK Party 'line' involved the transformation of Cambodia's traditional political, religious and economic structures. It was only by arranging people in a radically new manner, which implied new ways of living, working, behaving and thinking, that progressive revolutionaries could be produced. This is the first of two types of organisation discussed in a 1976 issue of the CPK party magazine, *Revolutionary flags*: 'The first...is to establish collectives, strengthen, expand, improve, purify our collective [organisation]...Live collectively, manage collectively, work collectively, lead collectively...Assault private property...It will not have time to breathe...This is a strategic measure, a basic measure'.[7] Proper organisation would lead to proper consciousness, and vice versa.

On the local level, 'organisation' implied collectivisation and obedience. The adult population was organised into sexually-segregated work 'forces', that performed a variety of agricultural and construction tasks. The work hours were extremely long and the labour physically arduous, particularly given that communal food rations were often minimal. Under such conditions, many people died of overwork, starvation or both.

These themes were emphasised by Ebihara's informants, and this is particularly interesting because, despite the fact that they were 'already familiar with agriculture and accustomed to manual labor, a spartan diet and meager living conditions', the villagers 'found life in DK to be as horrendous as did city people for more comfortable socieconomic strata' (Ebihara 1993a:152). The villagers complained to her that food was available, but was transported away instead of being given to them. By 1977, the villagers were subsisting on rice gruel and in constant hunger. One of Ebihara's informants told her:

> We worked so hard planting and harvesting; there were piles of rice as big as this house, but they took it away in trucks...We raised chickens and ducks and vegetables and fruit, but they took it all. You'd be killed if you tried to take anything for yourself. You could *see* food, but you weren't allowed to eat it (Ebihara 2002:101).

Despite minimal nourishment, villagers were required to perform backbreaking labour with minimal rest. Regardless of whether they were cultivating rice or digging dirt for an irrigation project, the Svay villagers emphasised the difficulty of their task:[8]

> You'd carry heavy loads, fall down, get up and fall again...Even when you were sick, you didn't dare stop working because they'd kill you. So you kept working until you collapsed. You'd come back at night, brush off your feet, and fall into bed...You'd lie awake thinking of all the people who had died...You lay there and wept (Ebihara 1993a:156).

Even when this incessant work was finished or the Svay villagers were given a day of rest, they were still expected to attend political meetings and participate in criticism and self-criticism sessions regularly.

Organisation entailed obedience, since only a person with regressive 'private' traits would try to avoid an assignment. Ultimately, the key to survival was to suppress any sign of 'privatism', which implied that one had a 'sick consciousness'. Interpersonal communication was severely curtailed, both because the populace didn't have access to telephones or a postal service and because terror curtailed interaction. One's personal connections were further diminished because family members often separated. Moreover, the DK regime took over many familial functions, ranging from the provision of food to the arrangement of marriages. To travel anywhere, one had to obtain a permit. In all of these ways, the DK regime regulated the bodies of their subjects, who were expected to work hard, survive on whatever rations were distributed and unquestioningly obey whatever orders were given to them. A progressive revolutionary didn't complain.

The Party Centre recognised that many people, such as the 'bad elements' who were too immersed in a 'private stand', would have trouble transforming their bodies and minds to the new system. Accordingly, the second dimension of 'organisation' involved surveying and punishing these regressive elements of the population. If 'mistakes [might] be straightened out by political-consciousness, by warnings, criticism and education', there also had to be organisational 'measures to purify our statepower so that it is clean, tough and strong. To purify out the enemy among the people, to be clean, to be good, to be tough, to be strong' (Jackson 1989:286, 282). Proper organisation, therefore, entailed constant surveillance. People were categorised at checkpoints and through the writing of life histories. Local cadres kept ledgers listing personal information about the people under their control, including their former occupation and class background. This biographical information was supplemented by close observation. Armed soldiers and cadres kept a close eye on the populace throughout and spies moved about searching for signs of subversion. The phrase 'Ângkar has the eyes of the pineapple' captured the atmosphere of constant surveillance during DK; the 'all-knowing' Party could see everywhere, even into the most private of spaces, even into one's mind.

The DK regime created new institutions to 'purify' the populace. Those people who displayed regressive tendencies might be 'rebuilt'—DK ideology was pervaded by metaphors of construction—through political education, manual labour and frequent criticism and self-criticism sessions. This process of reeducation was sometimes likened to the process by which metal is placed under intense heat and pounded into a new shape. Teeda Mam recalled, 'If, after heating and hammering into shape, [a person] still refused to conform, they were either "reheated" in the fire of evening political meetings and everyday struggle, or disposed of' (Criddle & Mam 1987:101). As these comments suggest, the Khmer Rouge also employed more lethal disciplines of terror to 'purify' the new society. Death squads roamed the villages at night, making arrests. Some of the victims were taken to one of the numerous local, regional or national prisons, where they might be tortured into confessing their 'crimes'. Other people were loaded into trucks, often with their entire family, and killed *en masse* at local extermination centres. In still other cases, a group of victims might be taken out into the forest, executed, and dumped in a mass grave. The death of the victims was often silently announced by their absence the next day. While no-one knows exactly how many people this Khmer Rouge network of death annihilated, it is almost certain that hundreds of thousands of Cambodians were killed in this manner. The 'bad compositions' who were targeted for purification included class 'enemies', 'traitors' from the ranks of the Khmer Rouge themselves, members of various ethnic minorities and people who had simply made 'mistakes'.

One of the striking things that emerges from Ebihara's research is the extremely high death rate of the Svay villagers, even if, as urban evacuees, the majority of them were considered 'new people' or 'April 17 people' and thus more likely to receive harsh treatment and come under suspicion during DK. She notes:

> In 1960, West Svay had some 159 inhabitants. Speaking now only of these people, sixteen died during the 1960s of old age or illness. Four died in the early 1970s because of the civil war. Thus, in 1975, at the beginning of DK, 139 people were left—of whom some seventy (fifty percent) died during DK…[meaning that] only sixty-four out of 139 people managed to survive the Pol Pot period (Ebihara 1993b:57, 58).

Some died of starvation; others were executed. In any event, Ebihara argues that this 50% mortality rate should caution us against assuming in any sort of straightforward way that peasants always had it easier than urbanites during DK.

The semiotics of terror

Semiotics is concerned with signs and semantics, and the semiotics of terror can be said to encompass those free-floating discourses—ranging from explicit ideology to colloquial idioms—and nonverbal behaviour that help generate an atmosphere of terror (see also Scarry 1985; Suárez-Orozco 1990). A saying here, a glance there—these words and gestures carve out spaces of terror in the flow of daily life. 'Be careful—bodies disappear'. 'Ângkar kills—but never explains'. These are injunctions to regulate one's behaviour in order to escape the ever-present threat of death.

What were some of the ways in which Khmer Rouge ideological discourse helped constitute this semiotics of terror? Violence, or the threat of it, pervaded Khmer Rouge discourse, which glorified those who 'defended' the country by 'crushing' hidden enemies. The DK national anthem began: 'Blood red blood that covers towns and plains/ Of Kampuchea, our motherland,/ Sublime blood of workers and peasants,/ Sublime blood of revolutionary men and woman fighters!/ The blood, changing into unrelenting hatred/ And resolute struggle…'. Similarly, the Khmer Rouge flag was red and exalted in 'The Red Flag' song, often sung in unison before meetings:

> Glittering red blood blankets the earth—blood given up to liberate the people: the blood of workers, peasants and intellectuals; blood of young men, Buddhist monks and girls.
>
> The blood swirls away and flows upward, gently, into the sky,
>
> turning into a red, revolutionary flag.
>
> Red flag! red flag! flying now! flying now!
>
> O beloved friends, pursue, strike and hit the enemy.
>
> Red flag! red flag! flying now! flying now!
>
> Don't leave a single reactionary imperialist (alive): drive them from Kampuchea.
>
> Strive and strike, strive and strike, and win the victory, win the victory! (Chandler, Kiernan & Lim 1976:14)

Other Khmer Rouge songs, as well as music and dance, contained similar themes and imagery (Marston 2002b; Shapiro 1994; 2002).

This ideological glorification of violence and revolutionary struggle extended to everyday life, which was often described in military metaphors that likened society to an army at war (Marston 1994:112; see also Ponchaud 1978). Just as an enemy would be defeated in battle, so, too, would the revolutionary spirit of the people 'defeat' the problems the country was facing and enable them to 'become masters of the lands, the rice paddies, harvests, indeed, of the fruits of their labor' (Pol Pot 1977:57, 60, 61). Units (*kâng*) of workers from the cooperatives were sent to 'launch offensives' (*veay sâmrŏk*), 'struggle' (*brâyŭt*) and 'fight heroically' (*tâsou*) on the economic 'front lines' (*sâmârâphoum mŭkh*). As Haing Ngor explained:

> 'Struggle' was military talk, like 'front lines'. It reflected the idea that the nation was still at war. On the front lines we didn't just work, we 'struggled', or else 'launched offensives'…The goal of this struggling and launching of offensives was 'victory' (Haing 1987:197).

As economic problems mounted and paranoia within the Party Centre heightened, DK radio broadcasts, speeches, and publications increasingly spoke of the need to root out hidden enemies who were subverting the revolution from within. On the one hand, such rhetoric 'manufactured difference' by constructing essentialised categories of identity and belonging. These reified images are a crucial part of violence, terror, and genocide, as they provide a set of binary oppositions that distinguish 'us' from the 'enemy' in situations in which there is often enormous uncertainty and ambiguity about identity. For example, the Khmer Rouge published an essay, later played on domestic radio, that attempted to lay out who belonged to the revolutionary community:

Who are 'we?'

> It is necessary to draw a clear line between us and the enemy and stand on our side to make the revolution. First of all, let us determine who we are. 'We' means our nation, people, worker-peasant class, revolution, collective system of the proletariat, cooperatives, trade unions, Revolutionary Army and KCP. The 'enemy' includes imperialist aggressors and lackeys of all stripes; the enemy has the intention of annexing and swallowing our territory; the enemy which is planted within our revolutionary ranks; the enemy in the for[m] of the feudal-capitalist and landowner classes and other oppressor classes; the enemy in the form of private and individualist system; and particularly, the expansionist, annexationist Vietnamese enemy.

While the language in this passage resonates with many dimensions of Khmer Rouge ideology (Hinton 2005), it quite directly invokes a series of simplified binary oppositions between 'us' and 'the enemy', who range from traitors in the revolutionary ranks to capitalist 'elements' that had not yet been eradicated from the new society.

Part of the power of this semiotics of terror comes from the way it uses metaphors of purity and contamination (see also Hinton 2002b). Yet another Khmer Rouge tract asserts that a person who was 'honest' (*smaoh trâng*) with the DK regime would continuously and relentlessly struggle to 'clean up' (*baos sâmat*) hidden enemies burrowing from within and purify various bad compositions so that they are completely gone, cleansed from inside the ranks of our revolution, Party and revolutionary youth. In this passage, as in so much other Khmer Rouge discourse, DK is metaphorically portrayed as being marked off by a permeable boundary, one that ideally separated 'us' from 'them' (Ponchaud 1977:138). Unfortunately, the tract argues, the proper state of order had been violated by 'hidden enemies burrowing from within' and 'bad compositions'. To restore a proper state of order, DK society had to be purified; the enemies had to eradicated so that they would be 'completely gone'. This, I argue, is a call for genocide. What helps make such ideology so effective is its resonance with bodily experience. Perpetrators have a powerful embodied understanding of what it means to be invaded by impure forces that threaten one's very survival, though these understandings take on culture-specific forms (for instance, Khmer conceptions of bodily equilibrium being threatened by a host of invading forces, ranging from spirits to obstructing substances (Eisenbruch

1992; Hinton & Ba 2001a; 2001b)). Such imagery was not just invoked by the Khmer Rouge leadership; it was reiterated on the local level by cadres and affirmed by frequent 'cleansings.'

The semiotics of terror, however, is not confined to spoken language; it also involves nonverbal behaviour, such as the way people move, walk, dress, look, stare, gesture and comport themselves. In Cambodia, such nonverbal behaviour is extremely salient, since much communication is indirect. Relative status, for example, is not just acknowledged through hierarchical speech registers, but also through gesture and posture (Marston 1997; see also Hinton 2005). While the Khmer Rouge transformed the social hierarchy, relative standing continued to be expressed in modified forms. When survival is on the line, such expressions take on an overwhelming importance, as one must take care not to give offence to those who have the power to let you live or die.

Many Cambodians responded to this situation, as I said, by 'planting a kapok tree', or erecting a wall of silence and attempting to avoid potentially dangerous interactions. Likewise, since spies might be listening underneath the bamboo slats of one's house at night, people had to communicate in silence through movements of their hands and eyes (see, for example, Moyer 1991:84). The gaze was another locus of terror, as a cadre's stare meant that one was visible and under threat. For this reason, Cambodians continue to speak of how they were afraid to even look at the Khmer Rouge's faces.

Terror was also encoded in images and events: the sight of a line of 'enemies' being led away in chains at twilight, the redistribution of the clothes of the dead or the experience of stumbling across a mass grave. One of Ebihara's informants recalled how, after the Khmer Rouge caught a man who had dug up some potatoes, they:

> made him wear the potatoes around his neck and beat him while he was paraded around the village. They...tied him up and got in a circle around him and struck him until he fell, and then they kicked and beat him some more; even female cadres hit him. He went almost crazy from the beating (Ebihara 2002:101).

For those who, like this man, were arrested and faced imminent death, of course, the semantics of terror took on an even more extreme form (see Hinton 2005:213–14).

Experiential terror

Foucault (1979; 1980) has suggested that the modern state characteristically creates a more completely 'transparent' society that it may oversee with its 'dominating, overseeing gaze'. This 'eye of power', epitomised by Jeremy

Bentham's panopticon, enables the state to impose its will on its subjects through the sorts of DK 'disciplines' I noted earlier—control over bodily movements and functions, over the arrangement and distribution of bodies, over appropriate forms of knowledge, over the very formation of the self. In this pursuit of legibility and control, however, the state is haunted by the 'fear of darkened spaces', the most invisible of which is, of course, the inner thoughts and feelings of people. Therefore, the state attempts to extend its 'eye of power' into even these dark recesses by forcing its subjects to 'interiorise' its gaze so that each person 'is his own overseer, each individual thus exercising this surveillance over, and against, himself' (Foucault 1980:155). It is at this point of interiorisation that the DK regime can be viewed as embodying a number of interrelated tendencies: the high-modern desire for the legibility and control that will enable it to carry out its ambitious social projects; the overseer's panoptic desire to expand his or her gaze so that it reaches into the darkest of spatial, corporeal and mental spaces; and the terrorist's willingness to use fear and coercion to achieve these goals. Meanwhile, the populace lived in a macabre liminal space that such millennial movements often create (see Ledgerwood 1990:209f).

What was it like to live in these spaces of terror and death? We can get a sense of this by examining the practice of discipline and the semiotics of terror, since these structured the lives of the terrorised. Foucault (1980) has argued that the condition of extreme terror is characterised by the feeling of isolation, loneliness and impotence. In the extreme case, the terrorised are incapacitated, unable to act. This is the point at which the terroriser achieves enormous control, though, of course, it is never complete and forever challenged by resistance arising out of new order.[9] The semiotics of terror captures these features of terror: the 'eye of power' parallels the saying 'Ângkar has the eyes of the pineapple'; atomisation is implicit in the DK saying 'plant a kapok tree'. And, of course, there is the fear, the 'trembling' that terror causes.

To understand the experience of terror, however, we must at some point turn to the accounts of those who have lived through the terror, such as Ebihara's informants. Fear and consciousness of death emerge as central themes (Ebihara 1993a; 1993b), particularly after the executions intensified in 1977. One man from Svay noted the effect these killings had upon people:

> From 1977 on, people were taken away to be killed (*veay chaol*). Many died at a prison [to the south] that was a headquarters of the Pol Pot people. [After DK] they found lots of corpses in a ditch; some of them still had ropes on their hands and feet and blindfolds on their eyes. [One day in 1977, seven men in Sobay (Svay)] were taken away. [The Khmer Rouge] said, 'Come on, load up everything, you're being taken to build houses.' They lied. They didn't tell you they were going to kill you; they said you're going to work. But I knew. C [one of

the young men being taken] also knew. He cried and embraced his father. I went up to C, and he said to me, 'We're about to be separated now; I'm going.' When people were taken away, I knew in my heart they were going to die. I knew when they were taken away with their hands tied behind their backs, but also when they were called away to work. I kept thinking, when will *I* be taken away? But you couldn't ask, and you couldn't run away—or even kill yourself—because then they'd get your wife and children (Ebihara 1993a:157).

I kept thinking, when will I be taken way? And there was nothing a person could do about it. As this man's remembrance suggests, the experience of terror during DK was closely linked to the constant threat that one would be killed. Suddenly a person would be told *you're going to work* and that was it.

Friends and family members disappeared at random, usually leaving uncertainty about their fate that mirrored the fear and uncertainty about one's own. As one woman from Svay told Ebihara, 'Every morning you were grateful to have survived another night, and on the way to work you stole glances at the other work teams to see if your children were still alive' (Ebihara 1993b:57). And then, as Haing Ngor describes in the epigraph that began this essay, people immediately began to worry about whether or not they would survive until the next day. Amplifying this extreme existential uncertainty were the broader conditions of life during DK: the constant hunger, the loss of basic rights, illness, the (real or perceived) sense that one was constantly being surveyed, the extension of state control over most aspects of life, the spies that eavesdropped under houses at night, uncertainty about who was one's friend or enemy, the loss of traditional pillars of stability (religion, village solidarity, familial cohesion, economic life) and so forth.

Plant a kapok tree. Be careful—bodies disappear. Ângkar has the eyes of the pineapple. This was the world of terror that Cambodians like the villagers in Svay inhabited, a world in which many people withdrew, became silent and trembled—fearful of a cadre's glance, of making a 'mistake', of being labeled a 'bad element', of being taken away, of being tortured, of being 'purified', of becoming one of the 'disappeared', of becoming another one of the bodies in the killing fields.

The phrase 'plant a kapok tree' takes on new significance in this light, epitomising the emotional and interpersonal constriction that was required to survive DK. Thus, Haing Ngor's father warned his son:

From now on, keep your mouth shut. Plant a kapok tree. *Dăm doeum kor*. No matter what happens, don't give them any excuse to take you away again...So plant your kapok tree, son. Be patient, be quiet and stay clam. One day, sooner or later, the revolution will be overturned (Haing 1987:253; see also 258, 266, 310).

Similarly, one of Ebihara's informants explained, 'I survived because I worked very hard and didn't say anything, so they couldn't blame me [for anything]' (Ebihara 2002:101).

But the phrase has other important connotations that demonstrate how, even in situation of atomisation and terror, people remain meaning-constructing beings, responding to and acting within their difficult conditions of life. Thus, although it had been officially banned, Buddhism nevertheless continued to provide an important reservoir of meaning upon which Cambodians drew during DK. Many people came to see their plight in terms of *karma*, as a cosmic consequence of their own (or sometimes even their country's) bad actions in the past (see, for example, Haing 1987:157, 312). Some viewed what was going on as the fulfillment of Buddhist millenarian prophecies, such as well-known Buddhist predictions (*put tŭmneay*). Many of these foretold a time when demons or members of the lowest rungs of Khmer society would take over and invert the social order, leading to an assault on Buddhism and widespread famine and death (see Ledgerwood 1990; Smith 1989).

In fact, the phrase 'plant a kapok tree' seems to have been taken from just such a prophecy, as Pin Yathay (1987:91) explains:

> Puth was a nineteenth-century sage who prophesied that the country would undergo a total reversal of traditional values, that the houses and the streets would be emptied, that the illiterate would condemn the educated, that infidels—*thmils*—would hold absolute power and persecute the priests. But people would be saved if they planted a kapok tree—*kor*, in Cambodian. *Kor* also means 'mute.' The usual interpretation of this enigmatic message was that only the deaf-mutes would be saved during this period of calamity. Remain deaf and mute. Therein, I now realized, lay the means of survival. Pretend to be deaf and dumb! Say nothing, hear nothing, understand nothing!

On a cosmological level, such prophecies played upon Khmer understandings of purity and contamination, which are in part structured in terms of the opposition between the Buddha and demons, *dhamma* and *adhamma*, order and disorder, coherence and fragmentation (Hinton 2002b; see also Kapferer 1988).

The phrase also had other ontological resonances as well. In Khmer, the feeling of terror is expressed in various ways, often through the use of compounds that signify an intensification of meaning (*phăy năh, pĭt phăy, phay khlach, ronthŭot, phăy ronthŭot, phăy tăk slŏt, slŏt slŭan, chĕtt ronthŭot, nhor ronthŭot*). The experience of terror is also experienced through somatic idioms. In Khmer ethno-psychology, for example, health is linked to the proper flow of wind (*khyâl*) through the body (Hinton & Ba 2001a; 2001b). When persons don't feel well (*mĭn sruol khluon*) or are 'dizzy' (*vĭl*), they will often 'coin', 'cup', pinch or massage themselves to remove obstructions and regain proper flow. In more severe cases, a person may suffer form 'wind overload' (*khyâl kor*), a culture-bound syndrome in which, in the classic version, 'a person lies supine, the eyes open and aware of the surroundings, but is unable to move or speak' (Hinton & Ba 2001a:419).

Interestingly, the term *kor* (meaning 'to pile up' in the context of wind overload) is the same term used in the phrase 'plant a kapok tree' (*dăm daoem kor*) that carries the double connotation of kapok tree and, through its auditory closeness to the consonant *ko*, muteness. Moreover, the classic version of the wind-overload syndrome mirrors somatically the state of terror and emotional constriction that so many Cambodians report experiencing during DK. In a clinical study of patients at an outpatient clinic, over a third (36%) of the patients had experienced wind overload and of these over half (56%) experienced wind overload during DK; many more had witnessed an episode during this period (Hinton & Ba 2001b).[10] What I am suggesting here is that this somatic syndrome ontologically resonates both with the DK saying 'plant a kapok tree' and, more broadly through the experience, witnessing, or hearing stories about episodes of wind overload, with the incapacitating experience of terror that many people felt during DK. And, at least for Cambodian-Americans in one clinic, wind overload continues to be a signifier of DK terror.

'Beyond suffering': Cambodians in the aftermath of genocide

To conclude, I would like to consider how DK terror has had an impact on survivors from places like Svay. As the above discussion of wind overload suggests, many Cambodians suffered from somatic symptoms after DK. While these may be linked to other factors, such as poor health care, poverty, continued war and domestic abuse, many Cambodians report suffering from ailments that they link to DK. This emerges clearly in Ebihara's research in Svay where, she reports, villagers suffer from:

Constant fatigue, difficulty walking, weak limbs, faulty memories, impaired vision and other physical problems that are due to the beatings or overwork endured during DK. They often note such difficulties as:

My legs are still weak; sometimes they collapse and I fall down. They beat me on the head, shoulders, and back; I never recovered, and now I can't lift heavy things. I've forgotten how to read or write Khmer since Pol Pot. I'm still sick in the chest.

People also explain the deaths of several villagers in the 1980s as due to illnesses caused by conditions under Pol Pot. They also say that one villager, who was relocated during DK to a distant province with especially harsh conditions and saw most of her family die, went 'crazy' from grief. At present, though she functions quite capably in daily life, she herself feels that DK made her emotionally unstable, noting that 'sometimes I laugh or cry for no good reason.' I see, however, no other evidence of mental instability in Svay, although many villagers doubtless carry deep psychic wounds from DK that are perhaps somaticized as various ailments (Ebihara & Ledgerwood 2002:102–3; see also Ebihara 1993b:59).

While cautioning us against invoking a common stereotype of post-DK Cambodia as a land of traumatised, dysfunctional people (Ebihara & Ledgerwood 2002), Ebihara notes that some of her informants appear to 'carry deep psychic wounds from DK' that are expressed through somatic idioms including, I suspect, syndromes such as wind overload.

After DK, people throughout Cambodia returned home only to find villages and homes that had been destroyed or radically change. Ebihara and Ledgerwood (2002) note that these 'landscapes of memory' were imbued with personal and cultural meaning. In Svay, like many villages throughout Cambodia, reminders of the civil war and DK were found at every turn (Ebihara & Ledgerwood 2002:95–7): a road now pockmarked by potholes and divots; an overabundance of small, thatch houses low to the ground (as opposed to the traditional Khmer houses made of wood and raised high on pilings); rice fields reshaped into a grid-like design and marked here and there by traces of Khmer Rouge irrigation projects; the ruins of a shaded temple that had once served as a key centre of social life; a disproportionate number of widows and female-headed households due to higher male mortality during DK (Ebihara & Ledgerwood 2002:278); and a former teacher-training centre, 'now roofless, crumbling walls scarred by bullet holes and artillery, their gaping window frames like eye sockets in a skull' (Ebihara & Ledgerwood 2002:97). Perhaps most evocative of all were mass graves where the bodies of the dead were found and the memorials in which their skulls and bones were placed, some still bound by cloth blindfolds or ties. When Ebihara returned to one of these memorials near Svay with a villager, he

> softly recited the names of his kinsmen who had probably been killed here. Gazing at the pile of skulls, it was devastating to think that some of the remains might be people we had personally known. At one corner of the platform stand a small statue of Buddha and offerings of incense, expressions of compassion and mourning in this grim scene (Ebihara 1993b:51).

Over time, this landscape of memory has shifted. Change accompanied the end of the Cold War, the initial State of Cambodia move away from socialism, peace accords, the arrival of UNTAC and elections, massive foreign aid, development projects and increased connections to the diaspora. In and around Svay the main roads have been repaired, new traditional-style houses constructed, temples rebuilt, the gender balance largely restored and the bombed-out teacher-training centre rebuilt (Ebihara & Ledgerwood 2002). Despite such changes,

Cambodians have by no means forgotten the terror of DK life—even if there was much talk about 'national reconciliation' during the 1990s. The memorials still stand and, on holidays like the 'Day to Remain Tied in Anger' and 'Day of Liberation', people continue to commemorate the genocidal past. And, most recently, the publicity surrounding the creation of the Extraordinary Chambers of the Courts of Cambodia has led to greater dialogue about DK in Cambodia. The post-PRK massive resurgence of Buddhism in particular has helped many people to cope with the past, as monks treat the afflicted (for example, by teaching them breathing and meditation techniques, by listening to and advising them or by sprinkling them with holy water) and provide ritual means to commemorate the dead during holidays like *phchŭm běn*, by reciting scripture and transferring merit, and by sprinkling holy water on the remains of the dead. Ebihara's invaluable work documents how village life changed during and after DK and provides us with a crucial, on-the-ground understanding of the experience and aftermaths of DK terror. For this, we all owe her our deepest thanks.

Notes

1   As Marston (2002a) has argued, it is too easy to simply say that the Khmer Rouge were 'modern'. For example, DK lacked many of the things commonly associated with modernity, such as advanced technology and telecommunications, industry, and an extensive bureaucracy, Moreover, personal ties remained central to sociopolitical organisation, and Khmer Rouge ideology glorified the peasant and manual labour. Marston's points are well-taken, though, as he notes, by no means do they preclude a reading of DK in terms of modernity. Any conception of the 'modern' requires a notion of the 'tradition' and, I would add, almost all societies, including the US, ideologically foreground the traditional in certain contexts. Here, I argue that Khmer Rouge discourse and ideology was heavily informed by what Marston calls a 'vision' or 'aesthetic' of modernity, one that had direct implications in policy and, ultimately, the creation of an environment in which terror was pervasive.

2   See also various documents in Chandler, Kiernan & Boua (1988).

3   The plan itself is translated in Chandler, Kiernan & Boua (1988:36–119). For an analysis of the plan, see Chandler (1999a:55–6; 1999b:114f.).

4   On the demographic and ecological changes caused by the war, see Chandler (1999b:115).

5   Scott (1998) argues that high-modernist schemes often fail precisely because they favour rationality and centralised control over local knowledge and practices. The DK case clearly supports his claim. See Pijpers (1989) for an analysis of how the Khmer Rouge creation of a grid-like system of paddy fields, dykes and canals often led to problems—both during and after DK—because they ignored local variations in soil quality, topographical conditions and climate. The Khmer Rouge also attempted to standardise rice, leading to the loss of strains of rice that were adapted to local

conditions; see also Yathay (1987:63). Many of these were later reintroduced into Cambodia by the International Rice Research Institute (Ledgerwood, Ebihara & Mortland 1994:3).

6   'Report of activities of the Party center according to the general political tasks of 1976', in Chandler, Kiernan & Boua (1988:207).

7   'Sharpen the consciousness of the proletarian class to be as keen and strong as possible', in Jackson (1989:286).

8   Their work included: 'building large irrigation systems with hard labor, reshaping paddy fields into huge plots of uniform size, serving as human draft animals to pull plows when oxen were not available, growing successive crops of rice in regions were irrigation enabled multiple cropping (in contrast to the mono-cropping that had been typical of pre-revolutionary Sobay), making fertiliser from a mixture of human excrement, cow dung and other ingredients, cultivating vegetables and fruit trees, tending animals and poultry, making mats and thatch and so on. No sooner was one task finished than people were dispatched to other work' (Ebihara 1993b:56).

9   Even in the extreme context of the DK, Cambodians also found ways to actively or passively resist the regime, an example of what Foucault calls 'revolts against the gaze'. Some forms of resistance, while extremely dangerous, were crucial to survival: stealing or foraging for food to supplement the insufficient diet, trading for food or medicine on the illegal black market; lying about one's past and adopting a poor peasant identity; forging a fake pass to escape a particularly harsh locale or, to save strength, not fully exerting oneself. In other situations, Cambodians resisted the structural transformation of the Khmer Rouge. If a loved one died or was killed, for example, the family would secretly mourn or even perform clandestine funeral rites. People often found ways to return home for brief periods to visit parents, spouses or children whom they missed. Some family members also rebelled against communal dining and reasserted the family bond by sharing precious food items they managed to procure. Still other Cambodians resisted the DK regime's attempt to rebuild their thoughts and emotions by mocking or deriding Khmer Rouge cadres or their ideology. These 'hidden transcripts'—which often involved indirection, innuendo and the use of puns—were most frequently said to oneself, muttered under one's breath or quietly shared with a few friends or family members. Such acts of resistance may also help people cope with the difficult circumstances in which they find themselves, showing them that they still have dignity and agency and providing them with the hope that, if such small feats of defiance may be achieved, ultimately the repressive system may ultimately be overthrown. Some people attempted more direct forms of resistance, such as, rarely, a direct expression of protest—most of these people were quickly killed—or escaped into the jungle to join one of a handful of resistance groups.

10   While no detailed studies have been carried out on the occurrence of wind overload in Cambodia, a preliminary study suggests it is a salient and familiar syndrome in Cambodia (Hauff 2001).

chapter four

Trust and distrust in a highland Khmer community after thirty years of war

Eve Monique Zucker

This chapter is about the concept of trust and about attempts to recover trust after the installation of radical mistrust in the village of O'Thmaa and its neighbouring communities since the early 1970s. Following a period of distrust that lasted from the civil war years through the period of Democratic Kampuchea (DK) and 1980s and 1990s, villagers today are taking steps to rebuild trust in the moral/social order and personal trust with each other. This process sees villagers contending with the residue of distrust that is the legacy of Khmer Rouge ideological policies and practice and 30 years of war, while they seek to rebuild their lives together in a radically changing social and economic context.

Exploring these issues of trust and distrust brings together two dissonant registers. On the one hand, there are major conceptual issues associated with the question of how communities ruptured by violence and betrayal are able—or perhaps not entirely able in the case of O'Thmaa village—to reconstitute social norms of trust and relatedness. On the other hand, there is the much smaller research moment that actually first drew the topic of trust to my attention: the numerous exclamations of 'distrust' articulated as '*ắt tŭk chĕtt*'—'I don't trust'— during the course of my field work. Why did I hear this phrase so often?

To draw these registers together, I found a formulation by Ernest Gellner particularly helpful. In *Trust, cohesion and the social order*, he distinguishes between two modes of trust. The first type, in Gellner's words, is 'coextensive with the very existence of a social order' (Gellner 1988:42). The second type takes place *within* society and would therefore include communal and personal relationships. Elaborating on this distinction, trust is fundamental to moral order and sociality itself; it is what allows people to form the continuing social relationships that, in turn, ground practical actions with the reliable expectation of particular results. Trust makes action in the present meaningful for the future, because it allows us to anticipate possible outcomes.[1] In turn, when individuals are willing to risk actions that imply trust in others, these could be seen as acts of trust analogous to speech acts (in the linguistic-philosophical sense), that is, performatives that *make trust happen* simply by being undertaken. I argue that it was because of the intrinsic interconnections between trust and moral and social order that the Khmer Rouge made trust the object of vehement attack, by installing a general climate of betrayal and suspicion and by seeking to dislodge even, and especially, the most intimate expressions of trust, in the sphere of family and kinship relations. What could re-infuse trust into interpersonal transactions after such corrosion?

The sentiments expressed as '*ạt tŭk chĕtt*' could be directed towards both people and situations. The objects of this sentiment were often strangers to the local area but were also frequently local leaders, the police and even other villagers. In respect to situations, the expression was used to convey a sense of uncertainty, as when the police stopped a man from another village who was smuggling wild game and a confrontation occurred. My neighbour softly said, '*ạt tŭk chĕtt*', meaning here 'I am apprehensive about this situation'. The phrase is also used when talking about the influx of foreign researchers and development people to the area and in relation to the political uncertainty accompanying national elections.

Listening to these sentiments of uncertainty, I recalled May Ebihara's observation that, in the late 1950s, the Khmer villagers she worked with held a general mistrust of strangers and strange places (Ebihara 1968:561–3, 625–6). The distrust she characterised is reminiscent of the insularity and suspicion of foreignness often associated with rural villages and small towns everywhere.

However, the distrust expressed in the village of O'Thmaa and surrounding communities seemed to me to go beyond this everyday suspicion and fear of strangers and strangeness. Was there something unusual, some underlying condition of anxiety, expressed in the sheer frequency of utterance: 'I don't trust', '*ạt tŭk chĕtt*'? Or was the statement simply a habit of used to convey only a vague apprehension? Even this would indicate a generalised uncertainty, such a significant part of the fabric of villagers' everyday existence that it has embedded itself within every day conversation. If this is so, when did this manner of speech emerge? Indeed, what is the 'trust' that the phrase 'I don't trust' counters? Clearly, I thought at the time, I needed to find out more about honesty, reliability and predictability, and how the villagers related to them. I needed to find out how, and by whom, trust is (re)formed in the aftermath of generalised violence. Such was the range of questions that I set out to answer, having noticed the extraordinary frequency of utterance of '*ạt tŭk chĕtt*'.

In this essay, I explore the notion of trust and distrust through everyday events and conversations as they occurred in O'Thmaa village and the surrounding communities in Prei Phnom and Doung Srae communes during my field work, concentrating especially on people's accounts of the past. My intention is to present a picture of how sentiments of distrust and trust are understood and mobilised by people in response to sweeping social changes, not only those incurred through war and genocide but also those incurred via 'modern' and global ideologies, practices and 'products'. I also seek to examine some of the outcomes of these responses as they illuminate the melding, dismantling or rebuilding of trust as an integral component of the moral ordering and interrelatedness, in the larger sense that Gellner says is co-extensive with the social order as such, and also in the 'performativity' of the intra-social sphere.

Theoretical background

In sociology, the topic of 'trust' has become a burgeoning field of study, focused especially on the emergent interest in the impacts of globalisation on societies (for example, Fukuyama 1995; Giddens 1990; 1991; Misztal 1996). In anthropology, 'trust' and 'distrust' have long been *implicitly* analysed in theories of exchange (Mauss 1967; Sahlins 1972), sorcery and witchcraft (Geschiere 1997; 1999; Wikan 1990), as well as uncertainty in modern, globalised and violent contexts (Appadurai 1996; Hinton 1997; 2005; Taylor 1999), egalitarian ethics (Overing 2003), or conspiracy (West & Sanders 2003). One of the few explicit accounts is the essay by Ernest Gellner (1988), to which I referred to earlier. Otherwise, within anthropology, trust or distrust has rarely been taken as a distinct object of analysis. This may be because trust is 'tenuous, even illusive [*sic*]' (West & Sanders 2003:11). Yet, despite this elusiveness, trust is also clearly a pervasive feature of human relations and the societies they constitute, as the studies above suggest—indeed, as Gellner argues, it is a vital part of social and moral ordering.

Moving beyond the disciplinary boundaries of anthropology, we find many echoes of Gellner. We have learned from psychology, for example, that trust forms one of the most basic foundations for human social interaction beginning from the time of infancy (Erikson 1995), providing us with 'ontological security', which the sociologist Giddens (1990:92) describes as the 'confidence that most humans [*sic*] beings have in the continuity of their self-identity and in the constancy of the surrounding social and material environments of action'. Giddens' focus on constancy of environment echoes, in turn, sociologist Bernard Barber, who sees trust as made up of three types of expectations, the first of which is 'the expectation of the persistence and fulfilment of the natural and the moral social order' (Misztal 1996:23). Barbara Misztal (1996:17), also a sociologist, tells us that trust underpins co-operation (but not the reverse), thereby underlining that trust is not merely a by-product of social processes but, rather, a prerequisite of social acts like co-operation. Misztal (1996:18) adds suggestively:

> What makes trust so puzzling is that to trust involves more than believing; in fact to trust is to believe despite uncertainty. Trust always involves an element of risk resulting from our inability to monitor others' behaviour, from our inability to have a complete knowledge about other people's motivations and, generally, from the contingency of social reality.

This may make trust something more akin to faith, as suggested by Giddens (1990:27).

The ethnography of trust and distrust in Southeast Asia

Spiro (1967:71–6) accounts for what he considers to be the distrustful nature of the Burmese, partly as a by-product of childhood experience, when parents shifted attention from the elder sibling to the younger[2] and partly as a conceptual reality where dangerous and harmful supernatural beings—such as witches, demons and ghosts—share the world with ordinary people. 'The Burmese say that no one can be trusted because, in the expression that came to me as a constant refrain, "How can anyone know what is in the mind of another human being?"' Spiro (1967:73).

Similarly, Unni Wikan (1990) describes how Balinese live in a perpetual state of anxiety over the hidden sentiments and intentions of others. Beneath the veneer of their 'smooth bright faces' lurk 'hidden hearts' that at any time may be aroused by jealousy or anger. A heart thus aroused may spur someone to invoke black magic to bring misfortune upon their hapless victim (Wikan 1990). Addressing relations with state and religious institutions, Schrauwers (2003) found deep suspicions in Indonesia among Central Sulawesi Christians towards the apparently transparent democratic state and church bureaucracy. First, the hidden machinations of power by corrupt officials led these people to produce a number of conspiracy theories. And, second, in contradiction of Weber's account of the demise of enchantment in the modern rationalised world, Sulawesi Christians are turning *towards* tradition, employing 'an indigenous set of magic and witchcraft beliefs' (Schrauwers 2003:144) to balance what they see as the Protestant church's failures. While Spiro and Wikan see people distrusting the generally hidden realms of people's minds and hearts, Schrauwers finds distrust directed toward the hidden power structures of bureaucracies. In these cases we see that a 'clear bright face' (Wikan 1990) or a 'transparent rational [enlightened] bureaucracy' (Schrauwers 2003) is a face or veneer that hides potentially malicious intentions and power. Indeed, as Spiro's (1967:74) ethnography tells us, the more dangerous the person or supernatural being is, the more benign they will appear.

Cambodia

In her ethnography of Svay in the late 1950s Ebihara observed villagers' wariness of strangers and strange situations. Such distrust, Ebihara (1968: 177–80) tells us, was instrumental in bringing about the institution of fictive kinship. This arrangement offered security and protection to people when they were away from home in a manner reminiscent of the security and protection offered by *kula* exchange partners in the Trobriand Islanders, studied by Malinowski (1922). Ebihara suggests that villagers generally trusted each other, the government and the Buddhist temple. However, in a recent study in contemporary Svay, Ledgerwood (2008) has noted a rise in distrust of the moral integrity of Buddhist monastic institutions. Finally, in Hinton's (2005:116–25) study of the executioners of Pol Pot's genocide, we see distrust in the form of suspicion towards potential rivals for power. This suspicion, he tells us, is informed by a Buddhist ontology that emphasises the notion of impermanence and a hierarchical patronage system. Those who have power occupy the upper rungs of the hierarchy, and yet that power is something unfixed and finite and fundamentally impermanent in any particular form. Hence a person's power may at any time be lost to another, particularly those who are ready to seize it from below. It is, therefore, the acute awareness of this impermanence of relations involving power that leads people to be on their guard and suspicious of others whose intentions are often hidden (Hinton 2005).[3]

Distrust: inculcation, expressions and persistence

Distrust during the first civil war (1970–75) and the DK period

Background: distrust and the Khmer Rouge ideology

At the start of the DK period most of the residents of Prei Phnom commune were moved to Doung Srae to work on the large agrarian projects that had been in place since 1973. These projects were part of a socialist leap towards modernisation aimed at creating a utopian future that would allow Cambodia to be completely self-reliant. As dictated in 'The Revolutionary Principles of Marxism-Leninism', as written out in a 1976 Khmer Rouge cadre notebook, the aim of the revolution was also to create a 'national democracy and revolution that provides rice fields for the masses' and rid the nation of all forms of feudalism, capitalism and imperialism (D2183 1976). The revolutionary program dictated that individuals should be ever vigilant against enemies of the revolution and the regime employed villagers to spy on one another. Such was the case in O'Thmaa and the neighbouring communities. This program of surveillance operated in part around ideas of clarity and transparency. The populace needed to be 'clear' of any forms of potential dissent. This meant that individual life histories needed to be transparent to the leadership and be 'cleared' of any conflicting elements. But while transparency and the demand to be 'clear' were placed on ordinary people, the revolutionary organisation itself (Ângkar) was administered by a different policy. Described as a 'tactic' (yŭtthsas) to achieve the revolutionary aim cited above, it is elaborated as follows: 'The image that the struggle must project is one that is half hidden and half out in the open' (D2183). Ângkar required total transparency of its people, but it masked much of its own behaviour. This 'tactic' echoed everyday social interaction, as noted by Wikan (1990), where people may 'protect themselves against malicious actions of others by presenting 'a clear bright face' and 'keeping a hidden heart'.

From the early days of the revolution in the 1970s, throughout DK and the 1980s and 1990s, a discourse of spies (kĕnh, kâng chlop, ronŭk knŏng)[4], traitors (chon kbạt), enemies (khmăng, sâtrauv) and 'bad elements'[5] permeated the everyday social relations of Prei Phnom and Doung Srae villagers. The Cambodian genocide was not primarily an ethnic war, such as the wars in Rwanda or Bosnia.[6] However, Arjun Appadurai's observation that ethnic violence is articulated in a vocabulary of (internal) spies and traitors is relevant here:

> The primary literature closest to the most brutal episodes of contemporary ethnic violence is shot through with the language of the impostor, the secret agent, and the counterfeit person. This discourse brings together the uncertainty about categories and intimacy among persons... (Appadurai 1996:155).

Of course, the spies, traitors and enemies existed, in smaller numbers than the regime suspected, but it is clear that the distrust and uncertainty that fuelled these accusations and searches substantiated them in a circular fashion. As Gambetta (1988:234) has noted, 'distrust 'may become the source of its own evidence' and, in Cambodia in general and O'Thmaa in particular, we see this in extremis.

The surveillance methods that the Khmer Rouge used involved enlisting local villagers to spy and report on their fellow villagers and family members, methods commonly used in dictatorial and totalitarian regimes, including in Stalin's Russia, in the Nazi concentration camps and against other political backdrops. An immediate effect of surveillance is to atomise individuals and families by breaking bonds of trust that normally exist, thus destabilising potential pockets of resistance and fostering Appadurai's 'uncertainty about categories and intimacy among persons' Enlisting the locals and encouraging them to report on one another created a confusion of categories; even the closest neighbours and family who would normally be trusted might be 'one of them' rather than 'one of us'. Later, during the second civil war (1979–99), this same confusion of categories recurred when government soldiers and the Khmer Rouge would repeatedly accuse villagers of working for one side or the other.

The discourse of spies, traitors and enemies became self-perpetuating, propelled by distrust and generating more distrust by making people increasingly uncertain about whom they could trust not to turn them in for real or alleged activities. In a broader sense, the degree of distrust was also increased as more alleged traitors were found and their real or alleged associates named in forced confessions. As enemies were arrested and tortured into producing records of their traitorous activities, they were also required to supply names of people they were associated with, who together formed part of their 'network'.[7] In the manner of a self-fulfilling prophecy, the distrust was sustained, rationalised and reproduced, creating a warped logic whose logical conclusion could only be total annihilation.

Distrust during the first years of the Khmer Rouge revolution (1970–75)

Distrust was inculcated in Prei Phnom and Doung Srae communes from the earliest years of the revolution. The phenomenon went through a number of phases. At first, many villagers concluded that, since they were already viewed as potential trouble-makers by Lon Nol, they would be better off placing their trust in the Khmer Rouge. As Ta Chan, a 64-year-old Buddhist layman and original resident of O'Thmaa explained:

> Lon Nol did not trust us. We also were very scared! Even if we didn't join the Khmer Rouge they might accuse us anyway. If we didn't run away Lon Nol wouldn't have believed us, so we had to run...We trusted the Khmer Rouge, that's why we went with them.

Villagers told me that the state government always distrusted them, regardless of who was in power, because of the village's mountainous locale and its reputation as the lair of fugitives, bandits, criminals and insurgents. In any case, many of the villagers were sufficiently wary of the government soldiers to take their chances with the Khmer Rouge and follow them into the mountains; however, a few remained and joined Lon Nol's forces. Some others say that they were not really following the Khmer Rouge, but ran to the mountains to escape the fighting.

But, following the villagers' subsequent descent from the mountains, circumstances were to change. It was clear that the Khmer Rouge became increasingly distrustful. This would have been partly due to the discovery that some villagers' relations in two interior villages were working for the renegade, anti-Khmer Rouge guerrilla group calling itself the *Khmer Sâr* (White Khmer). This led the Khmer Rouge to begin spying on the villagers directly and to employ certain villagers to spy on the others. Sau, a man in his early forties, who was the acting village leader at the time of my field work, explained what had happened to his father in the early 1970s.

> My father...He died in 1972...They accused him of being a *Khmer Sâr* [White Khmer]. It is very hard/difficult/complicated [*lŭmbak*]. I don't really know all of it. There were spies [*kâng chlop*]. They would go to people's houses to listen to what people were saying about the situation. If we said things that were considered good then it didn't matter, we were okay. But if we said something about them that could be taken as a criticism they would catch us and take us saying that we are spies/enemies [*kěnh*]. They just tied him up and forced him to go but I don't know to this day where it was that they killed him...So the Khmer Rouge were afraid that other people may come to know the full story and so they caught him and took him away...He just talked about whether or not there were any people who could come and help him to escape from having to eat as a group. He would just say things like that and they accused him of being the 'arms and legs' of the *Khmer Sâr*.

Sau's narration of the death of his father is not unusual; similar stories are told about the revolution and the DK regime itself. The story conveys the distrust the Khmer Rouge had for the villagers, as well as the distrust the villagers learned to have for the Khmer Rouge. It also indicates the emergent distrust between villagers themselves when he says 'in O'Thmaa here there was a group of spies...'. Looking back at the Khmer Rouge tactic of remaining half-hidden, we can see that Sau's story depicts his father as being able to see into the 'heart/mind' of the Khmer Rouge and this made him dangerous.

Hence in O'Thmaa, the first civil war years (1970–75), betrayed by the Khmer Rouge and then by each other, villagers' trust was rapidly eroded and replaced with a culture of distrust. Khmer Rouge propaganda made a further contribution by stressing self-reliance over dependence on others, including close family members (see Hinton 2005; Kiernan 1985; 1996; Mam 1998). Self-reliance meant that honesty and integrity were only found within—a theme that was extended to the level of the nation-state itself, which sought to cut any form of dependency on other foreign powers (Becker 1998; Chandler, Kiernan & Chanthou 1988; Kiernan 1985). In O'Thmaa there were undoubtedly betrayals within nuclear families, as well as between extended kin relations. Yet, no villager spoke about this to me and I could not locate evidence to support the possibility. From villagers' accounts, it appears that trust within the immediate (nuclear) family remained largely intact, despite the distrust between the extended families of the village.

Distrust in Democratic Kampuchea

In 1975, when Khmer Rouge military forces seized power, the majority of the villagers in Prei Phnom commune moved into the neighbouring commune of Doung Srae, where the search for enemies and traitors continued. Within Doung Srae and Prei Phnom communes, any male old enough to serve as a soldier worked in mobile work brigades that were dispersed around the country. Most of the other villagers were sent to different villages in Doung Srae and put to work on the dam and other large-scale agricultural projects taking shape there.

The stories I was told are generally similar to accounts of life elsewhere in DK. Villagers told me how family members, relatives and associates were reported for having the wrong attitude, stealing food or asking for more food, or were accused of being spies and taken away to be killed. In most cases the accused were never seen again. One Doung Srae woman, Ti, now in her fifties, survived. She escaped execution when she returned to her home in Doung Srae in the early stages of the Vietnamese invasion in late 1978. The Khmer Rouge, she explains, distrusted her because the area she had come from had just been captured by the Vietnamese:

> After I came back, I was nearly killed because they accused me of having the head of a *Yuon* [a derogatory term for Vietnamese] and the body of a Khmer... The *Yuons* hadn't entered this area yet so when I arrived back the Khmer Rouge saw me as someone who was coming from a place controlled by the *Yuons*... meaning that they saw us as having a relation to the Vietnamese that entered early on [in the war] in order to cause whatever. That is why on this side, Pol Pot didn't trust us.

The timing of events probably saved her. Had she returned earlier, she would almost certainly have been executed. As Sau's story also suggested, because it was impossible for the Khmer Rouge to identify enemies by their appearance, everybody was seen as potential enemies and not to be trusted. The Khmer Rouge did not trust who people really were. Or, put another way, they were not confident that people were who they said they were or who they appeared to be. Killing off such liminal identities may have relieved the anxiety of wondering whether someone was a White Khmer, a Vietnamese or, in periods of civil war, a government soldier. By the magic of backwards logic, by their definition as such through their execution, they must have been an enemy; this, in turn, warrants the perpetuation of distrust, for 'underneath the surface' they were essentially a traitor all along.[8] We will return to this notion of trust and confidence, and also to the idea of fixing identities as a remedy to the confusion of categories, later in the chapter.

A final aspect of the DK legacy is the existential distrust arising from the terror and betrayal that occurred under DK. Violence permeates, mars or destroys one's sense of trust in one's fellow humans, oneself and society as a whole. Among the people I worked with, it was clear that trust in the durability of the social and moral order had been severely shaken, as had the more intimate trust between people. In everyday discourse in Doung Srae and Prei Phnom, people would talk about how society has changed and how it may change again at any time, just as it did when 'Pol Pot' came to the area. In O'Thmaa, where members of the community had other people's relatives killed, there is a diminished trust between neighbours, many of whom are extended kin. People say that, although people may now act in a friendly manner, it is unclear what lurks in their hearts (*nôv knŏng chĕtt*) because, as they have seen in the past, people within the community have killed one another or been responsible for their deaths. More broadly, the violence and terror made the morally unfathomable fathomable in the everyday and implanted the cancer of negation. Society itself was shown to be impermanent and capable of being contorted into a kind of hell that was previously unimaginable and, as the institutions and foundations of society were turned on their head or destroyed, so too was the trust in their power, authority and longevity. The ancestral spirits, elders, and Buddhist monastery were stripped of their power and sanctity; ordinary men or women were stripped of their humanity. Moreover, those who survived were forced to live with these memories of the roles that they and others had taken, or had been forced too take, in the revolution.

The second Khmer Rouge civil war (1979–99), its aftermath, and social change: new and old sources of distrust

While the mass extermination of perceived enemies and traitors ended with the collapse of DK, killings of people named as enemies, traitors, spies and, later, sorcerers continued to some degree until the very recent past. The more recent events have been enacted locally between individuals rather than as part of an overarching state policy as before.

In 1979 most Khmer Rouge forces fled to the Thai border, where they regathered and began a prolonged war against the Vietnamese-supported Cambodian government. During the 1980s and early 1990s, Khmer Rouge guerrillas periodically returned to Prei Phnom and Doung Srae and were evacuated during the People's Republic of Kampuchea (PRK), and again in the UN Transitional Authority in Cambodia (UNTAC) period, to stay along the main highway for their protection and to prevent the possibility of collaboration. Nonetheless, there were significant periods when villagers lived within the battleground of the Khmer Rouge and the Vietnamese-led forces.

In the 1980s and 1990s, but in a manner similar to the civil war in the early 1970s, villagers of the two communes were distrusted by both sides, as well as by each other. As Ta En, a musician in his seventies and Doung Srae resident, explained:

> This was the tension zone...When the Khmer Rouge would retreat, the government soldiers moved in. When the government moved out, the Khmer Rouge would move in again...When there was war, the government soldiers would come and have lunch at my house, and then the Khmer Rouge would accuse me of being a spy for the government. And after the Khmer Rouge moved out from here, the government would then accuse me of being a spy for the Khmer Rouge!...Anyone who lived in this frontline (*sâmârâphoum mŭkh*) area was also accused of being a spy.

Residents were suspected by both sides of collaborating with the opposing force. During this time, being accused by the government or the Khmer Rouge of working for the enemy was no longer an automatic guarantee of execution. Many people were killed on that charge, but accusations and killings were not always motivated by politics. As villagers tell it, the charges often were simply a cover for soldiers (and possibly civilians) to kill, or have people killed, for personal reasons.[9] It was during this period as well that a new form of accusation surfaced—sorcery. Those accused as sorcerers were usually executed.

Sorcery, adultery, and AIDS

In early 2002, I was invited to a substantial wooden house in Doung Srae where a young man was hosting a *bŏn da* ceremony 'to send prayers and offerings to the Buddha and the Brahman spirits'. The man had been accused of being a sorcerer (*thmŭap*)[10] three years earlier and, as a result, had been shot at three times and hit once in the leg. People attending the ceremony told me that these accusations were similar to an accusation of being Khmer Rouge or working for the government and that people were using this new label to kill people they did not like.

In later interviews, I learned more about these accusations of sorcery and met some relatives of those who had been accused and murdered. Un, a 36-year-old, told me: 'They said that my father was a sorcerer. It was in 1987. They did a lot of that then. They did that to kill people.' Another young man told me his

57-year-old father, who had already lost his wife to a Khmer Rouge mine, was accused of being a *thmŭap* as recently as 2001.

AIDS has added another dimension. Another woman explained that it was during the 1990s that people started becoming sick with AIDS. The illness caused people to panic and to begin accusing neighbours of sorcery. In the 1990s, the development agencies and the market economy, along with AIDS, came to Doung Srae and Prei Phnom. The market economy existed to a limited extent in the years prior to the war and Pol Pot's regime, but people say that, compared to the Sihanouk years, things became more 'modern' in the 1990s. The move to market towns along the national highway and increased movement of persons to different locales to work or trade often brought villagers into intimate contact with new and different people, ideas and diseases.

AIDS is feared by the people in Prei Phnom and Doung Srae. In Cambodia it has particularly damaging consequences for the many families who cannot access or afford proper medical diagnosis, treatment, and support. Nga, a 32-year-old woman, was dying from what was probably AIDS when I met her. She was living on her own in a one-room wooden house with her three children. Her eldest daughter, 13, was supporting the family by working for people in their rice fields and gardens. Nga's legs were covered in sores and her thin exhausted face was almost without colour. Her life so far had been tragic. She had lost her father and her two uncles during the 'Pol Pot time'. Nga had married her first husband, a policeman, in 1987 in a village along the main highway. In 1994 she accompanied her husband back to her village in Doung Srae, where he was sent to work for a period of 20 days. The Khmer Rouge killed him, shooting him in front of their house.

Some years later Nga married again and she had another child, her third. Her second husband went to Aural to forage for aloe wood (*khlĕum*), but didn't return. In 1997 the couple divorced; six months later she received news from Aural that her husband had died, possibly from malaria. She has been ill ever since. She said that some say her husband died of AIDS and she thinks she may have it as well.

Since the end of the fighting in the area, life has changed, according to Nga, but, at the same time, she has observed that people are now extremely afraid of the sorcerers (*thmŭap* and *ap*[11]). 'If someone dies without reason they will blame it on a *thmŭap*', she told me. 'And if someone gets angry with someone else then perhaps in two or three years they will end up dead from a swollen stomach through black magic'. For her and for many others, fear of the fighting has been replaced by fear of sorcerers. She was unsure how many sorcerers there were, but reasoned that there must be many though the situation might have been be improving. She did not say whether she thought her own illness or that of her husband was a result of sorcery.

Nga's story speaks of several forms of distrust: her distrust of other villagers, who may be sorcerers and accountable for the deaths that are occurring in the area and from AIDS; her distrust of her husband (and perhaps, by extension, men in general) who betrayed her by sleeping with other women, possibly giving her AIDS, and leaving her without support. Her fear of sorcerers is a way of interpreting her present circumstances so that the question of her husband's loyalty can itself be transferred onto an external source, sorcerers. In this way, the intimate trust and security of the family is maintained, even as it is questioned.

Another example of distrust also involves adultery. In this case, however, the individual blamed is a woman. This episode is also a sad one. It took place in Doung Srae in 2001. I paraphrase the story as it was told to me by a group of villagers. One evening a young woman of about 20 years of age was taken into the forest by her cousin, two village security men and a relative of one of the village leaders and shot dead. Several days later, the stench from the rotting corpse wafted into the village, but no-one investigated until the dog of an old man living on the forest's edge returned home with part of the woman's body in its jaws. Alarmed, the man followed the dog's footprints to the corpse, and frightened, he notified the district police. The four men were arrested, but only the security man who shot the woman was held in police custody.

Later, the villagers telling the story explained that the young woman (who, they mentioned, was quite good-looking) was a *sâhay* (an adulteress), who was married but had sexual liaisons with several of the married men in the village. They said she was, therefore, considered a *chngrai* (someone who causes trouble and brings misfortune to society). The villagers said that, after the woman was accused of being a *chngrai*, but before she was killed, she had been placed in isolation. When two of her nephews fell ill and then died, she was accused by her family and other villagers of having invoked the wrath of her ancestors. A villager told me that her parents had said she should be killed. Her body was buried in the forest without ceremony, marker, or the Phnom Yong funerary tower (as is the custom in this village).

I would argue that the distrust and intolerance displayed in these stories indicates a very different type of distrust than the everyday suspicion and fear that Ebihara, Spiro and Wikan discuss. Here we see a rationale and a practice of eliminating what are considered to be bad elements within the community and the use of labelling to justify the killings. The concept of sorcerers or bad elements (*chngrai*) implies that those so labelled are exercising a secret aggression that undermines proper social interactions and the integrity of society. In the context of chaos and flux, causes and agencies of uncertainty must be identified and destroyed.

In their story of the woman who had committed adultery, there are some parallels to the introduction of AIDS. First, the killing was clearly gendered, the woman's behaviour was not to be trusted (nor that of the males, who clearly had a choice about whether to sleep with her). Second, the woman's behaviour violated the intimacy of marriage relations and endangered the offspring of marriage. In this way the institution of kinship itself was violated, hence disrupting a significant basis of the social and moral community. As such a threat, she was thus removed, first in life, by her exclusion, and then by her death and, later, in death, through being buried in the wilderness without mortuary rites.

In the context of extreme 'uncertainty about categories and intimacy among persons', violence fixes otherwise murky identities and creates a sense of order. Appadurai observes: '...the extreme violence which accompanies many recent ethnic wars is a product of radical uncertainty about key social identities, which produces a surplus of anxiety and rage about categorical betrayal' (Baldauf & Hoeller 1998). The 1990s saw massive flows of individuals, military forces, populations and foreign ideologies and diseases entering and traversing the area, with a dislodging of categories and an unsettling of intimacy. In such an atmosphere of flux and chaos, categories were being restored and social order buttressed by labelling people as traitors or sorcerers. These accusations echo other societies where strong links between charges of sorcery and radical social change have been identified. These studies have shown how the destabilising forces of modernity and globalisation are often articulated by locals as a discourse of sorcery, which provides a logic to the invisible machinations of capitalism (for example, Geschiere 1997; 1999; Schrauwers 2003). Here, too, accusations of traitorous activity and sorcery seem to provide a logic to the chaos of war and to the often mystifying sources of modern globalised products and ideas. But as Nga's story indicates, sorcery also provides an alternative logic to the distrust located in intimate and sexual relations between men and women, thereby placing the burden of blame outside the nuclear family, which appears to be the cradle of trust throughout social change. The story of the adulteress is, in many ways, another version of the same story, only in this case the nuclear family is the community and she, as sorcerer (in the form of a bad element or adulteress), is placed outside. She is like AIDS (or the AIDS-ridden woman with whom one had sexual relations) that penetrated the intimate security of the nuclear family and the newly re-established community, and threatened the trust implicit within the intimate domestic sphere and the trust co-extensive with the social and moral order. Because several families within the community were affected, she became a danger to the community as a whole.

The black market and the law

Another source of distrust for villagers living in the two communes is the ever-burgeoning black-market trade that brings villagers into ambiguous and, at times, dangerous contact with the state, outsiders (such as foragers and traders) and environmental development agencies whose agendas do not always match that of villagers. Today in the village of O'Thmaa, an outpost on the wilderness frontier, locals maintain a level of insularity and distrust that is unsurprising, given the illegalities that occur through and within their village. In the periods between planting and harvesting, convoys of two-wheeled wooden oxcarts, mostly originating from the nearby villages and neighbouring commune, emerge from the forest on a daily basis, carrying their illicit bounty of timber and wild animal carcasses. Warily, they make their way past the village police post, trying not to catch the attention of the officers ever ready to make an impromptu inspection and procure fines in the form of cash or a portion of the bounty. Occasionally, during these impromptu checks, the police uncover guns hidden under plastic tarps or bundled within clothes. Depending on the situation, the weapons are seized and/or fines issued, and the event usually would be reported to the commune headquarters.

In addition to police checks, there are also periodic raids by the military, as well as spot checks by officers working for the Ministry of the Environment. On one memorable occasion, an oxcart driver failed to heed the order to stop for inspection and the environmental officer ran down the road after him, waving his gun and threatening to shoot him if he didn't. The man decided he was better off taking the risk of continuing, and local police and others convinced the officer to put his gun away. Another day, an enormous military truck thundered down the earthen road into the forest, chock-full of ominous-looking, black-clad, armed soldiers on a mission to seek out and arrest illegal loggers, poachers and hunters. Not surprisingly, the ex-Khmer Rouge tank commander who owned the sawmill up on the mountain, also a recent resident of O'Thmaa, was not arrested; nor, so far as I was aware, was anyone else from the village arrested.

Although the villagers do not, on the whole, trust the local police, there appears to be a tacit understanding between them, whereby the police allow the villagers to extract a certain amount of products from the forest illegally, providing they pay a fine to the police in the form of money or portion of the goods.

Strangers and powerful people

My presence in the village ignited a certain amount of anxiety. Villagers and local authorities were unsure about me because I was an outsider and because of their fears about who I might really be. Seemingly, they concluded that I was someone with a certain amount of power, which meant that initially villagers and authorities alike distrusted me because my actions and intentions were unclear and unpredictable. At the same time, it was important to local authorities that I gain a good impression of the people in the village, and I was told repeatedly that the villagers 'love one another' (*srâlănh knea*). Most of the villagers, with a few exceptions, tended to avoid any interaction with me by keeping their doors closed and making little attempt to converse in public. Moreover, the police and administration told the villagers (sometimes in my presence and in spite of my protestations) that I must gain a good impression of them; should anything happen to me, or if I were to draw negative conclusions about the area, then the villagers might have problems. The uncertainty attached to me was so great that several villagers refused to allow me to accompany them to the forest, saying that it was dangerous and that I should have the police escort me because, if something were to happen to me, I might hold them responsible and they might be arrested. The police and administration, meanwhile, had concluded that I was working undercover for an environmental NGO in order to expose illicit operations in the village.

This personal narrative exposes one of the key forms of distrust in the everyday social sphere; both strangers and people with power are mistrusted. The logic behind such distrust derives from ideas of non-transparency of intention combined with the potential for lack of moral restraint—that is, a stranger or someone with power is not immediately accountable to the community, unlike someone who remains in the community or occupies the same level within society. The distrust ascribed to those with power is also informed by the knowledge of one's inability to respond effectively, should the holder of power act against them. It is important not to offend those with power so as not to make them angry, as villagers said to me on numerous occasions, explaining that they wouldn't dare approach someone with power. This is especially true for those who take issue with the government or those with greater power. In the words of Ti, 'If I speak out, I'm afraid that the society (*sângkom*) will turn against me'.

Distrust also runs in the opposite direction. As noted earlier, Hinton (2005:119–25) has shown how those with power in Cambodia distrust those without power for fear that they might one day be usurped from their position by those just beneath them. Another dimension of this distrust by those above of those below became clear to me during my field work. Some members of the community are wealthier than others—not by much, but 'they have enough for their family'. As Ya, an ex-Khmer Rouge and government soldier and his wife San, explained:

> They do not have relations with the poor. They are afraid that, if they have relations with the poor people, the next day their wealth will be finished. It is because the wealthy don't see [ât khoenh] poor people. They see only those people of equal wealth. These days they want to see only rich people.

Hence those below, if given the opportunity, may seize not only your power but also your wealth. This distrust of those with less indicates a perceived failure of the patron–client relationship. As San stated, 'The rich people, they don't take care of the poor people, they are afraid the poor people will ask something from them'.

In the longer term, there is a perceived loss of egalitarian principles within the communities of Prei Phnom and Doung Srae. People in both communes complain that, at present, if you want something from your neighbour, you have to buy it, whereas before, everything was shared. They also say that reciprocal relations have diminished from former times and there is less trust among members of the community nowadays.

Reformulating trust

What, then, is trust, how is it formed, and between whom? Because trust between people usually develops over time, my ability to observe its emergence between villagers was somewhat limited. Nonetheless, I had the opportunity to hear a number of stories in which people's characters were described or actions judged. I had the opportunity to see how trust developed between several villagers and me. I will be using all of these observations and experiences in the discussion and analysis that follows. Because much of my understanding of how trust develops has come from my own experience, I will, however, rely on these examples with an understanding of the limitations this implies.

What is trust?

Tŭk chĕtt (trust) implies having confidence in someone or something. This confidence implies predictability and reliability and is tied to a notion of integrity. One afternoon I was talking with Yeay Khieu, an 89-year-old woman who had become one of my closest friends in the village. She was telling me a story about how her ancestors were able to see an enchanted wedding party with the help of an enchanted forest hermit (nĕak sâchchâm). The party appeared riding on elephants in the forest. Yeay Khieu explained that her ancestors were 'were allowed to see this' because they were honest:

Back in those days people were very honest—if they were going fishing and planned to catch three fish, then they would only catch three and no more. It is because of this honesty that it was possible for them to see the people on the elephants.

In this explanation we see honesty as tied to predictability and also an implicit trust. Those who are honest do exactly what they say they will—no more and no less. This level of predictability makes them trusted by the *něak sâchchậm*, the enchanted forest hermit, who lets them see the beautiful enchanted wedding party on the elephants.

When Ya says then that the wealthier villagers do not 'see' those with less, he means that they don't allow those with less into their mind/heart (*chětt*). He, in turn, does not trust them because he cannot 'see into their hearts and minds'. In any case, as in the example of Ya, opacity of the heart produces and is produced by distrust. Conversely, in Yeay Khieu's story we see the link between seeing or being aware and trust. The ancestors were 'allowed to see' because they were trusted for their honesty (indicative of their transparency—they could see because they could be seen and also because of their trust, which here may be more akin to faith). It is also this trust, as faith perhaps, that enabled them to see. Therefore, to not see someone implies a lack of trust, whereas to see implies trust. Moreover, we also see how being honest (*smaoh trậng*) means to be predictable (if one says they will catch three fish they catch three and no more)—to do exactly what one said one would do; being predictable means their intentions are transparent or *clear*.

Before leaving the village to fly home to California to get married, I told the villagers I would return in a month. When I returned, several of the elder women made positive remarks about how I did exactly as I said I would—I had said that I would return in a month's time and I did. Thus, predictability allows a confidence in people and situations that enables a trusting relationship to develop. These remarks were often accompanied by a gesture of affection, such as placing their hand on my arm, indicating that my actions were socially embraced as the right moral action. Thus, one might say that trust, beyond predictability, implies confidence in a person's reliability, where this has connotations of integrity and competence to do the right thing.

For several months, the police chief, Phal, who occupied the police post near my house shared the post with another policeman, San, from the neighbouring village. This arrangement was then altered on orders from the commune police chief, who had San replaced with a much younger man, Nhim, from another district. Nhim seemed an amiable and honest character, so I did not understand it when Phal would continually complain that he wanted San back, saying he did not trust Nhim. When I asked Phal what he meant, he said he could trust San in a way that he could not trust Nhim. He explained that, if something were to happen, he knew he could rely on San, who was older and more experienced than Nhim, who was then only in his early twenties. In other words, he had a confidence in San to handle a problematic situation because of his knowledge and experience.

Therefore, we see that trust can be a confidence in someone's predictability and also a confidence in someone's reliability. But is it also something else? Reciprocity is an integral part of Khmer culture as a set of institutionalised exchange relationships between patron and client and within the more informal spheres of everyday interaction with one's neighbours and kin. Mauss (1970) has suggested that this form of exchange, which he calls 'gift exchange', compels the receiver of the gift to return the favour after some duration of time. The passing of time is integral to the process, for it cements a trust that the relationship is founded upon—without it there is no exchange. Villagers claim that there is significantly less reciprocity between villagers than in the past. Many add that the introduction of a market economy has led to villagers being less willing to help each other out without attaching a fee for their services. Nonetheless, it would be wrong to assume that reciprocity in village relations has disappeared entirely. In everyday practice, villagers on occasion share food, alcohol, care of children, stories and information with one another, if not on a universal scale, then at least between a few select kinfolk and neighbours. Also, on some occasions, they will help one another out with farm work or other tasks. Within these re-emerging networks of reciprocity, one finds trust in that there is the expectation that one deed will bring another in return, sooner or later. Reciprocity is not just a manifestation of trust in a particular set of social interactions; it is also a means of cementing or establishing trust, as I discuss in the next section, which looks at some of the ways in which trust is established (see also Kim's chapter in this volume).

How is trust formed and between whom?

Trust between individuals

On what basis does someone trust someone else? Spiro observed among the Burmese that 'since clearly one cannot know what is in the other's mind, one can only watch for cues' (Spiro 1967:73). Indeed, observation also seems to be one of the central means by which people in Prei Phnom and Doung Srae communes determine whether they will trust someone. This happens through their own personal experience and face-to-face interaction and also by observing how someone behaves over a variety of circumstances and with others.

I have already described how, in the early months of my field work, both villagers and the local administration treated my presence with apprehension. Villagers did not want me to accompany them to the forest and generally kept their distance. Over time, the situation improved. It began with Yeay Khieu (mentioned above). While initially hesitant about my accompanying her into the forest, after I had visited a number of times, she one day took it upon herself to show me the enchanted 'rock box' (*thmâ brâ'ập*) up in the mountains (see also Zucker 2007:ch 7), with her nephew accompanying us. On the return trip, he remarked that he had observed that, when I was tired or hungry, I did not blame other people. This seemed to indicate to him what type of person I was. He then proceeded to tell me how he had been cheated out of his family's land by powerful people in the commune and implored me to act as his 'lawyer' to get it back. Then, following this excursion, Yeay Khieu let it be known in O'Thmaa and surrounding communities that she had more or less adopted me. She took me along to visit some of the other elderly women in the village and to the forest river to bathe and, surrounded by her peers at a wedding, she showered me with affection. And so I was welcomed into the community of elderly women. Later on, another elderly woman from a neighbouring village made a similar gesture by placing her arm around me in the taxi truck (*lan chnuol*) for the entire length of the 30-kilometre journey to the market town, despite the fact that I really hardly knew her.

It was clear to me that, although my stay in the village was arranged through the men of the commune—the commune chief, village chief and police chief— the real entrance into the community was through the community's female elders and, to a lesser extent, through the younger females. Trust was extended along gender lines in a way complementary to how distrust, as demonstrated in the previous section, crossed gender lines. Furthermore, trust was also extended vertically, as elderly women in a sense adopted me into the community. The demonstration of trust on the part of these women then set an example for others in a manner that counted far more (and made possible) the trust extended by younger women in a society that values and respects age.

But *why* did Yeay Khieu or the woman on the truck come to trust me? And is trust a sufficient explicator of their behaviour towards me? I have used the word 'adopted' to describe my relationship with Yeay Khieu and other elder women. The choice of this term was not happenstance but is, rather, based on an institutionalised form of trust found in fictive kin relations, called *thomm* (pronounced *thoah*) relations. As Ebihara has shown, these relationships are invented to indicate a bond of trust with someone, often from an unfamiliar place, who can be relied upon for protection and who can expect to receive the same in return (Ebihara 1968:17–80). *Thomm*, meaning *dhamma*, implies a spiritual element to the relationship, but the relationship is modelled more on actual kinship relations rather than having much to do with spiritual matters. In the story above, it was me who was in the unfamiliar place amongst unfamiliar people, and it would seem that Yeay Khieu, the woman on the taxi truck and others took it upon themselves to act as my absent kin. Ebihara doesn't tell us in her account whether *thomm* relations are usually formed along gender lines, but I would guess that they often are.[12] And, while there is a reciprocal trust implied in the relationship, there is also a demonstration of that trust to others in the community, both male and female.

'Adopting' someone as fictive kin does not come without risk. Even if there is the expectation that a reciprocal relation—comprising exchanges of protection, food, and access to goods or services—will ensue, there is no guarantee that the other person will reciprocate. Moreover, the arrangement also immediately opens up risks associated with allowing someone into one's intimate sphere where one is more vulnerable to potential harm. In both respects, then, a significant amount of trust is entailed. So what is it that compels someone to take the risk of 'adopting' someone as fictive kin when they could get by (and perhaps do better) without forming the relationship? It would seem that the answer lies in a mix of factors: observations (objective and subjective); the possibility personal emotional or material gain; and a 'leap of faith'.

Villagers study each other and outsiders for clues and hints of another's character and intentions. In the words of one woman: 'I have watched you, how you are and have come to like you and trust you'. Although someone's face may mask their true motivations and intention (Zucker 2007:ch 5), it can, nonetheless, also be an indicator. A brief and humorous example of this occurred late in my field work. I was visiting in a village in Doung Srae commune when a woman came up to me and asked whether I had seen her husband passing by my house in Prei Phnom commune a few months earlier. I said I didn't recall seeing him, not knowing who he was. She laughed, saying that exactly at the time he was passing my house, my mobile phone rang, I answered and then immediately someone pulled up in a car and photographed him. She said that, at first, her husband (who was probably smuggling goods from the forest) was quite concerned, but then he saw that the expression on my face did not reflect the situation—there was a lack of concern or interest in the events—andhe concluded, therefore, that the conjuncture of circumstances was just a coincidence.[13] This searching for clues as to people's character and intentions is fairly typical. People's judgements to trust or not trust someone are often predicated on these often brief face-to-face encounters. Face-to-face interactions often allow a momentary impression that may compel someone to take a 'leap of faith' to trust someone. Nonetheless, the decision of Yeay Khieu and others to take me under their wing still carried a risk, even though they had had an opportunity to observe me beforehand. However, there is another element to this leap of faith which might be called adventure. To take the leap into trusting someone or a situation opens one to new experiences. It is no coincidence then that it was Yeay Khieu, of all people, who became the first to come to trust me, for she was generally considered to be an adventurous type—open to novelty and ready to enjoy herself, even if it meant laying prudence aside.

A final means by which trust is established or re-established is through commensality. I touch on this briefly, although I discuss it at length elsewhere (Zucker 2006; 2007:ch 6). Commensality, it can be argued, is a potent means for building trust, partly because there is an implicit risk—as Bloch (2005:56–7) has argued, with commensality comes the risk of poisoning—and also, more positively, because it helps form relatedness. In O'Thmaa this form of building trust and establishing relatedness is communally expressed in the village feast that occurs in the Bŏn Dalien ritual (Zucker 2006).

The examples I have drawn on to demonstrate these formations of trust have come mostly from my own experiences with villagers, but they are also supported by comments villagers would make about each other and of outsiders. Through these examples, I have shown how trust is tied to notions of predictability, reliability, honesty and transparency, but that it also carries risk and, therefore, often requires a 'leap of faith'.

Conclusion

The Khmer Rouge revolution and the DK period introduced an existential negation of self and society, which corroded trust in the world, in others and self. The regime did this by re-defining trust and distrust and their expression through the moral idioms of clarity and vision (the ability to see), visibility and invisibility. Destabilising fundamental categories and intimacies, the new relationships infiltrated kin and community relations and demonstrated their fallibility. Leaving behind this wreckage of moral integrity, the period left a residue of distrust that continues to destabilise the remaking of the moral and social order. Yet the end of the DK period also brought the opportunity, as well as the need, to rebuild the moral order and the trust that it implies. Trust, it seems, resurfaces and develops even in the most formidably inhospitable environments and despite grave uncertainty.

We have seen how the upheaval of war, massive movements of people and the introduction of globalised modernity brought the market economy, AIDS and new ideologies and have spawned novel forms of distrust at a time when people were attempting to re-order their world. A moral rhetoric of 'bad elements', dating from before the Khmer Rouge and used extensively by them, resurfaced in the late 1990s. Those people deemed 'bad' were, in fact, the new products of distrust, responding to greater uncertainties, whether infidelity, illness or the capitalist market economy. Uncertainty and immorality become interchangeable in this economy of elimination and eradication; the Khmer Rouge political executions transmuted into 'private' executions by village communities, bent on both making and securing the pure moral community.[14]

More positively, we have seen how individuals and communities rebuild and fortify trusting relationships with each other. Trust implies confidence in someone's reliability or predictability and, especially since the former is tied to a notion of honesty, it connects to a larger cosmology where an invisible realm may become visible through social and moral behaviour that enables trust. In this manner, it may be reasonable to suggest that people's hearts can become visible to those who are honest and/or, conversely, that those who are honest are also transparent in that their hearts are visible. In other words, what is transparent is trustworthy and what is trustworthy is transparent. While not a reflection of what people actually do, it seems that this is a moral ideal, whose moral opposite is that the non-transparent is not trustworthy—a notion that certainly played a part in the Khmer Rouge demand for clarity in their subjects' life histories.

Perhaps a closer match between theory and practice would be Giddens' (1990) observation that trust inherently carries with it risk and, therefore, a leap of faith. The decision to trust, despite overwhelming uncertainty, was apparent in a number of villagers' willingness to accept me into their lives and share their stories, hospitality and company. With little on which to base this trust, given my 'strangeness', one can only account for it by attributing it to a leap of faith, even if that leap was supported by observations.[15]

I end this chapter with a brief word concerning the larger issue of trust in the social and moral order, which, as discussed above, Gellner (1988:42) says is 'coextensive with the very existence of a social order' and predicated on the 'expectation of the persistence and fulfilment of the natural and the moral social order' (Barber in Misztal 1996:23). Trust in this order can only come through the re-establishment of a level of stability and security that makes it possible for people to engage in practices that help build trust, like making relatedness. Now that the wars have ended and villagers have returned to their villages, they are rebuilding their lives together and restoring trust through the making of relatedness through commensality and the making of kin relations through marriage. But the path towards rebuilding trust and re-establishing moral order is not without obstacles and in O'Thmaa reconciling the village's particular past presents the greatest challenge.

Notes

1   See also Barber (1983), regarding the relationship of trust to expectations about the future.

2   Ebihara (1968:453) also noted the enormous impact of this shift in attention, but does not link it to distrust.

3   Hinton (like Spiro) brings childhood socialisation practices into the equation, but suggests it is an area where trust in one's superiors (parents) is developed. This argument is different from that of Spiro, who suggests that children learn to distrust their parents' benevolence.

4   *Kĕnh* is the term used by the Khmer Rouge and Lon Nol, *kâng chlop* by Pol Pot and *ronŭk knŏng* by Lon Nol.

5   In a manner reminiscent of the Chinese during the nationalist period (see Wakeman 1996), Pol Pot and his cohort used the metaphor of illness and microbes multiplying and infecting the body of state (see Chandler, Kiernan & Chanthou (1988:336) for an excerpt from a Pol Pot speech that refers to microbes; see also Kiernan (1996)). A 'bad element' was any idea, act or person deemed to be counter-revolutionary. People were accused and killed for having the 'wrong philosophy', the wrong life history, the wrong associations, or simply the wrong attitude (such as wanting an extra portion of food).

6   Although ethnic minorities such as the Cham Muslims and Vietnamese were especially targeted by the regime (see Kiernan 1996), the overall nature of the genocide was far less ethnically specific than in the conflicts between the Hutus and Tutsis and between the Bosnian Serbs and Croats.

7   Many of these confessions remain in the archives at the Tuol Sleng Museum of Genocide in Cambodia and in those of the Documentation Centre of Cambodia in Phnom Penh. The translated confession of Hu Nim, Minister of Information under Pol Pot who was killed in 1977, can be found in Chandler, Kiernan and Chanthou (1988). For a rigorous and compelling analysis of the torture and confessions at Tuol Sleng, see Chandler (1999).

8   For an interesting sociological analysis of moral transformation of an individual occurring in this manner, see Harold Garfinkel (1956).

9   These 'grudge killings' may be similar to those discussed by Hinton (2001; 2005) in the DK period.

10 May Ebihara (1968:436) defines *thmŭap* as 'a special kind of *kru*, always male, who specialises in a unique form of malevolent magical murder: the *tmóp* [*sic*] can cause a knife, piece of sharp bamboo, scissor, razor or similar sharp object to enter and swell up inside a victim's body'.

11 *Ap* is a type of female sorcerer who flies with her entrails trailing behind.

12 Except, perhaps, in cases where the age difference is great enough to negate the potential for any sexual element to the relationship.

13 In fact, until she told me the story, I was never aware of any car driving up or of anyone taking photographs of anyone else.

14 See also Hinton (2002b), who explores the role ideas of purity and contamination played in actualising the genocide during the DK years.

15 Finally, while Giddens recognises the importance of kinship to trust, he frames his analysis, unfortunately, in terms of the sociological dichotomy of pre-modern/ modern which seems to elude places like O'Thmaa, which are neither pre-modern nor modern in the sense that Giddens describes. Moreover, the institution of fictive kinship in Cambodia and the continued relevance and importance of real kinship ties in midst of modernity would seem to challenge Giddens' suggestion that trust relations between kin members has diminished from pre-modern times.

May Ebihara returning to Svay in 1989. Photo by Charles F Keyes.

Elderly woman with her great-grandson in Stoung district, Kampong Thom province. Photo by John Marston.

Villagers harrowing and transplanting in Kampong Cham province.
Photo by John Marston.

Elderly man preparing betel in
Kampong Thom province.
Photo by John Marston.

Angkorean temple re-made into the form
of a stupa in the post-Angkorean period.
Choeung Prey hill, Kampong Cham.

Mother with daughter and neighbourhood children in Kampong Cham province. Photo by John Marston.

Elderly woman in Svay. Photo taken by May Ebihara in 1959/60. Courtesy of Northern Illinois University.

Girl sporting new jeans in Stoung district, Kampong Thom, 1999. The following year she went to work as a seamstress in Phnom Penh.

Villagers contributing labour at monks' dormitory of local temple, Batheary district, Kampong Cham province. Photo by John Marston.

Late 12th century bas-relief from the Bayon during the reign of Jayavarman VII.

The evacuation of Phnom Penh in 1975. Photo courtesy of the Documentation Center of Cambodia, Phnom Penh..

Massive work projects during the Pol Pot period. Photo courtesy of the Documentation Center of Cambodia, Phnom Penh.

Villager ploughing with oxen in Kampong Thom province, 2009.
Photo by John Marston.

The same villager ploughing the same field in 2010, this time using a
mechanical plough. Photo by John Marston.

Transporting timber in the highlands of Kampong Speu. Photo by Eve Zucker.

Boy transporting water, Kampong Speu province. Photo by Eve Zucker.

Wat Svay photographed by May Ebihara in 1959/60. Courtesy of Northern Illinois University.

Recent picture of Wat Svay taken by Judy Ledgerwood.

chapter five

A tale of two temples:
communities and their *wats*

Judy Ledgerwood

May Mayko Ebihara conducted ethnographic research in Svay (Mango) village in southern Kandal province, Cambodia in 1959–60. Her doctoral dissertation, completed in 1968, provides the most detailed description of pre-war, pre-revolutionary life in a Khmer village. Her descriptions of kinship systems, residence patterns, the agricultural cycle, land holding patterns, life cycle and other rituals and the activities of daily life have become the bedrock upon which her generation and now the following generation of scholars have understood Cambodian society. She could not have imagined, at the time that she lived in Svay, that only slightly more than ten years later the village she knew would lie in bombed-out ruins, the villagers having fled to the city for safety, or that, in the Democratic Kampuchea period (1975–79), that followed half of the surviving residents she had known would die of starvation, disease, overwork and execution.

Across the decades, Ebihara published work on kinship, social organisation, residence patterns, women's roles and relations between village and city (Ebihara1968; 1974a; 1974b; 1977). She was not able to return to Cambodia until 1989; only after 30 years of silence was she able to learn what had happened to the families of West Svay. Ebihara was able to make visits in 1990, 1991, 1994 and 1996; given the restrictions at the time, she stayed in the city and made daily visits to Svay. I was honoured to have accompanied her on these research trips as a research assistant. In the early 1990s, people were still living in thatch huts on the ground with dirt floors, not the lovely raised wooden houses with tile roofs that Ebihara remembered from her initial research. The interviewing process, particularly in the 1990 and 1991 field research visits when Ebihara was collecting data on what had happened to all the prior residents, was joyous at times, as well as emotionally agonising and physically taxing. We would sit in the shade, usually under the house of the village headman, while people wandered by or were sometimes sent for. Old ladies chewed betel and smoked cigarettes. And people would tell her their stories—of all the things that happened since she had left, of the terrible suffering that they had endured during the Khmer Rouge years and how they were rebuilding their lives. Ebihara had the genealogical records of the village on note cards. She would go through them family by family, learning the fate of each individual. Among the gifts that Ebihara was able to give back to the people of Svay were pictures of their lost relatives and of themselves in another time. They had all lost their photographs from before the war; it was a priceless gift to allow someone to see again the face of their lost mother, or husband or child.

Based on this research, Ebihara (1987, 1993a, 1993b) published on the horrors of life in the village under Pol Pot and on changes in the village since the Khmer Rouge period (Ebihara 1993a; 2002; Ebihara & Ledgerwood 2002). During her last research visit in 1996, Ebihara became ill and, since she was not able to get out to the village everyday, villagers came to visit her in the city. While Ebihara was not able to make the trip to Cambodia again, she remained in touch with the villagers through intermediaries and letters until her death in 2005. In July 2005, a funeral ceremony was held in Svay and her ashes were interred in the community *chetěy* at Wat Svay.

While she did not focus her research on religion, her dissertation (1968) has a chapter on religion and, in 1966, she published an article entitled 'Interrelations between Buddhism and social systems in Cambodian peasant culture'. In these two works and in her various descriptions of life in Svay village, Ebihara gave us considerable detail about the interrelationship between temple and community.

The central issue raised in this chapter is the relationship between local communities' and their *wat*s or temples. Recently Kobayashi Satoru (2005) has challenged Ebihara's (1968:382,398) commonly accepted idea that village temples are 'a major social center' of village life, asserting that this implies a one-to-one correspondence between village and *wat* community (Kobayashi 2005:514). Ebihara's early work, Kobayashi argues, should be considered as situated within the context of early ethnographic work on Southeast Asia, particularly Thailand (see also Sharp et al 1978; Embree 1950), that provided an inherent bias towards the notion of stable communities. And, he writes, Ebihara's descriptions 'should be carefully reconsidered today in light of the upheaval of society that occurred after the completion of her research: the civil war, the rule of the Democratic Kampuchea (DK) regime and socialist policies in the 1980s' (Kobayashi 2005:493). While Kobayashi notes that Ebihara revisited the village in the 1990s and did publish on subsequent social change, she did not provide much empirical data on the temples in question.

In particular, Kobayashi is interested in the overlapping situation of the *châmnŏh,* or supporters of a particular temple. Rather than a stable community based in one village, he finds the *châmnŏh* of the temples he studied in Kompong Thom province to be a 'multi-layered spectrum' of participants that varies over time and across geographical space. While a temple 'community' may have the outward appearance of calm and stability, in fact he finds Buddhist temples in Cambodia to be

> characterized by tension and negotiation among the participants of various backgrounds, young monks and old monks, the rich and the poor, the so-called modernists and the so-called traditionalists. The divisions sometimes emerge as criticism, and sometimes appear as compromised lament toward the current situation, while on the surface they are draped with the Buddhist ideals of peace (Kobayashi 2005: 515).

People attend different temples on different occasions and support temples in their communities and neighbouring communities to varying degrees. Kobayashi encourages us to explore the 'conflicts and compromises' behind what has in the past often been presented as the 'harmonious Cambodian Buddhist temple atmosphere' (Kobayashi 2005:516).

John Marston has simultaneously addressed the complexities of temple histories and loyalties in research at one temple in Kompong Cham province, particularly in a piece which explores the history of one historical figure and includes a discussion of the changing local and outside support for this temple over time (Marston 2008b). In this piece, I would like to rise to the challenge of the new work of Kobayashi and Marston and reexamine the relationship between the two temples near Svay village across the turbulent recent past. This includes a review of Ebihara's published work on the subject, her field notes and new research conducted by me and students participating in an ethnographic field school in 2003.[1]

In rising to the challenge I hope to address some of the larger issues of the meaning of community raised by this volume. While it certainly is true that Ebihara was a product of her time and, therefore, may have emphasised community stability, we can find in her early writings confirmation of the kind of overlapping complexity that Kobayashi analyses in Kompong Thom 40 years later. Ebihara's writing, so closely derived from her ethnographic data, recognised in 1959–60 that community members supported two different temples, and discussed in some detail the reasons people gave for doing so. Taking this ethnography as a starting point, this paper provides a history of the two *wats* across the intervening years and discusses some of the tensions that characterise the relationship today between the two *wats* and the surrounding communities.

Svay village

In her work in the 1990s, May Ebihara introduced the village where she conducted her research as follows:

> Svay, located southwest of Phnom Penh in Kandal province, had some 790 inhabitants living in three hamlets (called West, Middle and East). My original fieldwork was centered on West Hamlet with about 159 people in 32 households, and it is these villagers on whom I continue to focus my current research...In 1959–60, virtually all of West Svay's villagers were peasant wet-rice cultivators. They grew rice mostly for consumption rather than the market because they had only small landholdings averaging about one hectare per household. Men and women individually owned means of production (land, draft animals, tools and so on), as well as other kinds of property. The family was the primary unit of production and consumption; each cultivated its fields using mainly its own labor, buttressed with mutual, cooperative aid from kin and neighbors during the busiest farming seasons. Although most families were largely subsistence cultivators, they were also part of a market economy insofar as they depended on purchasing various necessities and selling produce or labor.
>
> Most families were poor but not destitute; they kept themselves afloat with various part-time pursuits to earn cash. The village formed a social unit as an aggregate of kinsmen, neighbors, and friends. Various bonds of affection, loyalty and mutual aid also extended beyond the village to relatives on both sides of the family. Religion was an integral and critical part of village life. Svay had its own Buddhist temple compound (wat), with resident monks, that served as a moral and social center...(Ebihara 1993a:149–150).

Ebihara chronicled changes that took place in Svay across the 60s, 70s and 80s (Ebihara 1987; 1993a; 1993b; 2002; Ebihara & Ledgerwood 2002). There was heavy fighting in the area during the early 1970s and most of the villagers were forced to flee to Phnom Penh, while some from other hamlets went to join Khmer Rouge forces in the south. So the area was largely empty of local residents during the heavy bombing in 1973 and subsequent fighting in the area in 1974–75. When the Khmer Rouge forces took Phnom Penh in April 1975, the residents of Svay were evacuated from the city with everyone else; they were labelled 'new people' or 'April 17' people, despite the fact that they were rice farmers. They were not allowed to return directly to Svay, but were sent to a nearby forested area. Over the course of the regime, the villagers were split; some were sent to other areas nearby and one group sent northwest to Pursat province. Like most of the population of Cambodia during this era, they suffered terribly, working long hours with very little food. Ebihara has written specifically about this period in Svay:

> The death toll was high. In 1960, West Svay had some 159 inhabitants. Of these, 16 died before 1970 of old age or illness, while four more died in the early 1970s because of civil war. This left 139 remaining villagers, of whom 70 (50 percent)

died during DK. Of these 70 deaths, 39 (56 percent) were male…Of the West
Svay families that lived in 1975, some perished completely, and others were
left with only one or a few survivors. There is no one who did not experience
the deaths of close family members—whether parents, grandparents, siblings,
spouse or children—during DK (Ebihara 1993a:158).

After 1979, the villagers returned to Svay and re-established the village,
although the centre of the community had shifted to what used to be Middle
Hamlet and the Middle and West Hamlets merged into the new 'West' Hamlet,
with only two administrative units, west and east. The new West Hamlet had
421 persons in 108 households in 1991, with a strikingly high ratio of women
to men. Of the 59 people that Ebihara had known in 1960, 36 (61%) were adult
women, 12 of them widows of men who had died in the DK period.

Ebihara has described the economic and social regeneration of the village
under the People's Republic of Kampuchea (PRK) (Ebihara 1993a; Ebihara &
Ledgerwood 2002), the initial use of communal systems of production and the
return to farming private holdings in the mid-1980s. She also wrote of her shock
at seeing living conditions when she was able to return for the first time in the
late 1980s (Ebihara 1990b; 1993b).

She spent much less time being concerned about the rebuilding of Buddhism.
While she has pointed out the rebuilding of the temple in Svay and the nearby Wat
Samnang, and argued that the re-establishment of Buddhism was an important
factor in understanding post-war society (Ebihara & Ledgerwood 2002), she did
not write extensively about Buddhism in Svay in the 1990s. We would always
visit the temple and sponsor a blessing ceremony during our stay as a way to
return something to the community. Most people in the village, especially the
elders who had known Ebihara before, would gather to make merit and enjoy
a meal together.[2]

Throughout the 1990s foreign aid increased, peace allowed for men to return
from the war, new forms of economic enterprise grew, roads were improved and
the economic boom in Phnom Penh trickled down to surrounding communities
near the city. The economic life of residents in Svay improved throughout
the decade, although the rewards have been unevenly distributed, as the main
source of income has shifted from agriculture primarily to a new combination
of agriculture and wage labour.

Only a few people still live in thatch houses on the ground, almost everyone
rebuilt traditional wooden pile homes a metre or more up in the air. The better
off people first got bicycles and then motorcycles. People started in the late
1980s to replant fruit trees; they were able to buy more and better clothing.
Now everyone has radios and bicycles, many households have small black and

white TVs that run on batteries. There is still no electricity in the community, although one city person who maintains a house in the village has a generator and his relatives living nearby run lines to their homes. The sub-district (*khŭm*) chief has a cell phone, as does the local policeman. Cash for many of these improvements, and particularly for many of the new houses, came in part from relatives abroad, mostly in the United States.

Today Svay is, in part, a bedroom community for Phnom Penh. Most villagers still grow wet-season rice, but this income is supplemented with wage labour (nearly 30% of households across the six communities surveyed had household members working for wages in the city). The most dramatic demonstrations of this are the truckloads of young women from Svay and surrounding villages picked up each morning and brought back each evening from the garment factories on the southern outskirts of the city. One villager told me he has two daughters who work in the factories; each earns about $45 per month, though they can earn as much as $60 per month with overtime. They can earn double time if they work on Sundays. One daughter is married and her husband *rŭat moto dŭp* (run a motorcycle taxi), so they ride together to the city each morning. The other daughter pays $7.50 per month to ride in one of the trucks (interview, 12 February 2003). Because these girls are not paying for housing and meals in the city, they are able to hand over most of their earnings to their families, allowing for significant improvement in the local standard of living.[3]

The income from their daughters' wages has allowed farmers to change agricultural methods. With additional cash available, most households own water pumps; those without them can rent from those who do. Now, if the rains are not sufficient, people can pump and, because water is more reliable, many people have added high-yield rice varieties. These high-yield varieties require more fertiliser and pesticides, which, like the fuel for the pumps, can be purchased with the additional cash income. Some of the most prosperous villagers have purchased land from their poorer neighbours, especially elders whose children or grandchildren have left the land and moved to the cities. Wealthier families now have landholdings of two hectares or more. Some urbanites are buying plots of land along the road that runs to Svay to build second houses in the countryside.

Besides the relatives who live abroad, several village residents or children of the village have now been abroad. One family in particular has several members who have travelled, including one son who trained as a fighter pilot in the former Soviet Union, a grandson who studied agriculture in the former East Germany and a schoolteacher daughter who has been to a training program in France. There are also a few village residents in Svay who have returned from the refugee camps along the Thai-Cambodian border.

As Ebihara pointed out in her early research, Svay was never an isolated place (see, in particular, Ebihara 1974a), but today it is tied into the capital city and the world beyond in remarkable ways.[4] Svay residents watch Mexican soap operas, dubbed in Khmer, with commercials for American cigarettes and Thai soaps and creams. Many of their children and grandchildren live in Phnom Penh and they come out in cars on weekends to enjoy relaxing in the 'countryside'. At some point Svay will be consumed by the city, as Bang Chan was by Bangkok decades ago.

Recent history of Buddhism

During the DK era (1975–79), Pol Pot and his colleagues set out to deliberately destroy Buddhism, the religion of more than 90% of Cambodia's people. In 1978, Yun Yat, DK Minister of Culture, told Yugoslav journalists that 'Buddhism is dead, and the ground has been cleared for the foundations of a new revolutionary culture' (cited in Keyes 1994). The exact circumstances and timing of this devastation varied throughout the country (see Vickery 1984; Harris 2008), but the goal with regard to religion was clear. Monks were forced to disrobe and return to lay life; refusing to do so could result in execution. Some temples were destroyed, in other instances they were converted to secular uses such as warehouses, clinics and prisons. Buddhist imagery was smashed, defiled and, in some cases, dumped in rivers and ponds. Religious texts were burned or otherwise destroyed (see de Bernon 1998).

When the Khmer Rouge were driven from power by the Vietnamese in 1979, the new Cambodian government, the PRK, permitted the partial restoration of Buddhism. Khmer Theravāda Buddhist monks were brought in from southern Vietnam to restart the ordination line of monks. By 1982 some 2,300 monks had been ordained. The restrictions on religion under the PRK included allowing only those over 50 years of age to become monks; young men were needed in the military and for agricultural production. As Keyes suggests, these provisions were probably intended to ensure that the Sangha (the order of monks) did not re-emerge as an independent institution (Keyes 1994: 62).

Major changes began to take place in Cambodia with regard to religion in 1989–90. During the process of political reform that would eventually lead to elections, the PRK (renamed the State of Cambodia (SOC) in 1989), made an effort to shed its communist pro-Vietnamese image. SOC leaders saw the re-establishment of Buddhism and support for religion as a key factor in the process of political legitimisation. The age restrictions on ordinations and taxes on temples were removed (Keyes 1994:63). In April 1989, Hun Sen, Heng Samrin and Chea Sim, the most senior members of the SOC government, participated in a ceremony to reinstall a Buddhist relic in the monument in front of the Phnom Penh train station. At the same time, Buddhist prayers began again on the national radio station and Buddhism was formally declared the national religion. Pali schools were reopened and, with funding from abroad, religious texts began to be reprinted. The numbers of monks began to rise, from 6,500 to 8,000 in 1985–89, to about 20,000 in 1991 (Harris 2005; Keyes1994:62–3), to 50,081 by 1998–99, 55,755 in 2003 (Ministry of Religion and Cults 1999; 2003) and 58,828 in 2005 (Khy 2008:259).

With the restrictions on ordinations and temple reconstruction removed, the 1990s saw an explosion of temple building; rural communities rebuilt temples that had been destroyed, damaged or neglected during the DK and PRK regimes. Rural families living at subsistence level set aside whatever small amount of surplus they could to contribute to restoring temples and performing rituals. Overseas Khmer made important contributions to this process, sending money to support the construction of temples or *chetěy* (repositories for the ashes of the dead) and ceremonies for their loved ones. Given the extreme poverty in the Cambodian countryside, it is remarkable that this restoration has taken place. Gleaming new buildings with tiled roofs and beautiful wall murals adorn the central plains.

Given the poverty of rural rice farmers, this explosion in construction might seem surprising, but one must consider that Buddhist ritual life is central to community wellbeing and cohesion. Ritual celebrations include life-cycle rituals, such as weddings and funerals and annual festivals, such as New Year, Pchŭm Běn (the festival for the dead) and Kathěn (the ceremony where new robes are offered to the monks). With the temples restored and monks re-ordained, more people have been able to sponsor ceremonies and, thereby, earn merit for themselves and for their deceased relatives. With the re-establishment of the temples and Buddhist ceremonies, the proper order of relationships in society and between social actors and the spiritual realm is restored (see Ebihara & Ledgerwood 2002:281; Meas 1995).

Two *wats*

The residents of Svay support two local temples: Wat Svay is located in the village; Wat Samnang is two or three kilometres west up the road towards the nearby market town. In 1959–60 Wat Svay had ten monks and, in 2003, it had ten monks once again. During the DK period, Wat Svay's *vīhear* and all the other buildings, except one *sala* and the monks' residences (*kŏdě*, pronounced *kŏt*), were completely destroyed; the villagers said mines were attached to the walls and exploded. Several villagers reported being forced to carry pieces of the destroyed structure to fill in the temple pond to level the ground. The remaining *sala* was used as a DK 'hospital'.

In the 1980s, the *kŏdĕ* were still standing, but were riddled with bullet holes; the villagers used the one remaining *sala* as a worship hall. In 1989–90, the villagers started reconstruction in earnest with the building of a gate and wall to enclose the compound. On the high ground where the *vĭhear* would eventually be rebuilt, three small Buddha images were placed in a wooden structure with a tin roof (Ebihara 2002:96). The *vĭhear* rose slowly over the next six years. Even when the structure was complete, in 1996, it took additional time to raise money for images and paintings. Since then, the building process has continued and has included the construction of a second larger *sala,* the restoration of the *kŏdĕ*, the addition of a new roofed area used for teaching, a cooking shed and the re-digging of the temple pond. Still ongoing is the construction of several new *chetĕy*, including one *chetĕy ruom*, or community *chetĕy* for the elderly who die without children or grandchildren and for those from poorer families who do not have the resources to build their own monuments. Before the war, the temple also housed a school and, in the early 1980s, the *sala* was used as primary school classrooms. These classes were shifted when a school was built in Svay and, subsequently, to a village to the east where a larger school was built to serve both communities. Donors for Wat Svay include local residents, some overseas Khmer who were born in the village and wealthy people from Phnom Penh with kinship ties to the area. Among this last group are the wife of a famous *ayai* singer, the wife of a former Minister and a powerful police official. (Their support is discussed further below.)

In 1959–60, Wat Samnang had 23 monks—today there are 18, eight *bhikkhu* and ten novices. Wat Samnang covers a much larger area than Wat Svay and includes a wooded area at the back of the property. Locals say that, before the war, the large trees on the site were so big you had to tie four *krâma*s (cotton scarves) together to reach around them. Monkeys played in the trees. Part of what made the *wat* so popular with city residents was this wooded character. During the Khmer Rouge period Wat Samnang was also destroyed, the *vĭhear* completely levelled; people reported the same process as at Wat Svay—that explosives were placed on the walls and detonated so that the entire building collapsed. People were put to work breaking up the rubble to retrieve the steel bars and larger pieces of broken concrete; these were then used in the construction of a dam and irrigation system just to the west of the town. The large trees were cut down to make charcoal. People are not sure what happened to the monkeys; they may have fled when the trees were cut or they may have been eaten. One *sala* was left standing and two of the larger *chetĕy*s, although both *chetĕy*s were damaged.

Unlike at Wat Svay, it was difficult for the supporters of Wat Samnang to get permission to rebuild. In the early 1980s, the temple site was being used by a businessman with ties to the provincial-level authorities for a brick factory. When locals raised the issue of rebuilding to *khŭm*- and *srŏk*-level officials, they could not get any support (interview, 21 July 2003). Between 1982 and 1986 a temporary *vĭhear* of wood was built east of the old site. Unwilling to give up, the temple supporters started a petition, which garnered the support of 460 families (who put their thumbprints on the petition), and took it to the provincial-level government. The provincial-level officials asked if they did not have a *srŏk* office; the petitioners replied that they did, but that the *srŏk* office would not join them in the petition. Eventually the provincial-level officials passed the petition up to national-level religious authorities. Representatives from the temple community met first with Um Sum, a high-ranking monk in the national administration of the monkhood and the matter was passed to Tep Vong. It was Tep Vong, the head of the Sangha, who finally granted permission to move the factory and allow the temple to be rebuilt in 1990 (interview, 21 July 2003). This story of struggle by local laypeople demonstrates the importance people placed on the rebuilding of temples in their own communities, and belies the sometimes voiced notion that temple reconstruction is only undertaken for the benefit of politicians or by overseas Khmer.

When Ebihara visited Wat Samnang in 1990, there was a temporary structure set back in the woods and the monks were living in a damaged *chetĕy*, built before the war, but never used to inter remains. Construction for the new *vĭhear*, on the site of the old one, began in 1991 and was completed in 1997. Today the temple has a large *vĭhear*, a large *sala* for eating and festivals (built 1999–2001), a smaller *sala*, and several *kŏdĕ*, including a large two-storey *kŏdĕ* for the abbot.[5] The back of the temple property is a wooded area where there are several *chetĕy* and others under construction.[6] The abbot reported that Wat Samnang has had several powerful government officials as donors, including the Prime Minister Hun Sen and businessman Kun Kim. A certificate attesting to Hun Sen's donations hangs in the abbot's residence. Other powerful supporters of Wat Samnang include a high ranking official at the Ministry of Interior and a Phnom Penh police official who is a native son of Svay. This official sponsored the Kathin festival at Wat Samnang in 2002. Before the war the temple also had a Pali school; this has not yet been re-established, although there are plans to do so.

In both cases the temples are almost completely rebuilt; laypeople said the process, throughout the 1990s, went forward when there was money available and stalled when there was less. Money to rebuild the temples came from the local community, from wealthy patrons in Phnom Penh and from overseas Khmer.

Locals say that the two temples now are as grand, or more beautiful, than they were before the war. Ebihara (2002:106) wrote after her last visit in 1996,

it was amazing and gratifying to watch the central temples (*vīhear*) being rebuilt literally from the ground up, on what were mounds of dirt in 1990. In both instances, the temples have been constructed in classic style and are, in some ways, even more magnificently beautiful than the pre-war *vīhear*.

Wat Samnang charges a fee for outsiders, including urban Chinese and overseas Khmer, who want to build *chetěy* for their remains in the forested area at the back of the temple grounds. Wat Svay does not charge for the area to construct a *chetěy*, but say that it is financially beneficial to the temple in the long run as those who build on the grounds then come to participate in ceremonies and make regular donations to the temple.

The abbot of Wat Svay is 72 years old. He was ordained twice as a young man before the war and re-ordained after the war. Of the ten monks at Wat Svay, three are *bhikkhu* and seven are novices. Only three had been ordained at Wat Svay; the others had come from other places. At Wat Samrong, the abbot is only 28 years old, whereas the *achar* at the temple are 86 and 65 years old and the head of the temple committee, who was also head before the war, is 73. Of the 18 monks at Wat Samnang, three are from the local communities and there was one additional ordination from a local village during our research in 2003. The number of years of ordination varies from one to 11; at that time there were 20 temple boys in residence, 19 of whom lived in the temple and studied at the local high school.

Wat Samnang is the larger and clearly more prosperous of the two temples and is located on the edge of a market town, which was nearly completely destroyed by bombing in the war years, but has now been rebuilt. It is supported by the residents of seven nearby villages, of which Svay is the most distant. When monks from Samnang go on alms rounds they split up. Some walk through the two villages closest to the temple, while others sit in the market on a raised platform and wait for people to come to them to make donations. At Wat Svay the monks walk west through Svay village (east and west hamlets) one day and east through the adjacent village on the next; there is a much smaller overall support base for Wat Svay, with only three villages directly supporting the temple. The residents of the next village to the east of Wat Svay are divided between supporters of Wat Svay and supporters of another *wat* further up the road to the east.

In 1959–60, half of the 30 West Svay households attended the two temples equally or had varying ties of loyalty within the family—for example, the wife went to one and the husband to another . About ten families in East Svay were devoted to Wat Svay; the other households in the west went mainly to Wat Samnang (Ebihara 1968: 380). Ebihara reported that the choice of where people attended services and made donations was generally determined by where their parents had attended, where a man had been ordained, or personal preference. This is still generally true. Most families interviewed in East and West Svay and a third community nearby said that they supported multiple temples. Those in the immediate area of Wat Svay, in East Svay hamlet, identified it as their primary temple, the one they attended most regularly.

What are the main reasons that might explain why villagers are members of one *câmnŏh* as opposed to another? Or why might people be, as Kobayashi explains, members of multiple *câmnŏh* that shift where they attend and provide donations over time? Ebihara noted the fact that people attended different temples on various occasions. She said that while villagers recognised this divided allegiance, it was 'relatively insignificant' and did 'not usually disrupt daily relationships' (Ebihara 1968:381).[7] The following discussion focuses on the differences between the two *wats* that might help us understand the choices of individual *câmnŏh* members.

Thommayut and Mohanikay

First, the main difference between the two temples is that Wat Svay is Thommayut and Wat Samnang is Mohanikay. The Thommayut order, introduced from Thailand in the 19th century as a reformist movement sponsored by King Ang Duang, claims to be more orthodox and stricter in practice.[8] In 1955, over 90% of the total number of permanent monks and 94% of all temples in Cambodia were Mohanikay (Ebihara 1966, citing Martini 1955:416–17). After the devastation of the DK period, only the Mohanikay order was reintroduced under the PRK. The Thommayut had always been associated with the royal family and was not re-established in Cambodia until after the return of Prince Sihanouk in 1991. Wat Svay was, therefore, also Mohanikay from 1979 until 1991, when it reverted back to Thommayut. The numbers of Thommayut adherents are even smaller today; only 3% of all temples and 2% of all monks are Thommayut (Ministry of Religion and Cults 2002).

There are not any significant differences in practice between the two orders:

There is little to distinguish the Thommayut and the Mohanikay in terms of Doctrine, but they do disagree over the interpretation of some elements of Monastic discipline (*vinaya*), such as the wearing of sandals, the carrying of the begging bowl (*bat*), and the consumption of drinks after midday. The most obvious differences to the casual observer relate to the wearing and composition of the monastic robe…There is also a marked lack of uniformity in the ways that the two groupings intone Pali…Bizot's major study (1988:107) of differences in the formulae and pronunciations connected to the lower ordination formulae and pronunciations connected to the lower ordination ritual (*pabbajja*) also demonstrates that the Mohanikay tend to interpret such formulae in an exoteric manner…In all of these matters, as one would expect from a group who claim to 'adhere to the law' (*dhammayutika*), the Thommayut believe that their observation comes closest to the Buddha's own practice (Harris 2005:106–7).

Wat Svay was originally Mohanikay, but changed to Thommayut in the 1890s; villagers were unclear as to why the change was made. There is a semi-mythical story about the history and name of the village that make a connection to royalty. It is said that a king long ago was out travelling in his kingdom and stopped to rest in the village in the shade of a large mango (*svay*) tree; the king, enjoying his time there, declared the name of the village *Svay Samnak* (the resting place of the mango tree). There is no specific connection made between this story and the fact that the *wat* is Thommayut. One retired *achar* said that one of the *sângkhoreach* (titled monks) of the Thommayut monastic order in the 1940s, named Uom Srey, had been born in Svay. After his death, the former King Sihanouk organised a procession of his remains to Wat Svay. His *chetěy*, considered powerful by local people, was completely destroyed in the Khmer Rouge period.

In Ebihara's doctoral thesis (1968: 381), she notes in a footnote that Sihanouk himself had been ordained at Wat Svay as a young man. This is not accurate; according to the former *achar* of the temple it was Sihanouk's uncle Norodom Monireth who had been ordained at Wat Svay.

Villagers who regularly attend Wat Svay are proud that their temple has a strong reputation for strict adherence to *vinaya* rules. Their comments closely paralleled those Ebihara had heard 40 years before: 'Thommayut adherents will often have a superior tone in their voices when discussing the allegedly less rigorous behavior of Mohanikay monks' (Ebihara 1968: 379). Today they note that Thommayut monks do not touch money, watch television or use cell phones. Some people linked the stricter practice of Thommayut temples with the fact that Wat Svay, unlike many other *wat*s, does not have conflicts about the handling of money. When talking to the young, mainly female, interviewers from Phnom Penh and the United States in 2003, both monks and laypeople at Wat Svay emphasised that Thommayut monastic interactions with women were strictly regulated, that the interviewers could never be alone with monks, that monks could never accept anything directly from a woman's hand and that they could not look directly at women when they spoke. Thommayut was taken as a sort of shorthand for being stricter in observance of *vinaya* rules in general;

while no-one said so directly, the contrast was, as it had been in 1959–60, with 'looser' Mohanikay temples and specifically with Wat Samnang, where they knew we were also conducting interviews.

The strictness is something of a double-edged sword, as it is said that few men want to be ordained at the temple and there is less general support for Wat Svay than for Mohanikay temples. Because the monks can neither handle money nor go out to solicit contributions, the temple is said to be poorer and, therefore, less grand than Mohanikay temples. While the suggestion was made in a few interviews that royal support for the Thommayut sect might compensate for this, there is currently no royal support for Wat Svay.

There were also no obvious political divisions within the village with regard to the temple. There was no obvious National United Front for an Independent, Neutral, Peaceful, and Cooperative Cambodia (FUNCINPEC) support for Wat Svay, and some of the villagers who were core supporters, including temple committee members, are staunch Cambodian People's Party (CPP) activists. One elderly man did say, in an interview in 2003, that villagers feared giving support to the Thommayut temple (Wat Svay) for fear of being openly-associated with the royal family.[9] There is mention in Ebihara's field notes from 1991 of a comment made by an important patron and loyal CPP member from Phnom Penh to the effect that, since Wat Svay had become Thommayut again, he would no longer support the temple. This patron has supported Wat Samnang more over the intervening years, including sponsoring one Kâthĕn ceremony there, but he has also on occasion attended festivals and made donations at Wat Svay, including—or particularly?—when foreign anthropologists were present. I also overheard one village elder from Svay who only attends Wat Samnang lobbying an older woman at holy day services to vote for FUNCINPEC in the upcoming elections in 2003.

Despite all these noted differences, in general, people in villages surrounding both temples voiced opinions that were much like those Ebihara heard in 1959–60—that there really was little difference between Thommayut and Mohanikay. So what other factors might be at work in decisions about which temple to support and when?

Other factors

Interestingly, given the importance that Kobayashi found in Kompong Thom province placed on the differences between *bŏran* and *sâmai,* this was not a distinction that was generally mentioned in informal interviews. When the subject was broached in the context of formal interviews—that is when we asked about it directly—people seemed either to not understand the question, or they would connect the meaning of the word *bŏran* to stricter adherence to the *vinaya* rules for monks. Thus some respondents said that the Thommayut temple was more *bŏran* because the monks there were perceived as being stricter in their practice. Other respondents seemed to take it to mean 'as before' (*dauch pi daoem*) and, thus, said that their temple was *bŏran*; Marston (2008a:102) has observed that this can be one of multiple and conflicted meanings for *bŏran*, 'the idea of continuity with the traditional practices of specific wats and spiritual leaders' (see also Marston 2002c). They did not seem to be describing the kinds of esoteric ritual focus or one-on-one student–teacher relationships that Marston, Kobayashi and others associate with this distinction.[10] Or it is possible that because the interviewers—young urban Khmer—did not themselves understand the complexities of the distinction, the questioning in this area was largely unproductive.

Ebihara (1968:381) noted that the families in East Svay who supported Wat Svay tended to be among the wealthier households. It is difficult to say if this is still the case today. There were some comments collected to the effect that, in order to attend Wat Svay, one had to bring delicious, expensive food, whereas all that they could afford was soup with *brâhâk* (fermented fish paste), implying the food of peasants. In an interesting way this might help make sense of the current CPP loyalist support for the temple, as they are now the wealthiest families in the community. With regard to this distinction, Ebihara (1968: 381) wrote:...

> Thommayut families are among the wealthier households in the village, and it may be that their criticisms of the Mohanikay on religious grounds are an expression of superiority that they may feel in other contexts but cannot ordinarily express in the egalitarian village life.

The distinction is not a clear-cut one, as there are wealthy and poorer supporters of both temples; when the monks went on alms rounds through Svay, their 'regular' stops included new raised wooden houses and thatched huts on the ground (see Rudasill 2004). And virtually all households, wealthy and poor, reported taking a turn (*vén*) at contributing to one or more temple during Pchŭm Bĕn, the festival for the dead, when families take turns providing food and special rice cakes to the temple (Ledgerwood 2008a; Spiegel 2006)

Another factor that might influence a decision about which *wat* to support concerns the abbots of the two temples. While the supporters of Wat Svay linked the strictness of practice there to the fact that it was Thommayut, they also specifically linked it to the religiosity of the current elderly abbot. At 72, he has been ordained for three different periods of his life, as a young man from the age of 13 to 20, from 22 to 25 and again from the age of 55. In his youth he had studied in the ecclesiastical educational system and finished Pali primary school. In the post-war era he is considered a learned and devout monk and, therefore, garners respect in the community. The abbot of Wat Samnang is only 28 years old and has been a monk since 1993. During the interviews with community members who were supporters of Wat Samnang, the issue of monastic discipline came up on a regular basis, more frequently than at other temples. One elderly nun specifically said that there were two main reasons why the young monks were not more disciplined: first, the central religious authorities no longer 'paid attention' (*yok chĕtt tŭk dăk*) of the behaviour of monks, and second, the new abbot was simply 'too young' to maintain control.

The young abbot was at that time presiding over an important period of building activity and renovation of the temple. This was sometimes controversial, such as when he decided to borrow money to complete the construction of the large new *kŏdĕ* where he resided; but the other new construction was very much appreciated by locals and outside donors alike as the temple was viewed as having been largely restored to its pre-war glory. The fact that the temple attracted funds from powerful donors in the ruling party, including Hun Sen, showed its importance. It was now again a 'fun' place for annual festivals that would attract large crowds, both locally and from Phnom Penh. The large numbers of young men in residence to attend high school in the market town and the current discussions of reopening the Pali school add to this sense of a *wat* that is on the rise.

Ebihara (1966; 1968) wrote that the decisions about which temple to support were generally inherited from their parents and grandparents, and included consideration of where men had ordained in their youth and where their ancestors' ashes were interred. These reasons were also given in interviews in 2003. Since rural Khmer tend to marry not within the same village, but to marry spouses from nearby villages (see Ebihara 1968; 1977; Martel 1975; Crochet in this volume), there might already be a tendency to have loyalty to more than one temple within a household—for the *wat* of the wife's family and that of the husband's. You attend where your *bâng b'aun* (bilateral kinsmen) attend, which may mean you attend more than one *wat*.

The issue of ancestors' ashes includes the literal remains of known individuals (it may be known that one's grandparents' or parents' remains were interred in a *chetĕy* at a particular *wat*) and the generalised notion of one's ancestors coming from a place. At the festival for the dead, Pchŭm Bĕn, the unfortunate wandering spirits who have not been reborn are said to visit seven different temples looking for their descendants to offer them food. People will want to return for this festival to the temples in the area where they were born so that they are in the place their ancestors will visit. The Khmer spirit world includes several types of spirits identified generally as spirits of those who previously lived as humans, including *meba* (ancestor spirits), who may take an interest in the proper behaviour of their descendants, and *něak ta* (territorial spirits), who are also thought to be the living embodiment of ancestors from that place (see Ang 1986). People may attend one temple rather than another to make offerings to a particular *něak ta* because they are seen as powerful spiritually, because they are said to offer assistance in particular situations (curing illness, for example), or because they are the descendants of a *něak ta* who is a believed to be a village founder.[11]

Men also mentioned attending a *wat* because it was where they had been ordained; the current head of the temple committee at Wat Svay, for example, had been ordained there as a young man for four years. The retired *achar*, who was 86 when interviewed in 2003, had not been ordained at Wat Svay, but at another nearby Mohanikay temple. His father, however, had served as *achar* at Wat Svay when he was young, and he served as *achar* at Wat Svay from its reopening in 1979 until recently when he could no longer walk to the temple on his own.

A woman in her mid-50s said that she attends both Wat Svay and another Mohanikay temple to the east; on holy days her mother goes to the latter because it is closer to her house. She said that there was really no difference, that both temples were Buddhist, and that the crucial factor was that people would go where their ancestors lie. Sometimes Mohanikay temples have more influential donors from Phnom Penh and, consequently, grow more quickly, she said, but reiterated the choice of *wat* you attend still depends on where your ancestors are.

Finally, there is the issue of individual personal preference. Ebihara (1968:381) noted that some people just said that they thought the monks were 'nicer' in one temple than another, or that they felt 'more comfortable' in one particular place. For example, one elder made the trip up the road to the more distant Wat Samnang and made a point of giving his donations there and to other more distant temples because he had personal conflicts with relatives in Svay who attended Wat Svay.

Discussion

Returning to Kobayashi's observations about *chậmnŏh* in relation to a given village, it is clear that he is correct to point out that the notion of the temple as a social centre may obscure the kinds of divisions and conflicts that can characterise temple communities, which cut across village boundaries geographically.[12] I think he is also correct in noting that the theoretical models in anthropology of the 1950s and early 1960s emphasised stability and social structures over a focus on processes of change and conflict, although a shift away from these static models was well underway by the time Ebihara's thesis appeared in 1968. Ebihara saw herself primarily as an ethnographer, and one of the key values of her work lies in the detailed descriptions that she provides of people and events. The fact that people of Svay attended both local temples, together with some of the flavour of why they did so, is already present in her early work.

In the original paper that I wrote for the Association for Asian Studies (AAS) panel in honour of May, I emphasised the degree to which her detailed writings demonstrate an intimate knowledge of the lives of individuals. She taught us about the village, not by emphasising structures but by telling the stories of individuals woven together through their daily interactions. She wrote about their personalities, their foibles, their joys and fears; and, in the aftermath of the Khmer Rouge destruction, we heard peoples' stories of loss and devastation. In his introduction to this volume, Marston makes reference to this characteristic of May's work; he writes, 'Her writing is beautiful, I have finally concluded, because of a dignity of restraint, which itself had a moral dimension, combined with a respect and love for Cambodians revealed in her joyous attention to the details of their lives'. Crochet, also in this volume, refers to May's 'healthy penchant for pragmatism'. She was not one who conformed to theoretical models for the sake of doing so or in the face of ethnographic data that even hinted otherwise.

Anthropological theory today is more focused on disjunctures, shifting perceptions and imagined identities, as opposed to stable communities or reified notions of cultural models, and this certainly affects the way that we as ethnographers describe what we see today. As contemporary observers, we are more inclined to focus on conflict and distrust, particularly if that is what we go into villages expecting to find. And, of course, the notion of the stable community of smiling, happy Cambodians was shattered by the extreme levels of violence that have characterised the last 30+ years of Cambodian history.

The concept of community was the focus of some debate over the last decade, framed in part as a response to Ovesen, Trankell and Öjendal (1995). The authors of that study argued that Cambodian society had been so atomised by the upheavals of the Khmer Rouge regime that social relations had still not recovered, that people only took care of themselves and did not assist others through networks of reciprocity as had been reported by Ebihara, Martel and others before the war. Some, including myself, responded that this was an exaggeration, that social networks, while they might be more truncated than they had been before the war, were still the primary social bonds that held together groups of kinsmen, networks of patrons and clients, and fellow villagers (see Ledgerwood 1998; Ebihara & Ledgerwood 2002; Vijghen & Ly 1996; Kim 2001; Ledgerwood & Vijghen 2002). At the local level, I have also argued (Ledgerwood & Vijghen 2002), that patron–client relationships are still based, to some degree, on moral responsibility that people have to one another as members of village communities.

In 1999 a conference was held on the meaning of 'community' in Cambodia that included a review of the Khmer-, French-, and English-language literature on the subject, discussion with a wide range of Khmer and Western participants, a keynote address by Meas Nee and concluding remarks by Serge Thion. One of Thion's conclusions from that conference was that, for most participants and certainly for the overwhelming majority of Khmer speakers, there was 'a square equivalence of "community" with "village"' (Thion 1999:27). But, while it might be taken as a shorthand 'given' that the community is the *phoum* or village, Thion points out that it is also more complex than this.

> In many places, the village is such a unit, a self-enclosed group, with its internal rules and large autonomy. But it happened that even this basic approach does not fit Cambodian society. A village is often more an administrative way of carving up a chunk of territory on a map than a fully comprehensive social unit. The village map and the map of the wat parishes do not overlap. Even the sacred cow of the concept of 'family' can be kept only if one does not inquire too much on the real kinship ties of the members, as all Khmer families comprise, at times, of a sometimes larger number of unrelated people living together as a family (Thion 1999:27).

Thion says that, for years, NGOs have been embracing the concept of community as simultaneous with village, even though it did not really fit; he credits the conference with (at last) trying to understand local conceptions rather than imposing from outside the conceptions of funders. Thion suggests dropping the 'ill-informed and untranslatable word' community and replacing it bluntly with 'village.' (Thion 1999:28). At the same time, he appeals to those doing development work to really try to understand existing social institutions; he notes that 'a significant part of the discussions (at this conference) had the wat committees as the center of the village' but he notes that 'the situation of these associations is extremely diverse' (Thion 1999:28).

Following from this comment, I would note another image from this conference, raised by Meas Nee in his keynote address—that of the four blind men who are asked to describe an elephant. As each man touches a different part of the animal, the descriptions are, of course, completely different.

> In this, I am not assuming that community development workers are blind and unreliable…Many of us are trying to hard to identify ways in which community

can be helped. Very often, we are unable to tackle the whole complicated problem, and instead, we can only touch some parts under the assumption that this is community development (Thion 1999:60).

Meas Nee is using the metaphor to say that the problem of community is 'as large as an elephant' and that is why development workers see only part of the problem. But I would use the same metaphor in a different way and argue that, in fact, we see different kinds of communities because we are doing research in very different kinds of villages, 'feeling' in a parallel way different parts of the elephant (see also Crochet in this volume).

In Cambodia, post-DK and post-PRK, there are many different kinds of communities across the face of the country (see Ledgerwood & Vijghen 2002). In the context of Svay, which is on the central plains south of Phnom Penh and has a relatively stable population that includes mainly people who lived there before the war—people who have known each other across generations—there is a kind of stability that is not generalisable to much of the country. The fact that Ebihara knew the community members from the generation preceding the current residents and, in her research in the 1990s, focused on kinship linkages has probably served to highlight these connections more than would have been the case for other researchers in other communities. Methodologically she started with note cards of kinship networks and built outward, tracing those specific connections.

Now that it has been possible for some years to do research in other parts of the country, we have village studies and new kinds of research from villages with very different kinds of histories. Crochet writes in this volume that, in most Cambodian villages, the post-war population is not homogeneous. She notes three patterns: the 'old village', which was largely populated or repopulated with its pre-1975 population (like Svay); the 'new village', for a place 'recently build, (mainly since the late 1980s) for a large group of displaced people, refugees or returnees'; and 'mixed villages' which comprise a pre-war population and some combination of displaced and returned refugees. After discussing these possibilities, however, she describes the village where she conducted research as having yet another pattern, wherein the original inhabitants of a riverside village returned and rebuilt their houses and former residents of another nearby village joined the village, grafting themselves on the outer edges of the original settlement. And 'although they were coming from nearby villages, 30 years later they were still considered as newcomers and called "the others" (*něak dâtei*)'.

Kim (2001, and in this volume) finds systems of reciprocity parallel to those described by Ebihara 40 years before, but sees them as being dramatically altered by a transition to a new cash economy that is developing with the tourism boom in the Angkor Wat region. Zucker conducted research in a village in Kompong Speu from which all the villagers had fled and to which both new and former residents returned as 'new' settlers (Zucker 2007). She has also written about the particular social patterns there that are tied to a lack of village elders (Zucker 2008). Biddulph's (1996) research on the northwest border presented even more stressfully-blended communities that mixed returnees from the border with suspicious village neighbours who might also have not been from that place before the war, in a context where warfare had only recently ceased and the possibility of violence still loomed.

In comments to the 1999 conference, Biddulph notes that certain aspects of the discussion of community by outsiders seem to be out-of-date, 'in particular focuses on the breakdown of trust resulting from the Khmer Rouge experiences and also on the central role of Buddhist religion and respect for the elderly'. He says, rather, that villagers describe a breakdown in solidarity in the past 10–15 years 'as they increasingly sell to each other eg, fish or assistance in building a house, rather than just helping each other out—this seems to be the impact of the free market economy' (Biddulph 1999:137). The main trends he had seen in the late 1990s included a reduced role for village authorities and an increased exposure to the wider world (leading especially to the emergence of a youth culture less focused on local community). He also notes that, in contrast to other observers, he has found, especially in smaller villages, a strong sense of community at village level (Biddulph 1999:137).

How can the notion of overlapping *chậmnŏh* help us to understand communities in this post-conflict montage? This leads us to the issue of how and why temples are important in the lives of Khmer today. Meas Nee has argued that Buddhism has been crucially important as a means to renew the social and moral universe in the post-war society. At the same time people may make peace with their own feelings of guilt and remorse for the suffering of loved ones over the last 30 years.

> ...religion, the teaching of the monks, music...are the way to build unity and heal hearts and spirits. They help to create community where everything can be talked about, even past suffering. They help create community where the poorest are cared about. They help to restore dignity (Meas 1995:70).

Buddhism provides a system of cultural models with which one makes sense of the world, even a world as confused and traumatic as Cambodia over the span of a current adult's life. At the core of this model are notions of merit and *karma*. Kobayashi (2008:170) calls merit-making ideology a major force driving the religious activities of Theravāda Buddhists. I have argued elsewhere that what remains the same from the pre-war years in Cambodian Buddhism is the practice of merit-making—the way that adult Cambodians enact the religion in their daily lives (Ledgerwood 2008a). They make choices from within a range of options that are their learned ways of thinking, feeling, speaking, moving and so on, that come from their cultural experiences, especially their experiences as young people.

Merit-making helps us to understand the role of the temple in the community, as a place to enact, to live out the cultural models of the pre-war years. It is a realm within which things can return to normal, or at least to the ways which things are remembered as having happened before. The temple is a safe place in this sense. People go there to do what Cambodians have always done; so the temple is a restorative place, even in the midst of other social upheavals. In some ways, therefore, the *chậmnŏh*, one's membership in a community of people focused on merit-making, may be key to understanding the re-establishment of moral and social communities, simultaneously with and in spite of the overwhelming political and other divisions in the secular world.

This is not to say that temples are not also sites of social conflicts—from political conflicts to conflicts over temple donations to conflicts over land claims. But understanding the social dynamics of a particular community will always involve seeing ideal versus actual behaviour (the temple as an island of peace in a world of conflict versus the temple as a place where arguments rage about some particular social affront) and seeing social patterns as opposed to individual actions (reflecting personal choice as opposed to a person being locked into particular relationships by patronage obligations or poverty).

Choosing one's *chậmnŏh* still allows people a measure of autonomy in a world of dependence and vulnerability. I would agree then with Kobayashi on two important points: first, that villagers may choose to participate in the activities of a number of temples, depending on their own personal preferences and beliefs, creating a 'fluid, flexible situation' (Kobayashi 2008:177); and second, that 'sharing merit-making ideology facilitates cooperative activity', even as 'questions of identity frequently lead to competition and conflict' (Kobayashi 2008:189).

In the enactment of merit-making activity, people rebuild their lives as individuals as well as a sense of community. The forms, the procedures, the patterns of action are shared, providing comfort and a sense of the social and moral order as restored. And, while there are conflicts within temple communities, as Kobayashi, Marston and others makes clear, there is flexibility for people to move across *chậmnŏh* and still practise their merit-making activities in another setting, or in multiple settings simultaneously, to search for where they are most comfortable living as members of Buddhist communities.

The ethnographic details of the situation at the two temples where the residents of Svay are *chǎmnŏh* members allow us a window onto some of the reasons that people choose one 'parish' over another: a preference for Mohanikay over Thommayut; a sense that one temple in a community might provide more status as a more wealthy member of a community; a preference for a more elderly and respected abbot; a sense that a *wat* is more lively—a more fun place to be on festival days—with many visitors out from the city; that the temple is the site where one's ancestors are found (either literally in the sense of their ashes are interred there, or in the sense of being the place where the spirits of one's ancestors might come looking for you when they return on Pchŭm Bĕn, or, generally, in that one knows that one's *bâng b'aun* came from this place). The decision can relate to a personal animosity, as in the case of the man who is avoiding relatives with whom he has a longstanding conflict, or it can relate toconvenience, as in the case of the woman's elderly mother who can only walk to the closest *wat* to take the precepts on holy days.

And changes are taking place rapidly. Elderly monks are dying and most monks are relatively young monks from the ranks of those ordained since the end of the PRK; will this have an effect on the devotion of worshippers? Even more importantly, as the elders begin to pass, as those who learned Buddhism by attending services as children in the pre-war years are gone, and as those whose learning of the practice of Buddhism was disrupted by the DK and PRK years become elders, will temple membership and the practice of Buddhism generally be affected, and in what ways? As their focus is turned outward to the ever-encroaching wider world, will young people participate in Buddhist communities in anything like the way their parents did?

These kinds of questions will be researched using a range of methods, but an important method will continue to be the kind of on-the-ground ethnography that May Ebihara's work exemplified. One way that we will be able to trace these changes iwill be through using the precious legacy that she has left us, the record of the lives of people in a single village across the cataclysm of the Pol Pot era.

It is clear to me that the people of Svay understand and appreciate the value of Ebihara's research. They remember her fondly from her earlier visit, but they also value her teaching and writing about their lives because she was their witness. She understood the scale of their loss, because she knew first-hand what their lives were like before. She remembered their bodies when they were young and strong, though they are now bent, not only from the years but also from the hardships they have endured. She understood the scale of the horror of those years, the time *huos vetonea* (beyond suffering), because it was not a story in the abstract but a personal story with a cast she knew. She recorded the stories of how each person died, or of how they suffered and lived, so that others could understand. Ebihara was the proper person to record their stories because she had respect for the memories of their loved ones. Each of us who follows in May's footsteps strives to maintain that sense of honesty and respect.

Notes

1   I conducted research in Cambodia from July 2002 to August 2003, with funding from the National Endowment for the Humanities to study Buddhist prophetic texts and a combined teaching and research Fulbright Fellowship. I would like to thank both funding institutions for their support and to thank Northern Illinois University for the sabbatical that made this research possible.

This paper is based in part on research conducted in the summer of 2003 as an ethnographic field school sponsored by Northern Illinois University and the Royal University of Fine Arts (RUFA). The students who participated from the Buddhist Institute were Cheat Sreang, Aing Sokroeun and Mech Samphors. The RUFA students were To Thanarath, Sirak Sivana, Yim Many, Eng Lekhena, Iv Panchak Seila, Chen Chanratana, Mak Kun, Khun Sathal, Chey Serivath and Seng Chantha. The American students were Gina Curler, Margaret Karnyski, Elizabeth Markle, Katheryn Rudasill, Susan Speigel, John Stavrellis and Ellen King. The Center for Khmer Studies (CKS) assistants were Heng Chhun Oeurn, Hak Siphirath and Run Sambath. Special thanks are due to Dean Hor Lat of the Faculty of Archeology at the RUFA, Heng Kim Van at the Buddhist Institute and Kim Sedara, supervisor of the Anthropology program at CKS. Across six villages (including Svay), the students conducted 141 surveys with questions on Buddhist practice and ideas about Buddhism and society. They conducted one exercise in structured observation, following monks on their morning alms rounds, and made maps and took photographs at the temples. The researchers kept field notes of their own observations, conducted structured and semi-structured interviews with monks, temple committee members, *achar*, nuns and community residents.

2   As the temple was rebuilt over the years, May and I also made contributions to the reconstruction. We sponsored one of the panels of paintings of the story of the Buddha's life inside the *vīhear* and part of the back steps and railings, and contributed to the building of the community *chetěy* where her ashes are now interred. My family also contributed to the building of the new *sala chăn* in 2000.

3   Young women who come from remote areas of the country to work in the garment factories often have a hard time surviving on the wage and find it difficult to send money home to their relatives in the countryside (see Derks 2008).

4   It is no longer the case, for example, that all villagers in Svay 'lack the education and networks of connections that would have made it possible for them to seek higher-paying jobs outside of the rural economy', a phrase Charles Keyes applies, in this volume, to both Ban Nông Tün in Thailand and Svay when he and Ebihara conducted research in these two villages respectively.

5   This abbot's *kŏdě* is controversial because the abbot says that the money to complete it was borrowed from moneylenders and is to be repaid with future contributions.

6   This paper does not address the issue of the relationship between spirit worship and Buddhism, but it should be noted that both temples have also rebuilt the shrines to *něak ta* spirits that were there before the war. In fact, Wat Svay now has two *něak ta* houses, whereas in 1960 it had only one. The second is dedicated to a Yeay Deb,

a female *nĕak ta* spirit who alerted residents to her presence first by causing several children to fall ill, and then by possessing a local medium.

7   Ebihara does note a divisive incident when the village was short of rice and wanted to do only one post-harvest ceremony rather than two. The villagers argued over whether the monks from one temple or the other should be invited if they could not afford to invite both groups (Ebihara 1968:382; ch 3).

8   For a discussion of the introduction of the Thommayut order, see Hansen (2007) and Harris (2005:ch 5).

9   This shows that the issue is present at Wat Svay, even if muted. At one of the six temples where we conducted research in 2003, the division between political parties had exploded; one temple committee associated with the royalist party had been ousted by another temple committee backed by local CPP political authorities. According to one account, the old temple committee was forced to step down under threat of physical violence. At another of the six temples there was ongoing conflict within the temple between the abbot and a group of monks and laypeople, but this was not clearly linked to politics. At a third temple there were smouldering rumours of a recent conflict concerning alleged sexual activity by one of the monks. In contrast, Wat Svay and Wat Samnang seemed relatively peaceful places.

10   It could also be that the characteristics of the two abbots influence whether certain *bŏran* practices are known; in the case of Wat Samnang the abbot is young and has spent his years under ordination in the post-war Mohanikay modernist tradition, while the elderly abbot at Wat Svay, as a Thommayut monk, would have been less likely to follow *bŏran* traditions (see Harris (2005:ch 8) and Marston (2002c)).

11   During interviews in 2003 we did not ask about particular *nĕak ta* spirits and only noted their presence. Territorial spirits across Southeast Asia (*nat* in Burma, *phi* in Thailand and *nĕak ta* in Cambodia) are generally understood to be in ranked hierarchies, as are humans, so the choice of which *wat* to attend could be linked to the desire to be associated with a more powerful *nĕak ta*. (I thank Andrea Molnar for this observation.)

12   This is even truer in the second district where we conducted research, where the villagers are *nĕak chămkar* (gardeners along the riverside). The very high population densities in such riverside locations mean that villages run together and temple *chămnŏh* seem to correspond even less clearly to residence in a particular village.

Catching facts or sketching the elephant? Village monographs on Cambodia, yesterday, today, tomorrow

chapter six

Soizick Crochet

In a collection of essays about ethnographic field work, Joan Larcom, 20 years ago, was pondering on the fact that '[nowadays] most ethnographers find themselves with precursors in the field'. She wrote: 'Each fieldworker may be viewed as harvesting a netful of "fresh facts", but...the relationship between these facts may change with each new catch' (Larcom 1983:193). The most famous cases of ethnographic revisiting generally involved at least two different researchers.[1] May Ebihara has been in the situation of realising herself a double 'catch' of facts 30 years apart. Other anthropologists have sometimes been granted that chance, but what is rare in her case is that her 'catches' were made before and after a major societal cataclysm. Meeting one of the only two early Cambodia's ethnographers[2] just before starting my own field work was an intimidating opportunity. She had only been a name, an 'anthropological ancestor', but there she was, back to a field left vacant for many years. The number of social scientists doing research in Cambodia has expanded considerably in the last decade, but it was still 'virgin again' in the early and mid-1990s. Ebihara had been calling for a return to research 'about local-level existence and the ordinary people who comprise the majority of the population' (Ebihara 1990a:44). Now it was mid-1994 in Phnom Penh, and, as I listened very attentively, she was asking me where and how I would choose 'my' village. In her dissertation she had dedicated several pages to this problem, wondering 'first how similar is the community investigated to the other villages in the country; and second, what (or how much) does a description of village life tell you about the culture of the nation...as a whole'(Ebihara 1968:8).

These dilemmas and pitfalls of 'community studies' had been exposed in the 1950s (Redfield 1955) and were still debated in the 1990s (Marcus 1990; Népote 1992). Addressing the first issue (the hazards of generalising observations from one particular group, unique in its history, geographical settings and economic specificities), Ebihara, with a healthy penchant for pragmatism, used phrases originally applied to theories of personality; Svay was together 'in some respects like *no* other village...in other ways like *some* other villages in Cambodia [and at the same time] ...probably like *all* other villages in several important respects' (Ebihara 1968:8–11). As for the problem of distortion between scales and whether Svay could be considered a microcosm of the Cambodian society, she elucidated the issue through an account of cultural elements 'common to both Khmer peasant and urbanites' (Ebihara 1968:12), while exerting caution on their suitability to represent the entire nation.

A local version of this quandary recounts how four blind men who had only been able to touch a leg, the trunk, an ear or the tail of an elephant, held contradicting conceptions about the animal's shape (Leclere 1984:7–8).[3] This fable, famed in other Asian cultures[4] is used by Cambodians of all walks of life to warn the common person against the mirage of assuming a 'whole' on the basis of a part, to recall the dangers of building a global plot from single sketches.[5] It leads to a call for re-analysis; would more blind visitors, exercising a greater number of strokes, help us get a better picture of a phenomenon that does not stay still? Comprehensive village monographs have not been undertaken since the 1950s and 1960s (what we might call 'before yesterday'). It is difficult to access the corpus of smaller, unpublished studies about village life in the 1990s ('yesterday') (Lemarquis 1992; van de Put 1997; Vijghen 1991) and detailed reports about changes in the early 2000s ('today') [(Long 2004)].[6]

My own work (from 1994 to 1996)[7] aimed at describing representations and practices of popular medicine among rural women, but it included a home survey. The information on kinship, household composition and landholding collected at that time could be used for a comparison with pre-war data. Moreover, like a growing number of social scientists in Cambodia, I am able to go back more frequently now to 'my' village, witness the transformations and foresee the need for a new in-depth study. This paper does not intend to prove or contradict any theory about social order and change among rural Cambodians. Rather, it should be seen as a modest contribution to a topic once thoroughly documented by Ebihara—residence patterns in a Khmer peasant village (1977).

Kampong Thom province

I shall describe the province (*khaet*) first, because it might explain some differences between my findings and those of the two pre-war studies, one set in Kandal (Ebihara) and one in Siem Reap (Martel). Since village analysis cannot be dissociated from the study of larger areas, the provincial level could be seen as a pertinent perimeter, because, despite the range of specifics of agro-economy in each *khaet*,[8] it works as an identity marker. Often the first territorial unit mentioned in discussions or biographies and, among Cambodians, a label associated with personality stereotypes, the *khaet* carries a world of images and expectations.[9]

For various reasons I had chosen the *khaet* of Kompong Thom, centrally located[10] and the site of one of the oldest capitals of the kingdom—the ruins of Isanapura date back to the seventh century.[11] I had been told that while it was ranked as the country's eighth most populous province (over, at that time, 19 others), it was also very rural and very poor. It was also, in 1995, rather isolated; the road was in such bad condition that it took more than six hours to cover the 160 kilometres from Phnom Penh to the prefecture (*ti ruom khaet*) of Kompong Thom town.[12] While many *volags* (non-government organisations) used to work in Battambang or the provinces close to Phnom Penh, there were only a handful of expatriates operating less than half a dozen NGOs, and they were mainly concentrated in the *ti ruom khaet*. One of the reasons was the sporadic fighting that was still going on in Kompong Thom, even though most of the country was at peace.[13]

The people of this province have always had a reputation as troublemakers (Dufosse 1918:87).[14] They were involved, over the centuries, in several rebellions, and provided not only the 'original khmer' (*khmaer daoem*), Pol Pot, who was born in Prek Sbeu, a village close to the prefecture, but also most of the cadres of the dreaded 'security' (*sântĕbal*) of the Khmer Rouge (Kiernan 1996:315). A French colonial administrator had even once said that Kompong Thom inhabitants were 'the most deeply Cambodian and the least susceptible to our [French] influence' (Kiernan 1985:38), which, of course, appealed to me when I was choosing a place for field work. Later, my assistant referred several times to 'the strong character' of the mothers we were meeting for interviews: 'They are not as sweet (*slaut*) and patient as the women of Kandal, or Kompong Cham,...' The memories of a famous anti-colonial resistant were still alive among the intellectuals, who would proudly signal his ambush spot.[15] Furthermore, in September 1994, at a time when challenging official authority was still exceptional,[16] angry Balang villagers rebelled against what they saw as an unfair distribution of food-for-work under the UN World Food Programme. They marched to the *khŭm* office in protest (*padĕkăm*), burnt it down and carried on to the governor's building in town.

Such remarkable hardness implied limitations, for I finally realised that many areas were off limits and too dangerous for a Westerner to live in.[17] 'Safety' (*sthanâpheap sântĕsŏk*, the security situation) was an omnipresent word at the beginning of my stay. A third of the houses and the temple in the nearby village of Roluos had been burnt down just a few months before, by the '*a-Pot*' (derogatory term for Pol Pot forces) and when I went there people were begging for rice.[18] Hence, after visiting several villages around the prefecture, I narrowed my quest down to Balang, located between the National Road number 6 and the river (*stĕung*) Sen, only six kilometres south of Kompong Thom town.[19] It was not the tiny, isolated and easy to encompass hamlet that I had envisioned for an ethnographic study. It was also considered a 'rich' village. But, in a poor province like Kompong Thom, it could mean an economic level on a par with most Cambodian communities at the time.

Villages of Cambodia

Growing disparities

The latest published figures indicate that there are about 13,046 villages (*phoum*) in Cambodia (NIS 1999:xi). Their mean size has grown since Ebihara's research in 1959–60, when she estimated it at between 200 and 500 inhabitants (Ebihara 1974a:359). The growth in mean size has, of course, to do with demographic expansion. Cambodia had a little bit more than five and a half million inhabitants in 1960 (Migozzi 1973:226); the last population census counted more than eleven million inhabitants in 1998 (NIS 1999:xi). Hence, the mean size of villages in Kandal province, where Ebihara worked, has grown to about 935,[20] whereas by 1995 the mean size of villages across the country had reached 692.[21] But, notwithstanding the differences of density population within the country, there are large discrepancies in the mean size of villages within provinces and districts. Because of the large movements of population during the war, the Khmer Rouge regime and the years of civil war in the 1980s, some villages have disappeared, while others have flourished, especially along the main roads and in the vicinity of provincial towns.

For instance, in Kompong Thom province, with around half a million inhabitants, the population density is supposed to be 41 people per square kilometre, which is low compared to the national mean of 64 and the maximum of 301 in Kandal province (NIS 1999); in this province the on-the-ground residency in the districts (*srŏk*) shows very different patterns.[22] Almost half of the province's inhabitants live in two of its eight districts. The mean size of the villages—654 inhabitants for this province(Aschmoneit & Thoma 1995)—shows important deviations according to the location of the *srŏk*; those in Kompong Thom may have more than 1,000 inhabitants, whereas some in Prassat Balang district have less than 300. Distance between settlements may also vary greatly. In Stoung district, west of the National Road, there are many villages strung along mud roads, most less than a kilometre apart. In contrast to this distribution of villages, the hamlets in Sandan district have no means of communication other than the river, whose meandering increase the distance between them.

New settlements

The urban population of Kompong Thom province is estimated at around 12% of the total provincial population.[23] The villages in the immediate vicinity of Kompong Thom city have been considered its suburbs. But those around Stoung, a market town could also be considered suburbs, for they make a 'street' on the river with 14,000 inhabitants. This spatial organisation can also be found along National Road 6, where numerous villages are mere extensions of market towns, such as Tang Kouk, Baray, Kompong Thmâ, whose populations, initially counted at 1,000–2,000, can then be multiplied by two or three. These localities stretch along the road, at intervals of one or two kilometres. In total, more than 30,000 people live along this axis which is less than one kilometre wide and 60 kilometres long. Most of them are peasants, but their habitat is a far cry from the hamlet that one would expect to find as a rural dwelling-place. Village oraganisation along the road, a type of 'social space' influenced by security concerns, had already been described in the late 1950s.[24] It is getting more and more common and its implications for feelings of cohesiveness or belonging, its impact on the making of alliances, or the new economic opportunities it allows, would require more studies.

What might be more important about villages in post-war Cambodia, however, is that their composition is not homogenous. Some authors have introduced a new typology to describe this situation (van de Put 1997:7).[25] I will use from this typology the terms 'old village' (for a *phum* made up of its pre-1975 population), 'new village' (for a place recently built—that is, mainly since the late 1980s—for a large group of displaced people, refugees or returnees); and 'mixed village' (for a villages that comprises the villagers who used to live there before 1975 and refugees, returnees or displaced people).[26] Because Kompong Thom was considered a 'no-go area' in 1992–93, when refugees went back to Cambodia (UNHCR 1992:5), there were almost no returnees in that province during my stay. The number of internally displaced persons (IDPs), however, was around 18,000 (Kant 1993; O'Leary et al 1995). Balang did not receive any IDPs and I found only two returnee families.[27] But it could not be considered a merely 'old' settlement for different reasons.

Balang, a mixed village

Balang[28] is an old riverside village, one of many such that are long established in Kompong Thom province. These are not *châmkar* (which are very specific garden or non-rice agricultural settlements). Found among orchards and trees, one after the other along one of the *stung* (river) where the population density used to be high (Delvert 1961:616), they were created by rice farmers coming up the river on a quest for new territories. This process, probably started at the time of the founding of Isanapura in the seventh century (Parmentier 1927:44–5), was related by Balang elders as having happened in the late 1850s. The families descended from the seven original couples who had arrived from Kompong Chhnang 'before the French (Protectorate)' know about their ancestors and consider themselves as the 'authentic' (*trouv*) Balang villagers, an aristocracy of sorts. They make the core of the 'old' village, together with some other families who arrived also at the end of the 19th century, from Takeo province. They tend to live in the biggest houses at the centre of the village, to which they returned in 1979, after eight years in exile.

Just like in Svay, the village is comprised of an Eastern and a Western hamlet, officially designated as such by the authorities in the late 1980s. But the villagers still talk of the 'upper' (*loe*) and the 'lower' (*kraom*) Balang, the former being upstream and the latter down the river flow. This type of habitat, reputedly the most common in Cambodia before the war, is made up of houses built next to each other ('like a rosary'), sometimes for tens of kilometres (Delvert 1961:214). Balang was only four and a half kilometres long, with about 200 houses, ten or 20 metres apart, in two parallel rows along one side of the river Sen. Because it was such a large location (with about 1,300 people and 200 households in 1995), it was too big for a comprehensive study. Consequently, I focused my research on East Balang, more specifically on a group of 74 households which were surveyed in depth.[29] This is a little bit more than half the number of families researched in Lovea[30] and twice the size of the hamlet in West Svay studied in 1959-60 by Ebihara (Ebihara 1974a:6–7).

History of land occupation

I did not research pre-war household composition and cannot make an assessment of mortality in the 1970s. Data on that topic and landholding changes cannot display the diachronic aspect Ebihara was able to provide. What is known about these riverbank villages, though, is that a large number of their rice-farmer inhabitants are usually of Sino-Khmer descent (Delvert 1961:217; Forest 1980:475.6). Indeed, I was told that the sawmill and the brick factory on the outskirts of Balang belonged to 'rich' Chinese owners, who left the village, as many rural Chinese did (Kiernan 1996:288), at the beginning of the war. They never came back. Balang was abandoned in 1971, during the Lon Nol regime, when it was bombed and, according to the villagers,[31] sprayed with napalm. The villagers fled to villages south and west of the road (Panha Chi, Phnom Santuk, Tropeang Veng) until these villages were also burnt. Then, they eventually headed to Kompong Thom town and its suburbs (Kompong Roteh).[32] In 1975 most of them stayed in the province, around Tropeang Veng, and the youngest were transferred from one site to another.[33] They were divided into categories of 'new people' or 'old people', depending on where they were when the Khmer Rouge came into power. As Ebihara pointed out, the distinction was not based on whether people were of rural or urban origin (Ebihara 1993a:153). During the Democratic Kampuchea (DK) period, Kompong Thom was considered an especially 'bad area',[34] but as I did not systematically collect individual life stories of that period, my research does not confirm this characterisation. The village, like many others along the river, had no civilian population until 1979. The Khmer Rouge had a garrison there, used the old sawmill and built a water station for irrigation purposes. They cultivated the river banks and let the trees grow again.

In 1979, the Vietnamese army secured a transit point at the entrance of Kompong Thom for Chinese returnees arriving from the Thai border: 'at a river called Stoeng [sic] Sen, they were separated out from the refugees' columns... while the Khmers proceeded on to Kompong Thom, the Chinese waited at Stung Sen'(Heder 1980:25–6). The former inhabitants of Kompong Krabao, where this occurred, did not get the permission to resettle, whether they were considered Chinese or not, and were finally, in late 1979, sent to live in Balang with a group of relatives from Pat Sandaï (a fishing village in Kompong Chhnang). Although they had come from nearby villages, 30 years later they were still considered newcomers and called 'the others' (něak dâtei). They got the plots at each end of the line of houses spread along the stěung, the same plots abandoned by Chinese and Sino-Khmer families at the beginning of the war. Later, as other displaced people were assigned to live in Kompong Krabao, it was usual to hear: 'They live in our houses, we live in theirs'. Meanwhile, the 'original' Balang villagers went back to their previous spots and rebuilt their houses where they used to be (generally in the curve of the river—dey lei—not affected by erosion).

During the People's Republic of Kampuchea, Kompong Thom province officially had the biggest percentage (50%) of Level 1 solidarity groups (krŏm samokki), performing the most integrated type of collective farming [(Frings 1997b:84)].[35] Ten groups of 20 families were created in Balang in 1979, but I did not get information on the way they operated. These krŏm samokki ceased to function in early 1988[36] and land was quickly sold and exchanged. (As one interviewee said, 'When I arrived in 1988 there was nothing left'.) Two families reported buying land as early as 1981, but this report needs further elucidation. Early in 1995, a new system (robieb thmey) was designed, of 20 groups of ten families, in a move often perceived as a political manoeuvre on the part of the CPP.[37] The group heads (me krŏm), who were all males, were 'volunteers' and their responsibilities unclear, even to them. Most villagers did not seem to care and could not name their group leader.

Land ownership

In 1979, the plots (*dey phoum*, or 'village land') devised by the new authorities were all the same size. The strips of land were more or less 25 metres wide, not unlike those before the war, according to the villagers. The difference was that those few villagers who had possessed larger properties before the revolution now lost them. In 1995, the mean size was 1,500 square metres, with wide variations, from 320 square metres to 7,500 square metres, for different reasons: the river angle gave more width to some plots; others, on the river bank became longer at low tide (allowing for orchard plantation) and some of these had been 'bought' by powerful civil servants. Conflicts about land ownership started after the 1989 land reform, when private ownership of property was officially re-established and former owners came back to claim their land, as they did everywhere in the country.[38] If there were no disputes about the houses built on the *dey phoum*, six of the 74 households surveyed had an argument about ownership of the land. Village land has become an important asset in this area; its value on the market has increased almost tenfold in less than ten years.[39] A piece of property of 700 square metres was sold for one *chi* in 1987; in 1995, a 400-square-metre piece of land was worth five *chi*.[40]

The mean size of the paddy fields for the 74 households who provided the information was less than one hectare (91.5 ares[41]). In the 1960s, in a province with a much greater population density, the mean size of paddy fields in the village studied by Ebihara was 88 ares (Ebihara 1968:221).[42] But in Kompong Thom province, in the same period, it was between two and three hectares per household (Delvert 1961:494).[43] In 1995, ten families in the 74 households surveyed in Balang East did not have any agricultural land at all[44] a figure similar to the 13% found nationwide in 2000 (Biddulph 2000). Fifteen families had more than one hectare, including three with between three and five hectares. But it must be said that these plots were far away in the 'lower plain' (*veal kraom*), close to the lakes and unworkable. Between these two extremes, 39 households had between ten and 100 ares and among them 23 had fewer than 75 ares. The people without land were not in the worst situation. Among them, only three families had to rent agricultural land (*brâvăs srae*),[45] while the others could rely on other sources of income. It was more difficult for the majority of East Balang villagers, being large families with small holdings. It has been estimated that an average family of six people (two adults and four children) needs around one ton of paddy to meet basic nutritional requirements,[46] which, according to Food and Agriculture Organization in 1999, cannot be achieved if the land holding falls under 0.75 hectare (Biddulph 2000:7).

Farming and economic organisation

Because most soils around Balang were considered mediocre, a lottery system had been designed in 1982[47] to distribute good land. It resulted in agricultural tenure being fragmented into very small surfaces, especially around the village, while the larger plots were one or two kilometres away, on sites called *lo*[48] one (one kilometre away), *lo* two (two kilometres away), and so on. It was not rare for a family with 50 or 60 ares to have 20 ares here, 10 ares somewhere else and 20 more in a third location. There were two consecutive bad crops in 1994 and 1995. In the worst case, some families got as little as ten *thăng*,[49] or 240 kilograms, on 60 ares, meaning yields of 400 kilograms per hectare. In 1996, which was considered a better year, a 'rich' family harvested 200 *thăng* on four hectares and 40 ares, with yields of around one ton per hectare, a yield common in other parts of Cambodia (Delvert 1961:357; FAO 1991:75).[50] Two families with plots with better soil were even able to get around 28 *thăng* on 45 ares (equivalent to a little bit less than 1,500 kilograms per hectare, an exceptional figure; even so, they had to buy one more *thăng* to be able to eat until the end of the year). In any case, the amount of rice produced was often insufficient for a family of six (the average size) and almost all of them, like most rice farmers in the Cambodian plains, could only meet a third of their nutritional requirements (FAO 1991:22).

Looking for other sources of income, about half-a-dozen families were collecting palm sugar as a cottage industry. Some others completed their food intake by fishing either in the *stĕung* or in nearby ponds (*bŏeng*). A few more were making furniture with left-over bits of quality wood obtained at the saw-mill. A handful of civil servants (such as the schoolteacher, headmaster and policeman) were better-off because they could invest their meager salaries, when they were paid, in pig production or in a water pump or a rice mill that they would rent out to others. Draught animals were important assets, because they could be rented ploughing and harvesting times. But, in Balang, a little more than one third of the 66 families who provided information about sources of income did not have any cattle—the same proportion as in West Svay (Ebihara 1968:307). The other two-thirds had two or three animals, either a cow or a bull; only two families had buffalos,as are of little usein the soil types around Balang. Labour exchange (*brâvăs dai*) was performed among kin and close neighbours and was often done for a salary (2,000 *riel* a day in 1995, when 2,500 riel was equivalent to about US$1).

Residence and family patterns

Village demography

The survey of East Balang showed that, in January 1996, it had a population of 1,303 (666 males, 637 females, with 387 of the total under five-years-old) living in 207 houses. These figures are high, compared to the mean size of villages in Kompong Thom province. The slightly higher number of males is interesting and is difficult to explain, since females usually outnumber males by 1–2%,[51]. A number of 'newcomers' in the village had been considered 'base people' by the Khmer Rouge, so the village may have been spared the high mortality for men of the so-called 'April 17' or 'new people'. Probably for the same reason, we did not find as many households headed by women as there were in Svay or in other parts of the country in the 1990s.[52] Eighteen women were accounted as 'family heads' over 207 households (7%) and among those, a third were older women living alone but next to a relative (son, nephew or nieces). A more precise definition of 'female-headed household' would permit comparison of our data with information collected in other parts of the country (Tuot 2003). In any case, it seems that Balang villagers had been less affected by a large decrease of the male population during the Khmer Rouge period.

For the 74 households surveyed in detail we found an occupancy rate of 5.8 people per house. Five houses had more than ten people and 12 had fewer than three. It is more than the national mean in rural areas, which is 5.1 per household (NIS 1999:10). We then tried to figure out the type of housing arrangement and found that the majority (45 families, or 62.5%) were nuclear families, defined here as including widows, widowers or divorcees with unmarried children or with an orphan niece or nephew. This figure for nuclear families is higher than the 50%found in Svay, which is based on the same definition of nuclear family and a similar number of households (Ebihara 1968:107). It is lower than the figure of 75% of 'almost nuclear families' found in Lovea in the1960s, using almost the same definitions (Martel 1975:201–2). Similar percentages (50–60%) were found in northeast Thailand in the late 1950s [Smith 1979:23–4], but this type of arrangement, as simple as it may appear, is not very stable.

Martel (1975:95) wrote about the 'fluidity' and 'impermanence' of marriages and family composition, and Ebihara (1968:147) stated: 'within a year's time in West Svay, numerous households changed in size and composition'. In Thailand, in the 1960s, it was said that:

> there are several other variations of the nuclear family…They reveal what appears to be an almost nonchalant willingness or acquiescence on the part of the villagers to make modifications and adjustments in their living arrangements whenever

necessary. Underlying…a fundamental assumption that the question of who lives with whom is not one of overriding importance…This rather flexible… approach to family organization is expressed in both centripetal and centrifugal ways (Phillips 1965:24).

In Balang, in half-a-dozen cases, several teenagers were moving from one house to another. Two children given by a woman to her childless sister were counted in both houses and were in fact living alternating between both houses. There were 22 'extended families', which included under the same roof one or more grandparents, one or several of their children and one or more grandchildren, or other people affiliated to the family either by blood or by alliance. This number was 30.5% of the total of surveyed households. In Svay, this type of arrangement involved 43% of the families, and only 17% in Lovea. These disparities might be explained by economics, according to Vickery (1984:176): 'Most families in rural villages were nuclear, with a few three-generation families interspersed…More extended families occurred where wealth accumulated, particularly in urban areas'.

But it might have to do also with the availability of village land. In Balang and Lovea, where there was more space, it might have been easier for the grandparents to live by themselves in a separate house on the same plot, than it was in a high population density area like Svay. We also found five 'isolated' people, living alone in Balang; in Svay there were three in Svay (Ebihara 1968:107). But all of those living alone in Balang had some family in the village, often living very nearby. Four were women, three of whom were. Only one was much worse off than the average villagers, because she had no land and no support.

Residency patterns

The survey revealed the presence of family groupings, called 'cluster' or 'compound' and defined as:

> a larger kin group made up of those who live in several 'households' in the same 'compound'. 'Compounds'…generally consist of a parental household (perhaps with a married daughter and her husband living with the parents) and one or more daughter households (Keyes 1995:133).

This type of land occupancy was evident in 33 houses (out of 74 households surveyed) grouped into 13 compounds, of which people said: 'It is the same plan' (*muoy plậng*[53]). Nine of these compounds had two houses—one for the parents and one for a married daughter. This is alleged to be the most common type of housing arrangement in Cambodia (Delvert 1961; Martin 1997:131–3) and was described in the 19th century (Moura 1883:347).[54] In two of these compounds, there were three family-related houses, while groups of four and five family-related houses on the same land were also found. The settlement of so many houses in one compound was facilitated by the distribution of 20-metre-wide land plots in 1979; large families have had enough space for dissemination around the mother-house. Such a layout was widely appreciated as people declared that they preferred to have their kin for neighbours. Since the trend for kin of extended families was also to settle in plots next to each other, some quarters in the village were mainly composed of relatives. It must have been so for a long period of time, judging by the correlation between land occupation and kinship. Consequently, the oldest and wealthiest families have kept hold of entire quarters where they have lived generation after generation.

Kin clusters and lines of inheritance

The correlation between land occupation and kinship is indeed displayed by the data about kinship gathered in the survey. The offspring of five of the seven founding families owned almost all the centre of Balang, which was probably the pioneer settlement at the end of the 19th century. Hence, of the 74 houses for which genealogy charts could be established (with the usual question marks and difficulties that such an exercise entails), 41 can say, more or less precisely, that they come from one of the five village founding couples, and nine have ancestors in two or more of these five original families. For the 30 households that can prove it, 11 say that they are 'from the village' for at least two generations.

The next information provided by the household survey data is that, amongst these 41 families of 'Balang origin' (*něak Balang*), 28 claim to be so by maternal descent; their mothers were 'from the village', whereas their fathers came from another location. And in 17 of these families, the village land (*dey phoum*) had been given by the mother to her daughter and these women claimed to be the owners of the land and assured us that it had been their mother's land.[55] This situation was described as a 'matrimonial autarchy' in Lovea: 'the village permanent nucleus...tends to...keep women and land' (Martel 1975:90). In the other 11 families, the land had been handed on by the father who had inherited it from his mother, although in two instances the land had been given by the husband to his wife. Still, the property was officially registered under a man's name (*chmôh brŏs*), that of either the husband or the son.

Kinship and marriage preferences

While most Cambodians cannot remember the names of their ancestors, they are often able to give the first name of their grandmother (*chidoun*). And if the grandmother's name has been forgotten, they can at least recognise their relationships to *bâng b'aun chidoun muoy* (cousins with the same grandmother).

Ledgerwood (1995:251) gives a more precise translation: 'older/younger [persons with] one grandmother'. This memory of matrilineal descent has been studied by Népote, who says that 'the focus of [kinship] terminology' is 'on the grandmother' (Népote 1992:96, my translation) and that the terms used make it difficult to identify paternal grandparents (Népote 1992:80). According to his analysis, the nomenclature would be evidence that 'any marriage relationship is considered as an alliance with a maternal younger sibling'. The best type of alliance would be among cousins, with a preference, on the side of the groom, for a parallel matrilineal female cousin.[56] This idea has been the centre of rigorous debate (Népote 1992:47–50; Ledgerwood 1995) to which I will only bring in my own field observations.

During the household survey, we asked 72 couples how they had met. Six declared that they had been married during the Khmer Rouge regime to a total stranger in a collective ceremony. About half-a-dozen more did not want to admit this because of the 'shame' such an alliance conveys,[57] but it was either known or suspected by the other villagers.[58] Seventeen couples did not give useful information, although both the husband and the wife were from the village and the family names implied that they were related. Six couples with established genealogies were cousins, four of them parallel cousins, and one parallel matrilineal cousins (*bâng b'aun chidaun muoy, khang mtay*).

The most interesting case, however, was a family in which the parents of the husband and wife were 'brothers and sisters on both sides' (*bâng b'aun bângkaoet sâng khang*), because two brothers had married two sisters. According to Népote, this situation, also mentioned by Ebihara who identified a case in Svay (Ebihara[1968:9–99]), is equivalent to a sororate and 'would apply to 20% of the Khmer population' (Népote 1992:150).[59] Interestingly, in this Balang family, the next two generations married within the family. One of the sons of the first union married his parallel cousin.[60] His daughter, in turn, got married to his brother's son (cross-cousin). When these explanations were given (with some embarrassment, it must be noted), the research assistant, an elderly schoolteacher with an authoritarian leaning, decried it as a backward habit and commented that 'in the old days it was forbidden, but now...'. Neighbours attending the discussion stated several times, on the contrary, how good (*l'â*) that type of marriage was if it could be arranged.

Exogamy or endogamy?

Among the 71 couples who provided information, 38—more than half of them—were from different villages. More than twice as many men as women had married outside; 28 grooms had come from outside Balang, or, for those couples who were not 'old Balang' villagers, from outside their village of origin, but only 11 brides had come from outside Balang or their village of origin. More often than not, the stories are about young men coming to Kompong Thom or Balang in search of a job, or on a mission (*besâkâkâmm*) for the army or the administration the unions of these couples were said to be predestined (*kou préng*). But the exogamic trend that these figures indicate is not conclusive, because I have discovered that, in some instances, the stranger was coming from the father's village and the 'fate encounter' had not been completely fortuitous.

The six cases of marriage among cousins constitute only 8% of the unions in one part of Balang village. But the endogamous nature of these unions was obviously valued. If preferential marriage is defined not so much by its frequency but by the fact that it is 'culturally highly regarded' (Ghasarian 1996:148), we can say that, in Balang, union between cousins was clearly appreciated by several families. We do not, however, have information for 17 couples of which both husband and wife were from Balang, but whose genealogies could not be checked. While figures in Lovea showed that for 186 couples, only a third of the spouses came from outside the village, in Svay, 90% of the marriages in West hamlet were exogamous (Ebihara 1968:99). Although the sample is too small to provide reliable statistical evidence, Balang provides us with the half-empty or half-full bottle; in two-thirds of the cases studied (after excluding the couples married under the Khmer Rouge), the groom came from another village. All authors agree that these trends must be considered in relation to inheritance of land (Ebihara 1968:102; Martel 1975:89; Ledgerwood 1995:254). In Balang in the mid-1980s and 1990s, village land was not a scarce commodity, and men could come to settle on their wife's property. But we do not have data for acquisition of farming land and we do not know if the availability of paddy fields would have played a role in attracting young bachelors. Moreover, the 72 couples interviewed included older men and women, married before the war, and younger people. The reasons for getting a wife in Balang probably differed over time. Other motives, such as the absence of land mines in the soil and a better security situation (*sthanâpheap sântĕsŏk*) could have been considered by the men who came in the 1980s and 1990s. There could be a relationship between these 'pull factors' and the slightly higher figure of male population in Balang, compared to national rates.

Social space and relations

The difference between old and new residents was probably not as significant as in some of the growing number of 'mixed' villages that emerged hastily in the country (O'Leary et al 1995), particularly in Kompong Thom, at the time (Kant 1993). Twenty years after the distributions made in 1979, marriages, division among offspring and sales had reshaped patterns of village land occupation. Nevertheless, the same families, after almost a century, hold the same spots at the centre of the village and, although there has been some intermarriage, the daily relationships and social networks remained divided according to the distinction between new and original people, to the point that quite often the new people did not even know the names of the original people, even though they were 200 metres away. At weddings and funerals, or at *bon* organised for the monks, a great number of neighbours and friends busied themselves preparing food, offerings, sharing pots and firewood. Close observation and some further questioning would show that they were all related, even if some of them had come from districts far away.[61]

While I would not call these families 'islands' isolated from each other (Ovesen, Trankell & Öjendal 1995), it certainly struck me that a location four and a half kilometres long could indeed be compared to a rosary, with beads physically connected to each other, but distinctively set and independent. This does not mean that villagers did not interact with people who were not members of their family; villagers certainly had friendships, shared tools, and, as mentioned earlier, engaged in political activities and protests with people who were not their kin. However, most social life could be achieved within the family compound and its surroundings and, at times of crisis (for instance, when a member of the group was sick), care and cure were organised by the extended family, in ways that has often been documented by medical anthropologists (Janzen 1995). The person that an outsider might have identified as a compassionate neighbour was actually a relative.

The fact that villages were composed of 'groups of kinsmen related by blood and intermarriage' (Ebihara 1968:93) has long been known and is by no means unique to Cambodia. But the survey of a large location like Balang has shown is that quarters in a village, or sub-villages, can be similarly composed. Kinship, in the late 1990s was shaping land tenure in Balang. The villagers meant it when they stated that they enjoyed living with their *bâng-po-on* (brothers and sisters, kin), as Ebihara repeated about Svay.[62] Today, when Balang dwellers travel to Phnom Penh in search of jobs and decide to remain together in rickety sheds in the capital suburbs of the capital city, genealogies show that they are *bang b'aun*. Furthermore, in the case of a growing number of families recently arrived from Balang in Phnom Penh, I discovered in 2004 that they tend to live next to each other. Those renting rows of one-room huts on Tuol Kork dyke come from the same part of East Balang, the sector allocated in 1979 to the 'newcomers'. Other studies of female migrant workers record the same pattern of employment found through relatives and accommodation shared with relatives (Prak 2004; Derks 2005).

Catching new facts or revisiting old data

Kinship studies, unless they are crafted in rich theory, do not capture the imagination. At a time when anthropological work gained value through 'thick description' (Geertz 1973), village monographs that accumulated hard-core, 'dry' data were dismissed as a 'stutterers' speech' and compared with insipid 'filing cabinets' (Jaulin, quoted by Bromberger 1992:485). Ethnography, now and again at the centre of absorbing debate among professionals on its making and authority (Clifford 1983; Laplantine 1996), rarely makes sensational reading and has a limited readership, 'from document of the occult to occult document' (Tyler 1986).[63] Therefore, few reasons and mechanisms propel the 'flat' objective account of an obscure peasant community to the forefront of history books and political reviews. Furthermore, ethnographic 'revisiting' would only happen every other generation to the most famed field work, either using a new conceptual framework or putting together a new survey on the spot (Copans 2002:45).

In Cambodia, both approaches have been called upon. Pre-war data have been scrutinised in the light of what happened between 1975 and 1979. Could village and family organisation explain these events? In the 1990s, old studies about village organisation and family structure were exploited again. For the sake of 'community development', NGOs constructed models and theories of village harmony (since villagers were *brothers and sisters*), while some scholars argued that this very system of restraint socialisation was at the root of the Cambodian society's failure (Kemp 1988; Ovesen, Trankell & Öjendal 1995; Frings 1997b). A new compilation of facts about Svay and Balang might not provide conflicting information with pre-war residence and socialisation patterns. However, this is when Larcom's remark, quoted at the beginning of this chapter, rings true; it is the relationship between old and new facts that has changed. In Svay, after the fall of the DK regime, 'families also reconstituted themselves with whatever members survived' (Ebihara & Ledgerwood 2002)—a process observed and recorded all over the country from January 1979 to the late 1980s. In places like Balang, where land was available, the ancient practice of compound residence resumed, attested both in 'old' and 'new' families. My comprehension of intra-village dealings relies on crossing observations with genealogies and residence. It gave sense to some patterns of social interaction in East Balang, in ordinary situations and more specifically when disease struck. People who are related live together, or next to each other, and relate to each other, more than they would do with people to whom they are not related. What does it *mean* and can we presume anything from that?

Ebihara concluded her paper on 'Residence patterns in a Khmer peasant village' by stressing that dwelling and household composition fluctuated in response to local and larger demographic or economic contexts. But, she added, '...it is also important to note that Sobay villagers' perception of residence choices emphasize familial sentiment and morality rather than economic advantage or necessity'(Ebihara 1977:67).

A daughter's attachment to the mother or her obligation to care for aged parents, or a feeling of security among siblings would have been neglected in the 1970s, when functionalist theories focusing particularly on economic factors were applied to kinship and residence patterns (Murdock & Wilson 1972). This emphasis on the role of feelings, emotions and ethics runs in all of Ebihara's papers, for example: 'Various bonds of affection, loyalty, and mutual aid also extended beyond the village' (Ebihara 1993a:150); 'Non-kin friends are also important and may be treated virtually as kinsmen when affection runs deep' (Ebihara 1974a:364)

Her interpretation of residence facts, based upon an 'economy of affection' (Hyden 2004) can be accepted for pre-war Cambodia and for post-DK Cambodia. But the reasons why family members would 'cleave...close...' to each other (Ebihara & Ledgerwood 2002:11) have changed, because, as she noted, quoting Marston, 'in the aftermath of genocide, personal and kin networks become all the more important because other kinds of institutions have proven unreliable' (Ebihara & Ledgerwood 2002).

Conclusion

Is ethnographic description just 'explanation by the causes' (Wittgenstein 1992:79–86)? As questions about cohesiveness and reciprocity in rural society still excite social workers and scientists (Kim 2001 and also this volume), as they did in Thailand in the late 1990s (Kitahara 1996), the demand for village monographs, old and new, has been strong throughout the 1990s. It would appear that they can be used to prove opposite points of view—Cambodia was a segmented, loosely-structured society where co-operation is limited to the extended family (McAndrew 1999); or, on the contrary, informal institutions were present and survived in Cambodia (Aschmoneit 1995)—because, as it was demonstrated, readers are the active makers of ethnographies (Clifford 1983). The elephant remains formidable and its blind keepers should probably aspire to a very modest, yet indispensable goal—avoid assuming, keep exploring. If May Ebihara has set an example, it is in her meticulous collection and neutral reading of empirical data.

Notes

1   The 'revisiting' of ethnographic field work, as a methodology or as an accident, has been long described and debated (Garbett 1967; Garrigues-Creswell, Jamard & Picon 2000). The most famous cases are the stuff of legend (Tepoztlán in Mexico by Redfield and Lewis; Samoa by Benedict and Freeman, and some French-speaking African settings by Copans).With longitudinal studies of Cambodian settings yet to be done, Svay is becoming an exception. It is hoped that a new study of some Cham villages visited in the 1960s (Baccot 1968) will provide the same overview (Stok E. December 2005, personal communication).

2   As far as mainland ethnic Khmer are concerned. Village and cultural monographs of Cambodian ethnic minorities were conducted in the 1960s but were published much later (Wilmott 1966; Matras-Troubetzkoy 1983; Martin 1997)

3   Ebihara alluded to this fable as well and often expressed the view that peasantries, being 'part-societies with part cultures', must be considered within their larger context (Ebihara 1974:358).

4   It is reported as told in Java but might also be used in non-Asian contexts; as Beatty wrote (1999:201), quoting Schimmel (1975): 'The parable, now something of a mystical commonplace, derives from Aesop, via the poet-mystic Rumi'. I am indebted to John Marston for this information.

5   It was used by participants of the 'Conference on the Meaning of Community in Cambodia', who made use of a cartoon illustrating the fable (WGSOC 1999:65).

6   I have not been able to get an English version of Kobayashi Satoru's comprehensive thesis on village organisation in Sankor district, north of Kompong Thom, investigated between 1998 and 2000. There is also a rich collection of unpublished works by Khmer students lying untapped in Cambodian libraries.

7   The field work, supporting a doctoral dissertation, was financed by a grant from the Lavoisier Foundation, under the auspices of the French Foreign Ministry.

8   The large disparities in soils, topography and occupations within the same province are acknowledged, particularly in Kompong Thom, which can be divided into at least three distinct 'terroirs': the forests (*prei*); the valley (*veal kraom*) which, in Kompong Thom, borders the Tonle Sap; and the highlands (*srŏk loe*). Stereotypes are devised for people living in these sub-regions as well. For instance, those living up the river (*srŏk loe*) were depicted as rougher and more inclined to use black magic.

9   In the 2000s, beggars in Phnom Penh markets were all supposed to come from Prey Veng and derogative comments about people from this province are not uncommon. We also know that the political connotations attached to the province of origin sometimes meant life or death during the DK period. Questionnaires devised for interrogation at S-21 and used all over the country for self-confession (Chandler 1999a:91), or those in use for *brâvâttĕroup* (life history) under the Vietnamese regime, included place of birth (*srŏk kâmnaoet*) as an entry. Almost all the workers at S-21 came from a small region north and northwest of Phnom Penh, in Kandal province (Chandler 1999a:35). In the 1980s, elites from Prey Veng and Svay Rieng, attached to the Chea Sim political clan, had to give way to the Hun Sen clan, who originated in Kompong Cham (Népote 1995:195).

10 This spatial configuration overlapped with administrative and religious meanings until the 19th century and the *stech trŭang* (overlord) his province was given a leading role in court ceremonies (Aymonier 1900:367; Leclere 1917:299–300).

11 At the time 'the most extensive complex of stone buildings in all Southeast Asia' (Chandler 1993:22)

12 Travel time was slowed not only by a terrible road surface but by the ominous presence of rogue soldiers 'guarding' every bridge and imposing 'donations'.

13 In 1994, an estimated 3,000 Khmer Rouge were still fighting 16,000 'regulars' of the 4th Military region that included Kompong Thom (Thayer 1994:5). In August 1993, the Khmer Rouge had started to defect and the government had set up 'reception centres' for them.

14 Some medical workers still ponder what they perceive as a paradox: 'Patients from Kompong Thom are always the best: observant, polite and obedient. But when the newspapers report on an horrible crime, most of the time it has been committed in Kompong Thom! Why?' (Oum 2003).

15 A small bridge called after him—*spean* Pou Kombo.

16 The 1993 elections gave a majority to Funcinpec (45%). The vice-governorships were distributed among the opposition parties, whose weak or absent authority was often lamented by city and village people.

17 In 1994 and 199,5 several Westerners were kidnapped or killed in other provinces of Cambodia. In 1995, having heard of some similar abduction projects in their area, the provincial authorities decided to provide special 'protection' to all the foreigners living in Kompong Thom. As late as 2002, another anthropologist doing field work in Sankor, 20 kilometres north of Kompong Thom, sensed that he was in danger after 'bandits' kidnapped local villagers during the run-up to the communal elections (Kobayashi Satoru, personal communication, 9 December 2002).

18 It eventually came as 'food-for-work', under the UN World Food Programme.

19 The important point made to foreigners was: 'Do not settle north of the main bridge'.

20 With a provincial population of 1,016,861 people, excluding the population of the market town, Takmau, and 1,087 villages, the number of people per village is estimated at around 935. (This calculation uses figures from the General Population Census of 1998 (NIS 1999).

21 This figure, certainly underestimated, is drawn from the electoral lists set by the UN Transitional Authority in Cambodia (Aschmoneit & Thoma 1995).

22 I use the present tense, even though these figures are drawn from data available from the end of 1994 to mid-1997, as nothing more recent can be found.

23 This urban population percentage is lower than the national average of 15.7% (NIS 1999:96).

24 Between 1947 and 1957, large groups of the population were resettled by the authorities along the roads, to escape either from the Issarak (Independence) or the Vietminh guerilla movements (Delvert 1961:208–10).

25   The terms proposed in this typology were common in development literature during the 1990s , but have disappeared or acquired a different meaning now that the integration of returnees is no longer an issue.

26   The terms 'returnees' or 'refugees' apply to the people who returned from the Thai border camps. 'Displaced persons', or 'internally displaced persons (IDP),' refers to people who have moved within Cambodia because of conflicts or the presence of mines on their land.

27   The returnee families had come to resettle in Balang temporarily because they had relatives in the village; they left within a year.

28   I did not give a pseudonym to this village. Most of the time, rural settlements in Cambodia get their names from vegetal or geographic elements (Lewitz 1967:397). This one, rather unusually, refers to the old Khmer and the Prakrit *pallanka*, a statue pedestal, that those who came first found on the site. Of more than 12,738 locations in Cambodia, only ten are named Balang (Aschmoneit & Thoma) and five of these are in Kompong Thom province. It is also found in some former Khmer provinces in Thailand such as Surin (Bizot 1993:15).

29   We measured village land for 139 of the 207 houses. The survey for the 74 households was undertaken from December 1995 to February 1996. It included questions on house occupation; identification of each inhabitant and a genealogy; surface, ownership and inheritance/acquisition of village land; enclosing and use of garden/village land; surface and situation of rice fields; cattle and livestock possession; identification of relatives in the village; and each couple's matrimony history. Because the survey happened during the harvest, we often met old people or nursing mothers at home. Contrary to what has been documented (Sovannarith et al 2001:20), all the women knew the size of their paddy fields. On the other hand, almost nobody could tell us the size of their village plot, so we measured them ourselves.

30   One hundred and thirty-three households were surveyed at Lovea, in Siem Reap province in the 1960s (Martel 1975:88).

31   I could not verify this assertion.

32   There were between 35,000 and 50,000 IDPs in Kompong Thom town in 1973 (Debre 1976:187).

33   One woman summarised that period: 'And after 1975? I traveled a lot!'

34   The mortality rate between 1975 and 1979 was among the highest for nine provinces, with 22.4% of deaths related to the regime (Sliwinski 1995:58). Only 10.2% of the population were deported (Sliwinski 1995:33). Early statements by Vickery hinted at a very high violent death toll (Vickery 1983:123). It was challenged by official figures which indicated 281,816 deaths from hunger and 42,731 killings (DPC 1996). Important differences of leadership existed between the north and the south of Kompong Thom province (Kiernan 1996:338–44).

35   Frings (1997:85) warns of bias in these statistics. It could be that these figures apply to the most remote areas in the province.

36   In Svay, 'it is said that by 1984 *krŏm* existed only on paper' (Ebihara 1993:160).

37 That this was the opinion of my assistant Mr. Nol, a retired Cambodian teacher. (See also Ebihara & Ledgerwood (2002:127)).

38 'Disputes over property ownership are clogging Cambodia's judicial system, with land disputes making up as much as a quarter of all cases before the courts' (Watkins 1996; see also Guillou 1994; Sovannarith et al 2001).

39 This is probably because of Balang's closeness to Kompong Thom and the National Road. Proximity to such locations has been linked to large increases in land value since 1989 (Sovannarith et al 2001:21).

40 In 1995, one *chi*, the equivalent of 3.7 grams of gold, was worth about US$50.

41 An are is equal to 100 square metres, or one hundredth of a hectare.

42 In Lovea, inSiem Reap province, the mean size of landholdings was much bigger, at around seven hectares per household—'...landholdings considered are around seven hectares...more than 72%...have from 50 ares to more than seven hectares' (Martel 1975:115, my translation). In the entire country, average landholdings in the 1950s were between 2.2 hectares (Delvert 1961:470) and 1.9 hectares (Delvert 1961:491), with important variations between the central and the eastern part of the country (Delvert 1961:491–5). In 1956, nationwide, 55% had less than one hectare (Delvert 1961:495). But other authors stated that in 1962 around 30% of farming families had less than one hectare (Tichit 1981:50), while landholdings ranged from 0.9 to 5.8 hectares (Tichit 1981:74). Accurate figures are always difficult to obtain for the local level if we want to make any distinction between ownership and actual exploitation of land (Delvert 1961:469). In the 1990s, the national average of 12 hectares was not met in Svay, where 70% of the families had less than one hectare (Ledgerwood 1992:47).

43 Delvert (1961:473), however, also gives the figure of 1.8 hectares in Baray district and 2.3 hectares in Kompong Svay district. Other data indicate a mean of 3.6 hectares in 1962/1963 (Tichit 1981:74).

44 These landless households were two families of returnees, one old single woman (*krâmŏm chăh*), three young couples living on their parents' village plot, one old couple without children, two civil servants and a former village chief. The last three had sold their land to cover health expenses. It fits with data showing illness as a cause of landlessness in 21% of cases nationwide (Biddulph 2000).

45 They had to give half of the harvest to the landowner. This rate was considered usual in the 1950s (Delvert 1961:505), although in Siem Reap there were no rules (Martel 1975:138). In Svay 'sharecropping gives complete usufruct and responsibility for cultivation of one's field to someone else' (Ebihara 1968:241).

46 Estimates vary from '180–270 kilograms per year' (Ehihara 1968:272) to 220 (Delvert 1961:154) or 230 kilograms per person per year (Tichit 1981:72). In Lovea, it was considered that a family with less than 60 to 80 *thăng* (20 and 30 kilograms of paddy) per year would starve and that 10½ *thăng* per person per year was required (Martel 1975:150).

47 That date seems early, as similar systems were introduced in other provinces between 1984 and 1986 (Ebihara 1993:160; Frings 1997:81). This distribution system differs from the allocation of 'private family plots' described in 1983 (Boua 1983:269–70),

because, according to my informants, it was performed on all the land available to Balang and everybody could take part in the lottery.

48   From the French 'lot' (meaning portion).

49   A *thăng* is between 20 and 30 kilograms of paddy (Delvert 1961:229; Ebihara 1968:232; Martel 1975:19) or 50 to 60 pounds (Headley et al 1977:353). I have chosen to consider a *thăng* equivalent to 24 kilograms, after discussion with the villagers.

50   These yields are considered quite low for Southeast Asia.

51   Women comprise 51.9% of the Cambodian population in urban areas and 51.1% in rural zones (NIS 1999:14). They constituted 52.84% of the population of Kompong Thom province.

52   Percentages of households headed by women vary from 20% (UNICEF 1996:5) to 50%, depending on the area (Ledgerwood 1992:7; UNICEF 1990:111).

53   From the French 'plan', (meaning plan).

54   In Svay, it was noted that 'neo-locality involves residence quite near a spouse's natal home, usually because there was room to build on land that is part of or adjacent to a parent's house' (Ebihara 1977:58).

55   The question was: 'whom is this land coming from?' The most common answer was: *dey khnhŏm* (my land) or *chmôh khnhŏ* (under my name). We also found: *dey mtay* (land of my mother) and, less often, the expressions *dâmnael* or *morodâk* (heritage) or *dey ker* (inherited land), as opposed to *dey tĭnh* (land bought) or *dey rodth* (land (given by the) government). Of 74 lots, only 11 had been bought, three of them by one family member from another between the 1970s and 1995, and two lots recently exchanged.

56   There is a preference for the parallel cousin among Khmer people, whereas Sino-Khmer families would rather choose the cross-cousin (Népote 1992:147).

57   These people cannot, for instance, hold the *popil* <a definition of this would be useful in parentheses here> during a wedding ceremony.

58   This means about 15% of the married people interviewed in the village had married total strangers. It has been proposed that 250,000 women were forced into marriage by the Khmer Rouge (McGrew 1999), but further research is under way to establish the number more precisely (UNHCR 2003).

59   Unfortunately, Népote mentions neither the source for this information nor the ways by which this percentage was determined.

60   We can say bi-parallel cousin here, since she was the daughter of his maternal aunt and paternal uncle.

61   Ebihara noted, in her observations of interaction between Svay and other villages, that trips were made to visit kinsmen and friends acquired through exogamous marriages (Ebihara 1974:364).

62   'The former residents of West Hamlet Svay belong to overlapping kindreds such that everyone is kin, friends of kin, or kin of friends' (Ebihara & Ledegrwood 2002).

63   Tyler used this phrase with a different meaning in a different context, but the image is used here to describe what happens to most ethnographic texts.

chapter seven

Reciprocity: informal patterns of social interaction in a Cambodian village

Sedara Kim

Alternations between war and peace have inscribed themselves deeply on the history of Cambodia for over 30 years. Since 1970, Cambodia has undergone several changes of political system: it has had a monarchy, a republic, a communist genocidal regime, Russian style communism and electoral pluralist democratic government. In the 1980s Cambodia embraced a centralised state command economy, and in the early 1990s switched to a free market economy— at the same time that it shifted from authoritarian rule to democracy. These social polarisations, from one political regime to another, have been harmful to the traditional cultural ways of Cambodian citizens.

A number of studies in the 1960s argued that socio-economic relations in Cambodia are based on ties of kinship and result from influence of interpersonal relationships. A well-articulated study conducted by May Ebihara from that era maintains that 'kinship is the principal social tie in structuring social relationships, and the religious system is built around the Buddhist temple, animistic beliefs and ancestor worship' (Ebihara 1968:22–92). During the pre-war period, there were no formal permanent social organisations, economic, religious or other 'institutions' in Cambodian villages beyond the family, household and close friends (Delvert 1961; Ebihara 1968).[1] Conducting research in 2000, I observed that informal social patterns of interaction or reciprocal relationships shaped the forms of household economy in Cambodian society. These are determined by kinship, religion and the organisation of production and distribution (Hefner 1998; Tanenbaum 1984; Wilk 1996).

Given the political instability in Cambodia for many decades, some scholars have argued that after the revolution and civil war, Cambodia became a 'bare bones society', and suggest that its entire social infrastructure was wiped out. The title of one study, *When every household is an island*, itself indicates that the researchers viewed the village as nothing more than a collection of houses:

The common picture is that the traditional social cohesion and self-help mechanisms in the villages that were destroyed under Pol Pot are now slowly returning to normal. There is an element of wishful thinking in this view, for it is questionable whether such a 'normal', traditional social cohesion on the village level ever existed in the first place. It is less questionable, however, that the deterioration of social solidarity appears to be continuing still, and that it is reinforced by the liberalization of the economy and the consequent monetarization of most social relations beyond the nuclear family (Ovesen, Trankell & Öjendal 1996:66–7).

Frings, in her work on the PRK period, takes this idea a step further by arguing that Cambodian people are not concerned about each other because of their past social experiences. 'When Cambodians do help, they always try to take some advantage from it, even if the persons they help are their relatives. They do not help for free and do not think they have a moral obligation to do it' (Frings 1994:61).

These works on the atomisation of Khmer society are all the more powerful because so much of the academic literature on Cambodia has focused on the alleged destruction of Khmer society during the Khmer Rouge period. This chapter demonstrates that such judgments of Khmer society are unfounded. Cambodian rural integration most visibly emerges only at the intra-village level and that this integration does not link villages to outside communities.[2] Therefore, from an outsiders' point of view, cohesiveness may appear to be weak or non-existent. I argue, however, that the stance taken by Ovesen and his colleagues is overly simple and does not offer a sound basis on which to judge Cambodian society. I will use my own ethnographic work to shed light on the norms of reciprocity and interdependence at the grassroots level in a rural Khmer village.

I believe that even though Cambodia has undergone extensive social fragmentation for many years, the patterns of social interaction have returned to those of the pre-war era, although it is also true that the influence of a market economy is encroaching and changing the nature of reciprocal relationships in the village milieu. The aim of this chapter is to address the nature and extent of reciprocity in a village in Cambodia. Reciprocity plays an important role in maintaining social solidarity and the rural economy in contemporary society, which Hefner (1998) calls 'market culture'. I will explore the nature of reciprocity in the village of Angkor Krau in terms such as: intra-households relationships, intra-village reciprocal activities, balanced reciprocity and exchange of labour for rice cultivation, rice borrowing and the use of rice banks and exchange in the raising of animals. Generally speaking, reciprocity is directly influenced by Buddhist concepts, so I will also discuss the importance of the ordination ceremony, the *kâthin* ceremony and the *bâng kâk chmâb* ceremony.

Reciprocity in the Cambodian context

Most research in Siem Reap province has tended to focus on archaeology and art history (because of the famous ruins at Angkor). Only a small number of studies have been conducted in Cambodia at the village level, and there are few examples of detailed and holistic local-based research. Some of the most valuable research was carried out during the pre-war period: Ebihara (1968) focused on rural life in the central part of the country; Delvert (1961) approached nature of Cambodian village life from a geographical perspective; Martel (1975) conducted anthropological research in Siem Reap province, addressing some of the aspects of village life I am concerned with, including Buddhism and village labour exchange. She observed that people made numerous offerings to the Buddhist temple because they thought it represented 'nourishment of life and sources of moral authority' (Martel 1975: 251). Further, she contends that religious teachings encourage people to integrate for natural benefits through various forms of labour. 'In Lovea village, transplanting or harvesting are done by co-operative labour, the villagers share in a village a destiny in which they are constrained to solidarity of fact' (Martel 1975:153–4). Exchanging labour for rice cultivation is the principal theme of reciprocity in a Khmer village.

> Animal rental is not the usual way in Lovea of compensating for lacking a yoked pair; more often, a work animal is exchanged for human labour; this practice is called 'provas' [*brâvâs*]…the principle is established by custom, and there is no exception: a morning of labour with a pair of animals (ploughing) for a day of human labour (Martel 1975:127–8, translation by Carol Mortland).

These ethnographic accounts describe norms of reciprocity that still exist. Aspects of Khmer farming still rely upon the same kinds of reciprocity networks they used in pre-war years (Collins 1998; McAndrew 1997). Ledgerwood provides examples of how people still help one another in a number of ways, including sharing food, lending cash, exchanging labour and providing emergency financial support to one another within the family and at the village level (Ledgerwood 1998:141). Her work shows that the 'traditional' Khmer way of providing mutual assistance is still active in these communities.

Collins's work on the role of civil society actors in a Khmer village in the northwest part of the country recalls that there are various exchanges, including 'reciprocal' labour for farming, house building, cow exchange groups—owners can have an animal tended by another person in exchange for one of the animal's offspring—draft exchange groups by which people lacking one of a pair of animals needed for work in the fields share an animals, cooking groups for community feasting and 'dish associations' for community ceremonies (Collins 1998:15–16). According to Marston (1997:106), the reciprocal systems in Cambodian communities seem difficult to measure. People feel attached to those who have helped them before and have to reciprocate. Thus gift giving builds connections. But Marston also points out that the obligations can sometimes be overwhelming and even impossible to repay. (He was looking, however, at exchanges taking place beyond the level of the village, within the government bureaucracy and in urban areas.)

Some researchers, such as Curtis (1998:128), consider the Buddhist temple (wat) the most important social institution in Cambodia; it has multiple functions, including education, rural development, public charity and conflict resolution. This is an important village-based social institution and its role in stimulating social solidarity, part of a larger process of national development, is only slowly recovering its former importance. Many temples were rebuilt in the 1990s and only in the late 1990s did the number of monks return to the pre-war levels. (Many of these monks are younger and less experienced than their pre-war counterparts.)

Vijghen conducted research on the central plain in Kompong Chhnang province on community development and the issue of money lending. He notes that only relatively small amounts of money are available. It is mostly richer families who will lend money to their fellow villagers or relatives for social events on an honour basis. The need for payment of interest varies with the degree of affinity or friendship, but in most cases there is little or no interest. People can pay back the loan in rice when the harvest is completed (Vijghen 1991:19–20). People borrow money only when they have an extreme situation, such as a wedding, health care, a funeral or buying a cow. This exchange requires a high degree of trust and group cohesion; it would not be possible without long-term trust among friends and relatives.

A study by Hiroshi Komai (1997), 'The role of Buddhism in the reconstruction of the Cambodian rural village', provides some fundamental insights into Buddhism and community development. Trying to understand the role of Buddhism in Cambodian communities, one may ask why . According to Komai, people spend money and donate time to help rebuild the religious tradition mainly because of the reciprocal relationship between laymen and Buddhist monks regarding 'merit making' or 'seeking nirvana'; these two spheres are extremely significant and are integrated in the consciousness of Cambodian farmers (Komai 1997:23). Komai found that most donations to the wat were from the private sector and, in particular, from individuals. At the time of his study, there was no state funding to support wat construction.

The literature from pre-war and contemporary Cambodia reflects the nature of reciprocity in the village where I conducted fieldwork. These studies illustrate consistent patterns of social interaction in the Cambodian village to the extent that, after decades of civil war for, these indigenous systems have reverted to their original patterns. Since then, the cash economy has brought about some changes.

Existing patterns of reciprocity in rural Cambodia

According to my research, the scope of reciprocal relations frequently coincides with existing kinship groups and relations of close friends. Although some villagers believe the level of mutual help and social morality is now weak compared with the pre-war era, such patterns of reciprocity have not disappeared. Instead, reciprocal activities have shifted into new forms because of the new sociopolitical context and the initiation of a cash economy in the village. In looking at some cases of generalised reciprocal activities in the village, one needs to raise the following questions:

1. Why do villagers carry out reciprocal exchanges?
2. What role does reciprocity play in assisting community social and economic life?
3. What happens if recipients find it impossible to return gifts?

Generalised reciprocity: emphasis is on B receiving from A, in the context of an ongoing relationship, with little calculation of return or return with the same values

Balanced reciprocity: emphasis is on direct exchange, A giving to B and B return to A with equal value and within a time limit.

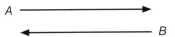

Intra-household relationships

Villagers think that the family relationships are the same as they were in the pre-war period (*dauc pi daoem*). During my fieldwork, I focused on two families. The first (Mr Chourn's family) is a normal, nuclear, village family, with rice fields and living conditions that would be considered middle class if compared to other families in the village. The second (Mr Poeun's family) is a refugee family who returned from the Thai border in 1992.

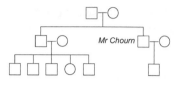

Mr Chourn's family

Chourn, married in 1995, has one son about two years old. He is one of three villagers who finished high school in the town of Siem Reap. He is working with a Japanese restoration organisation, where he makes about US$70 per month. He and is wife are unlike other married couples because they reside in his parents' home. His wife's parents live close to the great lake (Tonle Sap). After marriage, he received farmland from his parents-in-law, and he is responsible for the farmland of his parents. His wife sells groceries in front of his house in the village; she can make a small income and still have time to take care of her son. Chourn's father is working with an American restoration project. Chourn has one older brother with five children, who now stay in his wife's village. According to Chourn, his brother is very poor because he has nothing to do besides farming, and has only a small plot of land.

Every day, after finishing work at 3pm, he goes to work in his rice fields. He produces enough rice for the family and has some surplus to sell to cover clothing, health care and other family expenses. He does not plan to build his own house because he wants to stay with his parents and take care of them when they get old. His parents have a wooden house with roof tiles, which is typical of the middle class *(nĕak kuor sâm)*. Every weekend he takes his son and wife to stay at his her parent's home for one or two nights, to help work in their fields. On the way back from his parents-in-law's home, he stops at Siem Reap market to buy some groceries to re-sell at home.

I asked him how he feels about taking care of both sets of parents. He answered that 'this is part of my responsibility being a son in the family for my parents also for my in-laws' side. They are old, and have no-one to lean on besides me and my wife, especially as they get older.' Moreover, he has taken in one of his nieces and he sends her to school. 'I try to help my brother as much as I can, providing and lending him rice or money. I also go to visit him often. Sometimes, when my nephew comes my mother and I give him some fruit, clothes, and possibly money to send back to his parents.' Chourn has one motor bike to commute, his father also owns one. His rice lands allow him to grow different cash fruits in the dry season for extra income.

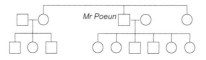

Mr Poeun's family

Mr Poeun, 41, is a returnee from the Thai border. He has four daughters and two sons. His eldest daughter is 15 years old; she is disabled because of polio. Poeun works with the government authority as a temple guard (Chmam Prasat), where he makes $25 per month. He works only six hours a day, so he has time to work in the rice fields. His wife makes a meagre income sells drinks to tourists. The family's living conditions are poor compared with Mr Chourn's. Poeun has two sisters living together in the same village, which is their natal village. The younger sister is single. The elder sister, Thy, 51, was married and has three children, two sons and a daughter. Her husband used to work with a Japanese organisation, but he died a year ago. Now she has no means of subsistence except rice cultivation. Her eldest son went to the Thai border to look for a job, but he failed to find one and has returned home.

Mr Poeun lost contact with his sisters after 1979. In 1992, when the United Nations (UN) repatriated refugees from the Thai border, he decided to return to the village.

I told the UN to send me back to my natal village, this village near Angkor park because I would have some relatives who survived the Khmer Rouge. I sent a letter via the International Red Cross; then I found out that my two sisters survived and were in the village. I was very excited to hear this news. I had a lot of hope that I would be getting assistance from my relatives and other villagers there.

According to Mrs Thy:

I was very happy to hear that my only brother had survived and would return to the village. I tried to prepare a plot of my parents' land for him to build a wooden home, gave him some money, and also gave him a small plot of rice land. I also lent him some money without interest to buy more rice land and finish building the house because we are brother and sister (*bâng b'oun*). If I do not help him whom should I help?

Poeun explained:

When my family and I arrived, my sister helped me a lot; for example, she helped me with money, land, taking care my children, and food, and she asked other villagers to assist me. Without relatives and friends my first settlement in the village would have been extremely hard. Many villagers showed up to help build this wooden house. We also went into the forest for many days to cut wood for building the house because I did not have enough money to buy wood. I will not forget their kind support to my family. Now if they need me for anything I must help them in return. My family at the present time is not that rich but we have enough rice to eat.

Since his brother-in-law's death, his sister has been in a difficult position.

I really pity my sister. She once helped me a lot, and now she is having a hard time managing the family. I helped her fix the house, organise the funeral and plough the fields and also, when I can, give her some money.

Thy expressed the same emotions: 'I have no reliable future; my brother and the villagers are my only hope as persons who will help me if I have an emergency; this is a time when my brother has to help me.'

From these two cases of intra-household relationships, we see a norm of assisting relatives that still prevails in the village. I would argue that these intra-household reciprocal activities are embedded in almost all Cambodian family relationships. This intra-family relationship is still characterised by generalised reciprocity, though this relationship is beginning to change because of the introduction of a cash economy, which affects the balanced reciprocity of rice cultivation in the village. These generalised reciprocal relations among kinsmen are grounded on two assumptions:

1. that each kin member has an 'obligation' to assist his or her own relatives, with the purpose of improving economic conditions; and,

2. that the basic well-being of their relatives must be ensured.

From this reasoning we can see Chourn has gained respect in the village. He is an educated person and relatively well off (*něak kuor sâm*), and to maintain his good reputation among the villagers, he has to help alleviate the economic burden of his brother. He is fulfilling his responsibility as a brother, his 'moral responsibility in the family'. My limited research suggests that reciprocity occurs in poor and rich families, although the scale of reciprocity will depend on degrees of wealth and personal sympathy each individual has for his or her kin. Ledgerwood (1998) writes that the poor, who are struggling to have enough rice to eat, do not have the resources to help relatives, but they will endeavour to assist relatives and friends through participation in different ceremonies where they can provide labour instead of money.

Villagers still borrow small amounts of rice and money from relatives without interest. All the types of reciprocal activities noted during the pre-war years are carried out by the villagers at the present time. But older villagers who have lived through many regimes report that things have changed:

I see in general people helping each other in terms of provision of financial support among their relatives. However, assistance to friends or co-villagers appears to be weak compared with the pre-war time, because many good *chǎs tǔm* (respected old people) died during the Khmer Rouge regime. They normally gave good advice to the villagers. Villagers are now more individualistic, they are busy making their own living. As you know, many people here in the village are working with different organisations. They make at least $50 per month and some can make money from tourism in Angkor. As long as they have money they can afford motorbikes, television sets, repairing their houses, hiring labour to cultivate rice, new clothes, and they have the ability to help their own relatives. (Mr Kiey, 60, Chourn's father, field notes, May 2000)

When people are involved in a cash economy, the scope of mutual help is transformed and could even be decreasing. Curtis (1998) argues that mutual assistance in rural Cambodia has survived through many traumatic regimes. Nevertheless, he also sees the practice weakened by fiscal relations. People in some areas, he writes, were 'refusing to perform public work, even if such work was of direct personal benefit, because of a lack of social cohesion and the consequent emergence of self-centered and self-interest me-first attitudes, including rampant greed' (Curtis 1998:125). This idea is similar to what Mr Kiey and some other villagers told me. This is a concern of the villagers in contemporary times. From my research findings in the village, I would argue that villagers have not abandoned reciprocal activities, but rather have altered them because of the introduction of a monetised economy that leads to increased self-centred or self-interested attitudes.

Intra-village reciprocal activities

Besides intra-household relationships, units of communal social cohesion constituted by neighbours and close friends are created by years of association in social networks. Households help each other in farming, building houses, lending money or rice at no interest, contributing time, food and money to local *wat*s, helping with household tasks such as babysitting and helping to prepare food or building shelters for ceremonial events. These kinds of activities, over time, even over generations, build favourable communal relationships, friendships and trust among villagers. As expressed by an elderly woman:

Usually in our Khmer village life we try to maintain good relations with all the villagers (*rǒap nheat*). Sometimes if you do not have many relatives living in the same village, if you need help or assistance only your neighbours will help you. If you do not have many friends around, people might regard you as a stranger or a bad person. The only way to keep good relations is to be frank and help the one who has helped you and not be selfish; this is the way we can build up good friendships. I do not know about the feeling of the other villagers, but for me when I have many good friends around I feel confident (author's field notes, May 2000).

During my stay in the village, I did not see any house construction because it was the cultivation time. However, people told me that normally house building occurs during the dry season when farmers are free from the fields. I interviewed some villagers about this reciprocal activity. A village house is typically constructed of a wooden frame with a gabled thatched roof and walls of woven bamboo. Family members and neighbours work together to build houses. The houses of poorer individuals usually have only a single large room. The house of the rich or middle-class villager is built with a wooden frame, roofed tiles and possibly with a concrete base on the ground floor. To build a big wooden house, the owners might have to hire construction workers and carpenters. But poorer villagers spend their free time working with friends and neighbours. A man in the village said:

> Poorer individuals and especially widows can afford only a small thatched house, so it is impossible for them to hire labour. In these circumstances, the house owners have to come and ask friends or neighbours to help whenever time is available. But now it is different from the past; we prefer to help only on the weekend, because most of us are busy with other work. I once helped put up the house of a widow's family; she organised a lunch and provided some cigarettes and cold drinks. At least ten villagers showed up in order to complete one house. It took many days. This is a traditional task, helping each other put up a house for our neighbour. This time we help them, and next time, when I need help, they will not say 'no' to me (field interview, July 2000).

I was told that it takes a few years for owners to save enough money to build a small wooden house. When they have the money, they gradually buy a certain amount of wood, cement, bricks and so on. They do not have enough money to build a house all at once. Sometimes people borrow money from their relatives without interest to complete the house.

Another example of village co-operation involves the case of a policeman who works in Angkor park. He has six daughters and two sons, all under 20. In 1994, he had an ox-cart accident and broke his leg. A number of his relatives took him for treatment with different traditional healers in other districts. Some villagers helped his wife plough the fields, transplant and harvest. It took almost one year for his leg to heal. He says:

> Without assistance and help from my relatives and other villagers, my life would be very difficult. All of my children are very young and not strong enough to plough or help in rice cultivation; that is why I would prefer to have many sons rather than daughters. I like my relatives and villagers very much, they are still very helpful to my family; having good neighbours (*nheat*) is good in case of emergencies such as the one I faced (field notes, June 2000).

He invited me to watch the cultivation a few times. He seemd to me very helpful to all the villagers. He knows how to fix ploughing tools and ox carts;

he helped to fix tools for farmers without charging money. I prefer to call such village social reciprocal systems generalised intra-village reciprocal interactions.

Spatial constraints keep me from addressing all the generalised reciprocal activities that I observed in the village, such as well and pond digging or building the local school. Occasionally some villagers lend rice to poorer neighbours in exchange for a few days of work in the rice fields, or grant loans that allow for repayment after harvest. They also engage in conflict resolution processes, help with cooking or building shelters for different ceremonies, and aid each other in emergencies. All of these reciprocal acts are common in the village. These examples confirm my belief that generalised reciprocity is still widespread. Villagers still have a strong sense of attachment and desire to help one another. This represents a difference in social atmosphere between urban and village society. Village general co-operation is still very much alive. Social networking takes place and close friends develop in dyadic relationships, usually between people of the same sex. People still have a strong sense of villagehood, and bond together to protect the village.

Balanced reciprocity in the village

Practices involving balanced reciprocity are common in the context of rice cultivation. In my research village, people exchange labour for rice cultivation because this is the only way to get the field prepared on time during the rainy season. Villagers also lend and borrow money and rice to/from relatives or close friends without interest, and since not all villagers have capital to buy a cow or a pig, they exchange animal raising. This balanced activity helps to generate economic income for individuals, improves social cohesion, and helps to alleviate village poverty.

Exchange labour for rice cultivation (*brâvăs* and *chaul dai*)

According to my fieldwork, people exchange labour for ploughing, pulling rice seedlings, transplanting, and harvesting. *Brâvăs* refers to a complex set of arrangements made between two parties to exchange labour and equipment so that each party is able to farm: sharing and offering what one has in exchange for something one needs. This is a way of combining household resources in mutually beneficial ways. In essence, it is based on a principle of mutual assistance and reciprocity. There is also a form for sharecropping where people exchange the use of rice land for a percentage of the harvest. Individuals who have many hectares of arable land reciprocate with other farmers or relatives to cultivate their land in return of a certain amount of rice at harvest time. According to a woman in the village this is called *brâvăs*.[3]

Another system of exchange labour for agriculture is called *chaul dai* (put the hands together), which means exchanging labour in an exact amount and at set times. For example, if someone comes to help transplanting my field for three days I will help him transplant for three days. Some farmers think that these two systems are similar. As one farmer said:

> *Brâvăs* is slightly different from *chaul dai*. For example, if I have rice fields and my husband is sick, and no-one in my family can plough the field, I must *brâvăs* the field with someone who can do it. If I pay the seed they must give me back the exact amount of seed, and the rice yield must be equally divided between him and me. This is called *brâvăs*. *Chaul dai* is if someone comes to ask me to transplant for two days, then when I need to transplant or harvest my field, s/he must come and help me for two days (field notes July 2000).

There are not many farmers in the village conducting *brâvăs* exchange of rice lands. Among the 35 households I interviewed, only two have engaged in *brâvăs*. Nevertheless, many villagers say that *brâvăs* and *caul dai* are the same; there is no clear-cut distinction, and many families are practising *chaul dai*. Sometimes, during my stay in the village, it was confusing to me. I tried to differentiate between the two systems, but the explanations overlapped.

In the village where I conducted fieldwork, no-one owns huge rice fields, so the number of people transplanting and harvesting may be fewer than ten at a time. The system of labour exchange has always been mainly used at the busiest times of the agricultural year. *Chaul dai, brâvăs* and hired labour are still found there. This formula offers various advantages. Work is completed in several hours that would require several days if it were done only by family members. Moreover, it also offers a chance for villagers to meet, demonstrate social cohesion and forget the cruel servitude of work in the enjoyable atmosphere of working in a team.

All villagers practise rain-fed rice cultivation with traditional techniques, primarily using oxen for ploughing. Many household heads say that '*brâvăs* and *chaul dai* are very important for all of us in the village because this is the only way we can get the fields done on time in the rainy season'. This system helps provide widows and very poor families with rice for the whole year. Without this system many farmers would face a lot of difficulties in having food for daily subsistence.

Villagers borrow bundles of seedlings (*sâmnab*) from relatives or friends when they need them urgently to transplant, and return the favour later. Some farmers buy *sâmnab* from a neighbouring village. A villager in Phong (west hamlet) says:

> Sometimes we borrow *sâmnab* [pulled seedlings] from relatives or friends if we need it urgently to transplant, then when they need it back I must pull it out from

my fields. If I do not have it, I have to buy it for them. *Chaul dai /brâvăs* is very helpful; everyone in this village has to use it during the cultivation time. They have to make sure that they will have enough time to go repay the work. If I do not have time, I can send my son or daughter to help them in return. This is a good way to maintain our relations for the future (field notes, June 2000).

This reciprocal system is carried out mostly by the villagers who are not working with non-government organisations. Villagers who are busy with NGOs prefer to hire labour instead of exchanging labour (see discussion below). The advantage of *brâvăs* and *chaul dai* is in allowing farmers to get agricultural tasks completed on time, particularly ploughing and transplanting. It allows poorer villagers, such as widows and elderly people who have no adequate labour sources or equipment, to reciprocate with another household so both will meet their needs.

Exchange in raising animals

Another labour exchange venue is 'exchanging is raising animals'. Frequently, villagers exchange the raising of pigs and cows. Pig exchange is less common because villagers can afford to buy piglets from relatives or friends. Normally, villagers who own rice mills are able to raise many pigs because they have the bran from processing rice. Processing rice at the rice mill is free but the rice millers keep the bran. The price of bran is 800 Riel per kilogram during harvest season and 1,100 Riel per kilogram during the rainy season. The pig feed consists of bran mixed with chopped banana trees and some leftover family food. It takes at least eight months for pigs to grow big enough to sell. At the time of my fieldwork, the price of pork was 8,000 Riel/kg. Some families used the money from selling pigs to fix their houses and buy clothes or for medical care. Pig raising is the job of women, usually the family's daughters. Most pig exchanges are conducted between relatives. For example, if one has raised a female pig bearing many piglets, one might give some piglets to relatives and in the future, if one needs piglets, the relatives will offer some back.

Among the families I interviewed, many had the experience of exchange in raising cattle. They do so if they have many children to herd the cattle. Some villagers say:

I want to have a cow or an ox to use for the rice fields, but I am not able to afford it. The only way to have it is *brâvăs kô*. However, I have no time to herd them and all my children are too young to take care of cattle.

Usually, the cow owner will take the second calf and the herder will keep the first calf (the cow owner will take the cow back after the calf is big enough to live independently). This is a very effective method for providing oxen or cows for use by the poor and widows. This cattle exchange occurs mostly with relatives and close friends in the village. Some households exchange cattle raising with friends from other villages. In this case the herder must be responsible for raising, feeding and proper treatment of the cattle. The cattle owners come to check on the condition of their animals from time to time; if they think the herders are not raising them properly they have the right to take them back.

In sum, patterns of balanced reciprocity in the village still prevail. The primary form used is the exchange of labour for rice cultivation. But many people prefer to get a paying job and combine this with farming rice. They realise that money can replace some of the hard work in the fields. The influence of the cash economy is changing the nature of village reciprocity. There are many opportunities for villagers to get jobs with NGOs, in the construction industry in Siem Reap town and in the tourism industry (hotels and restaurants). This influence of money and wage labour began in Cambodia in the late 1980s with the gradual emergence of a market economy. There is a large-scale pattern of rural villagers seeking jobs in the cities, especially Phnom Penh. Cash flowing from urban migrants back to rural areas changes the social environment and the nature of agriculture—people can afford pump generators, fertiliser and so on. But will this lead to fundamental changes in traditional agricultural techniques? Will a cash influx improve local employment and help alleviate poverty? Some well-off farmers might be able to buy more arable land and other villagers end up as their hired workers, thus increasing social stratification.[4] In this the village may reflect more general Cambodian patterns of economic changes in Cambodia. It is important to note that even with a shift to a completely monetised economy, some forms of social reciprocity will still be practised, as we find, for example, in neighbouring countries, where market-oriented agriculture co-exists with local systems of exchange.

The influence of Buddhism on reciprocal activities in the village

Buddhist concepts are important in understanding the notion of reciprocity. Three fundamental concepts (*nirvana*, *karma* and merit making) influence practice. One of the most important roles of the monk is to be a vehicle for merit making on the part of the lay community. From a Buddhist point of view, reciprocal exchange activities in the village or in the family constitute forms of 'right livelihood' since they do not involve the taking of life, but rather are seen as 'merit making'. This also has an impact on Cambodian notions of wealth accumulation. The accumulation of wealth is highly valued or appreciated, from a Buddhist perspective, if the wealth is to be used for merit making. Given limitations of space, I will not describe in any detail how merit-making ceremonies can explain Cambodian processes of reciprocity. But among the important ceremonies are:

- Monastic ordination, which involves a son trying to gain Buddhist merit for himself and for his parents in return for their having given birth to him and raised him from childhood.

- *Kâthin*, a crucial ceremony, celebrated every year in each wat to raise money. It shows the social cohesion in Khmer society and the ways organisers can reciprocally gain merit from their efforts and the money spent for the ceremony.

- *Bâng kăk chmâb*, a ceremony that parents commonly organise to allow their child to thank the midwives who attended their birth.

The Khmer term *kŭn*, according to the dictionary, means 'good deed, favour, kindness and merit'. This is best understood in context. For example, *tâp kŭn* means to repay a favour. In this context it has a positive meaning; it refers to someone who has helped or committed a good deed for you. *Dŏeng kŭn* literally translated means 'realise one's favour' or to recognise one indebted to another for a past kindness or service. *Bâmphlech kŭn* or *romĭl kŭn* means to forget or ignore someone's favour or to break a connection with someone who has helped you (Headley et al 1977:125–6). It makes intuitive sense to consider *kŭn* as a Buddhist concept connected to *bŏn* (merit). The concept of *kŭn* has obviously become in itself a social norm and belief in Cambodian society. As Rahula's elaboration of Buddhist teachings put it, 'human qualities and emotions like love, charity, compassion, tolerance, patience, friendship, desire...' need no sectarian labels; they belong to no particular religion (Rahula 1996:6).

Conclusion

Daily social reciprocal interaction is a means of maintaining social cohesion and morality in Cambodia. This interaction sets certain constraints on interchanges between people in rural society that are informal and yet pervasive. In our interactions with others, whether with family members or neighbours, social relations are overwhelmingly defined by informal codes of conduct, norms of behaviour and conventions. These codes inform patterns of social relationships and informal economic processes. I think that norms of reciprocity can ensure the economic survival of individual families and of village social networks. The process of sharing must be balanced or negotiated as time goes on. These norms of behaviour and mutual trust characterise the relationships of villagers. The prevalence of mutual trust can build strong community relationships within non-kin groups, such as intra-village relationships. Informal social institutions exist without state enforcement or interference. Informal social institutions have been working in Cambodian society for centuries. At the present time, these patterns draw on and contribute to social morality and village cohesiveness. However, we need to add that these systems are changing with the introduction of a market economy.

All of the reciprocal activities in my research village fit with the classic literature on reciprocity and the ways it explains how reciprocity maintains social stability and economic standards. As argued by Mauss (1990:33), all kinds of exchange are intermingled with larger patterns of material and moral life. Gift exchange functions as a social practice involving legal, economic, moral, religious and other dimensions of society. With each gift, in a system of reciprocity, the honour of giver and recipient is engaged. Gifts must be returned, though not necessarily within a particular time frame, and this can even take generations.

Nowadays, social change includes the influence of monetarisation from the introduction of a cash economy and the introduction of international organisations such as NGOs. Many villagers are working as wage labourers for NGOs, some have small businesses selling food and souvenirs to tourists, and some seek employment in a provincial town, in Phnom Penh or even in Thailand. These sources of money are changing the nature of balanced reciprocity in the village. Even though Cambodian villages are finding themselves caught up in new economic systems, traditional social reciprocal norms are nonetheless continuing in modified form. Such changes are taking place earlier in the Angkor region than many parts of Cambodia because of the influence of NGOs and tourism.

The main social change is a transition from family farming to hired labour, which in the future will take place increasingly throughout Cambodia. The monetisation of patterns of exchange is resulting in a shift away from mutual assistance in rice cultivation; however, at the present time mutual exchange and wage labour co-exist in ways consistent with cultural norms. In the long run, as the cash economy spreads, there may well be improvements in agricultural technology and augmentation of household wealth and land holdings for some. However, it is also likely to result in a widening of the gap between the rich and the poor, a gap presently still moderated by reciprocal exchange systems.

Notes

1   This chapter is drawn from a master's thesis from Northern Illinois University and draws principally on field research in Angkor Krau village, Siem Reap province, carried out between July and September 2000.

This was the terminology used by anthropologists in the 1960s referring to Cambodian community. At the present time, some anthropological literature considers that dyadic, personalised relationships, kinship relations, or other small scale linkages can be called informal institutions.

2   Some recent studies by the author reveal that inter-institutional interaction in Cambodia remains weak.

3   Sharecropping is unusual in this area because there are no large concentrations of farmland. This practice is more common in the neighbouring provinces of Battambang and Banteiy Meanchay.

4   This has not happened in my research village. But according to my work in Battambang province, many farmers lost arable land when they faced urgent problems such as illness or drought.

chapter eight

No longer a 'happy balance': the decline of female status in Khmer village culture

Kate Grace Frieson

Before the war, there was better balance in the family, husbands and wives were in better balance. So violence may have happened before the war but it was much less than now. The family structure was destroyed during the war so it caused unbalance. We are hearing about domestic violence during our Public Forums everywhere in Cambodia now, even in Ratanakiri, people are asking for help to end this crisis. (Chea Vannath, Director, Center for Social Development, Phnom Penh)

Before the war, women were respected, they had status that was valued whether in roles as mothers, or daughters, or as teachers or nuns. But since the war years, women have lost their value, and women and men in villages do not have the same relationships that they once did. (Female Khmer teacher)

Right now we can see a growing problem in Cambodia with the lack of respect for girls and women, with increases in the numbers of rapes of girls by family members and the selling of girls by their families into trafficking rings to make money for the family…Politicians and high ranking officials often have young girls around them as their mistresses, and this is the role model that poor villagers, especially men, are exposed to. We are losing our values and human rights and morality…We had such problems before the war, but following the Khmer Rouge period, it seems that the misuse and abuse of girls by men is growing. (Ung Vanna, Poet, Activist, Officer of UN Inter-Agency Project on Human Trafficking (UNIAP))

Life out of balance is a common reference made by Cambodian intellectuals and writers in their reflections on social relations between the sexes. There is a poignancy to this point because, for Cambodian elders at least, there was a time after Cambodia obtained its independence from France when life exhibited a fair degree of harmony, when predictable behaviour and sanctions for disorder among kinsfolk were regulated by village elders, Buddhist priests, laymen and nuns and by the ancient laws and wisdom of the *chbăb* that had been passed down from generation to generation in villages that were more or less autonomous. This period of relative harmony existed from 1960 to 1975, a short time span in numbers of years, but, as a historical reference point, a pivotal period for Cambodians. Put simply, it was the time before 17 April 1975, the date that the Khmer Rouge took control and ended all that was familiar. This chapter highlights the singular importance of May Ebihara's early ethnographic findings on the social and economic status of girls and women which stand in stark comparison to the evidence of decline of their status in rural Cambodia since 1975. While Ebihara was not sanguine about an editorial decision to place the phrase 'happy balance' in the title of her chapter in *Many sisters* (Ebihara 1974b), her data on female–male relations in the rice-growing village of Svay, based on social, economic and cultural indicators circa 1960, does suggest complementarity and relative harmony, rather than grave inequality.

Demographic and human-development indicators today register most graphically the vulnerability of women in Cambodia to the possibility of slipping into unending poverty, losing their land, becoming chronically indebted or becoming marginalised as less valued and respected members of society. While the statistical mix of adult men and women is slowly evening out (about 52% of the adult population is female and 48% male), in the immediate post-war years, adult women comprised 65% of the adult population (NIS 1998). This skewed sex ratio subsequently led to a disproportionate number of households headed by women—some 29% of the households overall (NIS 2004). Among rural populations, estimates from the government's interim census report of 2004 indicate that 65% are women, and 80% of these women are active in agricultural work. Moreover, women have dual responsibility for the farm and for household management. The economic indicators of decline in female status show up in surveys of landholdings, land distribution and rural poverty, where women are disproportionately worse off than men. According to the April 2008 Cambodia Gender Assessment by the Ministry of Women's Affairs:

> In rural households with five or more family members, 69 percent of the population in female-headed households with no adult males is poor compared to 50 percent in rural female-headed households with at least one adult male and 45 percent in rural male-headed household. The average poverty rate in rural areas is 40 percent (MWA 2008).

In terms of social factors, 40% of adult women are illiterate compared to 20% of men; (MWA 2008:82) and child prostitutes, it is alleged, number 10,000–15,000, mostly from rural areas and desperate to find sources of income for their families (Brown 2007). Moreover, human rights advocacy organisations and social science researchers are reporting dramatic increases in domestic violence and pornography and alarming rates of males deserting families, sexual assault, rape and trafficking of children and women. (MWA 2005; Fordham 2006; ADHOC 2006).

What is painfully evident, when talking to adult and elderly women in Cambodia, is that the social disruptions provoked by long years of war, economic deprivations and social revolution have had negative consequences for male–female relationships in almost all respects. The dignity and respectful social standing that women had in the 1960s, they say, have been eroded since the years of the Khmer Rouge.

Ebihara's early work on village life, social organisation and economic structures is, therefore, critically important for providing the historical starting point for a preliminary investigation into the decline of female status in rural Cambodia. The thoroughness of her village study and her careful documentation of male and female roles in agricultural production, family organisation and social relationships are particularly valuable in establishing foundational knowledge of gender relations in a rural context. As Scott (1986) argues, gender differences are a 'primary way of signifying relationships of power'. The changes in female status evident in Cambodia, therefore, need careful documentation for advocacy policy and planning by NGOs, women's movements, and government planners.

The objectives of this chapter are to review Ebihara's research into significant status markers for male–female relations in rural village life, to indicate areas where these have been forcibly altered by state and political interventions, and to suggest some possible areas for future research which could deepen our understanding of complex social and sexual phenomena. To help frame these issues, it is useful, first, to comment on how gender is situated in Cambodian society generally.

The chapter draws on research carried out in Cambodia in the 1990s and between 2003 and 2006 on gender relations in politics and nation building, based on archival research and interviews with active members of NGOs, commune-level leaders and women in leadership roles in health, education and women's affairs in the government sectors(Frieson 2001; McGrew, Frieson & Chan 2004:4).

Gender relations in Cambodian culture

Cambodia is a hierarchically ordered society and sexual difference is diffused in power relations (Nhiek 1962; Ebihara 1968; Frieson 2001; Ledgerwood 2002). Gender identity fits within a complex ranking system of social status markers that include age, wealth, education, rural–urban backgrounds, access to powerful patronage networks, social reputation, ethnicity, concepts of beauty and religious merit. Women are generally in subservient positions relative to men, even when they are equals in age and have similar social class and educational backgrounds. This is because at all levels of government and within the Buddhist order—the sources of the country's political and moral authority—women are denied equal access on the basis of their 'inferior' sex status.

Women lack access to the powerful patronage networks that mediate entry into the public domain of politics, religion, private sector and financial institutions, military, government, and even media. These male-dominated domains are interconnected through personalised relationships based on family ties and reinforced through patronage networks. Such domains have evolved their own cultures of power over decades that generally exclude women.

In contemporary Cambodia women and girls face many problems: unequal access to education, health care and other public services; lack of equal economic and political opportunities; marginalisation into feminised sectors of the globalising economy, such as garment factories, the sex industry, and and labour and sex trafficking; abandonment by husbands after marriage; and widespread domestic violence. In addition, during the many years of conflict, gender roles had to change when men were away at war, and society has still not dealt with these shifts now that the men have returned home.

Cambodian society reflects a general pattern of gender relations, reinforced during the French colonial period, whereby women figure prominently in family matters and are socialised to have a dominant position in the family. This is reflected by the title *me phtĕah,* 'household head', that is ascribed to women. Traditionally, women household heads took responsibility for household expenditures and management, making the decisions on debt loads, selling or renting household assets during the various agricultural cycles throughout the year, taking care of the moral education and physical needs of children and being important guides in marriage choices and bride price worth (Ebihara 1968; Delvert 1961).Classical Khmer morality literature was used as a pedagogical tool during the expansion of secular education during the post-independence period. Separate and complementary male and female codes of conduct were reinforced in the classroom and through their expressions in novels, cinema, poetry and proverbs (Ledgerwood 1990; Ung 1998; Ebihara 1968). One of the most frequently quoted Khmer sayings used in socialisation of disparate gender roles and values in society is, 'While men are gold, women are cloth'. While the relative value of gold and cloth suggests that men have greater social worth than women and are, therefore, more privileged in access to schooling and in carrying out public roles and responsibilities, more subtle interpretations are often attributed to this saying—of women's fragility, in that cloth is easily soiled and vulnerable to being torn or damaged. Another interpretation of the saying is that, like cloth, women need to be carefully handled and protected to avoid being soiled (MWA 2005). By 2003, the Ministry of Women's Affairs reframed this popular saying through an information campaign called Neary Rattanak (Women are precious gems).

Sex roles are premised on spatial divisions of power, wherein women reign in the domestic realm and men rule in the public sphere. As husbands and fathers, men are taught to earn wages, provide for the family's financial needs and represent the family in public matters, such as tax collection, land registry and civil registration with the state. Women are taught to run the household, take care of the children and provide the correct moral teachings to family members, in order to ensure their respectful standing in the community. For girls, this means staying well within the confines of the household, not venturing outside alone and, preferably, from the onset of adolescence to marriage, being chaperoned when they do venture out (Frieson 2001).

Women in Cambodia have always been active producers in local and national economies, as farmers, marketers, petty traders, gold and currency converters, and handicraft producers. As in much of mainland Southeast Asia, women were thus pivotally placed within local markets and earned important reserves of cash for their families although this activity was rarely acknowledged in the didactic verse or popular culture.

May Ebihara, ethnography and gender relations in pre-war Cambodia

Two salient observations made by Ebihara in her ethnographic study of village life in 1959—the relative equality of impoverishment and the autonomy of the family unit—are of particular interest, as they provide the historical starting point for considering negative changes in gender status of females in the post-war period.

The relative homogeneity of village poverty was certainly in flux throughout the 1960s, with increasing disparity in landownership patterns, particularly in the northwest. However, when Ebihara conducted her 1959 village survey, she found that, overall, Svay villagers were more alike than disparate in their economic circumstances, landholdings and access to resources, all living in relative shared poverty. Most villagers had ownership of limited cultivable land, averaging about one hectare per family unit, permitting a subsistence livelihood. All were essentially subsistence farmers linked to a national economy, but still, in the 1950s and 1960s, functioning in a domestic mode of production. The villagers themselves noted disparities amongst each other, but also recognised that, in absolute terms, they were all poor rice farmers. As Ebihara (1968) noted:

Although villagers recognized degrees of relative wealth among themselves, *there also existed simultaneously a general ethic of fundamental egalitarianism*. This was manifest not only in the villagers regarding themselves as 'poor people of the rice fields' (even those who were relatively well off spoke of themselves as such), but also in the fact that material wealth in and of itself was not the basis for high status among fellow villagers [italics added].

In gendered terms, what is significant about Ebihara's findings is that women and men shared poverty relatively equally and participated in equal, but differing, aspects of agricultural labour and ventures for generating cash income. That is not to say that men were equally tasked with household management—clearly women's labour hours were longer than men's in the village, precisely because the domestic sphere was considered female work. But women were equally active and important as male counterparts in the agricultural work cycle. In *Many sisters*, Ebihara (1974b:321) wrote,

> The wife is the necessary coworker in the rice-fields, for while men do the heavy work such as repairing dikes and plowing and harrowing, women do the sowing, transplanting, much of the harvesting and the winnowing and pounding of the rice.

Women were also equally partnered with men in the formation of collective work groups (*brâvăs dai*), which were necessary for completing arduous cycles in rice agriculture. 'For example,' wrote Ebihara (1987:18), 'several men might form a plowing team to work one another's fields in turn, while groups of women did the same for transplanting, thereby completing tasks more quickly and easily than could family members alone'. The pooling of labour and resources among kinsfolk at crucial times of the rice-growing cycle and women's active participation in agricultural production, coupled with equal opportunities for women and men in petty-trade income-generating opportunities, meant that gender disparities in economic and agricultural production were not evident. Moreover, women's ownership of property, including residences, cattle and farm equipment ensured protection in the event of widowhood, divorce or separation from husbands or estrangement from male household members. A summary comment on this point is that, with so few communal activities beyond the reciprocal labour exchanges among villagers during planting and harvesting cycles, gender asymmetry may not have been as visible as in more complex economies with stronger ties to national and global economies.

The second important contribution Ebihara made to our understanding of village culture in Cambodia was that the main sociological pillar was the family unit. The family unit, as Ebihara defined it, was a 'unit of parents and children (and often other relatives as well) who lived and worked together, shared resources, and were emotionally attached to one another'. Family units then were the main source of identity for villagers. As she emphasised in her PhD thesis:

> A striking feature of Khmer village life is the lack of indigenous, traditional, organized associations, clubs, factions, or other groups that are formed on non-kin principles...there are no enduring, well defined groups beyond the family or household that differentiate individuals; and status differences within the community are not extreme (Ebihara 1968:181–7).

The status of women vis-a-vis men in the family has special significance in this respect, since there were virtually no other social markers of status for women outside of their family roles. While patriarchal authority was acknowledged by villagers as the *de jure* system, the *de facto* practice was much more flexible, with women playing a critical role in the family's social and economic life. Ebihara (1968:113–14) explained that in village life the relations between the sexes and spouses are 'virtually equal':

> The husband is technically the supreme authority who is owed deference, respect, and obedience by his family. But the peasant wife is by no means a totally docile and submissive creature. Her role in the maintenance of the family is critical and her activities are varied; she has primary responsibility for the care of the children and household; she is coworker in the fields; she oversees and keeps the family budget; she shrewdly handles many financial transactions and often undertakes her own commercial ventures to earn money; she owns and can dispose of property in her own right; she assumes explicit legal authority over the household when her husband is dead, absent, in capacitated, etc. As a result, the wife and mother exerts considerable authority, both overt and covert, within her family.

The notion of the male as the *chef de famille* may have been a product of the French colonial period, when family law and marital status were formulated and defined by colonial legal frameworks. The feminine associations and linguistic genealogy of the term *me* (chief, or head), as in *me phtĕah* (household head) are sometimes used to exemplify female power in Khmer society.

Women were responsible for the management of the household, domestic chores and family finances, keeping an iron hand over the family budget and treasury. Women were also the main providers of care for children and had considerable authority in decisions on marriage partners for sons and daughters. In matters of fidelity women were noted for outspoken views. One example Ebihara draws upon to support this observation is the foiled attempt of one of the village husbands to take a second wife.

> Over a period of days, as we all breathlessly watched the drama, Luan subjected her husband to such a torrent of tears, remonstrations, reproaches, threats and more tears that he finally caved in under the pressure and broke off with the girl (Ebihara 1974b).

This starkly contrasts to what I encountered during field work in 1998, when many women respondents were quick to voice their resentment and bitterness about the changed nature of male–female relationships. 'It was as though war brutalized men, making them violent and disrespectful of women now', one respondent explained.

> Before the war, before Pol Pot, women had status in the family and her parents could protect her if her husband was abusive. But now families are torn apart, women are sometimes forced to marry bad men because there are so few among whom to choose, and who can protect these women when things go wrong? (Chan 1997).

Another respondent explained,

> Men now take two or three 'wives', spend money on prostitutes, and gamble away the money their wives earn, and women are powerless to do anything because they are afraid of not having a husband. For a woman to be single in Cambodia is not a socially acceptable thing, so we think, wrongly, that it is better to be married to a bad man than not to be married at all (Em 1997).

Finally, the bilateral kinship system in Svay and throughout most of Cambodia meant that males and females could inherit land, houses, cattle and other possessions equally. Ebihara (1974b:322) observed within the hamlet she studied circa 1960 that, in fact: 'more women than men own houses, village land and rice paddies—the most important items of property—because of the tendency toward uxorilocal residence'.

In summary, many of the above characteristics contributed to what Ebihara called a 'happy balance' in the relative status of males and females in Svay. With the expansion of primary and secondary education throughout Cambodia in the 1950s and 1960s, Svay boys and girls between the ages of six and 16 spent much of the week in school. This was the beginning of a push to combat illiteracy, especially among females; in Svay, for example, Ebihara found that all except two of the adult women in the hamlet were illiterate. She also noted that formal schooling for girls and women was not culturally supported, as gender roles prescribed domestic duties for females and these were learned at home.

While schooling for girls was expanding throughout the 1960s as part of the government's massive investment in secular education, a gender gap in the enrolment of boys and girls persisted throughout the country. Only 32.4% of students enrolled in schools were female in 1964, and only 21% of secondary school students were female (Smith Hefner 1999). By 1970, when civil war erupted and led to the closure of most schools in the countryside, the rate of school enrolment of females had risen to 70% of the level of male enrolments. However, the dropout rate was significant and the majority of girls did not finish primary school (Smith Hefner 1999).

The future of the girls and women must have seemed uncertain, but not overtly negative, in 1960 when Ebihara finished her ethnography of the village and returned to the United States to begin writing her dissertation. But Svay's nearly complete destruction by bombing, civil strife and communist revolution must have been unthinkable. The shattering of village autonomy with the takeover of rural areas by Red Khmer militias, the breakup and separation of the family unit and the unparalleled use of violence to force a social revolution upon a largely unwilling society have provoked a considerable body of scholarly research. However, the gendered dimensions of the Red Khmer revolution and its impact on female status have not yet been comprehensively studied.

The reconfiguration of female roles during the Democratic Kampuchea era

A gendered analysis of the state of Democratic Kampuchea (DK) is important, not least because social levelling, equality among the sexes and a rigid regulation of sexuality and relationships between men and women were prominent social policies of the Communist Party of Kampuchea (CPK). Traditional roles of girls and women formally ended when, beginning in 1975 and 1976, families were forced to break up, form into work brigades organised by age and sex, and live communally. I will briefly discuss two issues of particular significance for changes in gender and power relations during the DK period—food and female identity, and the newly-created political role for women at village level as guardians of the revolution.

Food and female identity

With the collectivisation of food consumption, begun in 1975 and implemented en masse in 1977, the state undermined women's status in several ways. As Ebihara has observed, the collectivisation meant 'greater control over the population by preventing storage of food for escapees and by allowing a means of daily "rewards and punishments" for individual conduct. Finally it undermined the family as a social unit' (Ebihara 1987:28). If we analyse this in gender terms, we can see that women in particular were denied their honoured status in the family unit as the provider of nourishment to their children and extended kin members, for whom they cooked on a daily basis. Women took pride in food preparation for Buddhist and animist religious occasions. Women earned special merit for preparing food for the Buddhist monks (Keyes 1984). With the abolition of religion and the breakup of the family unit, women were thus deprived of their respected status as providers of food. As Ebihara (1987:30) noted, the:

imposition of communal dining was not simply a means whereby the state controlled distribution, it further demonstrated that the work team or co-operative had superceded the family as the basic social unit in Democratic Kampuchea. It is possible that women had particularly strong negative reactions to communal dining because it symbolized the shattering of the domestic domain in which the wife/mother was a key figure exercising considerable authority over familiar matters.

What is noteworthy in this context, however, is how female authority in the domestic sphere was mirrored in the communist design of the social communes and work brigades for youth and small children. For example, the gendered dimension of women and food production and distribution is evident, as communal dining halls were predominantly staffed by women, especially in the most important positions of food preparation and distribution and the guarding of food supplies. Men working in the communal food halls performed traditional tasks of hunting for small animals and making charcoal, but only on the orders of the women.

While many women complained bitterly of having this important status of provider for the family taken away from them, forcing them to eat en masse with other workers and not in family units, the actual monitoring and controlling of food production and consumption remained with female and not male cadres.

Female guardians of the revolution

As in pre-DK times, the village and commune chiefs were typically men, and women were rarely placed in these positions. However, women did hold important security positions, such as *brâthean chlop*, the security chief responsible for determining the political background of villagers and their loyalties to Sihanouk and Lon Nol 'cliques' at the village, commune and district levels. Women in high-ranking security positions could order men below them to investigate. Mostly they were loyal members of the Red Khmer revolution, recruited in the late 1960s and early 1970s when the grassroots organising of the party was done in earnest. These women were mostly single, or related by marriage or kin ties to male members of the revolutionary Ângkar (the CPK organisation). Most of the women who were elevated to powerful positions controlling supplies, food, medicine and work groups came from poor peasant backgrounds, meaning they were landless or tenant farmers. These women were part of the generation who had missed out on the expansion of education for girls and women that took place in the 1960s. Female food-supply chiefs also tended to be married rather than single, ranging in age from late 20s to mid 30s. These women were addressed as *yeay* (grandmother), signifying not their age but rather respect for them as elders. Supply chiefs needed some education and basic literacy skills to read lists and to calculate amounts (Frieson, Siem Reap interviews 1997).

Village work teams, including those comprising children and elderly and adult men and women often had female chiefs overseeing them. While young men and women were put to work together on a project they were separated according to their gender during mealtimes and when sleeping. Children, although they slept in one room, were divided according to their gender. Women were always in charge of groups of children who were separated from their families and forced into production brigades.

The majority of chiefs in charge of goods and food supplies were women. These positions, known as *bráthean sedthâkěch*, were powerful in the distribution of food, in decisions about the portions of rice distributed to villages and about other commodities, such as salt, sugar, radios and batteries. These chiefs had authority to decide on specialised rations for those with illnesses, with or without consultation with the barefoot doctors working in the makeshift clinics. As so many people suffered from malnutrition and other illnesses related to overwork and lack of food, these women had enormous power over life and death.

Youth group chiefs at the commune level were always women. Their responsibilities were to instruct the young workers on tasks such as cutting wood, making compost and gardening.

How the gendered aspects of the DK regime were experienced by the villagers of Svay is a worthy research project for the next generation of anthropologists. The village itself had been largely abandoned by 1973, when the area nearby suffered some of the worst shelling of the entire war. After 1975, returning villagers were associated with urban social classes and classified by the label 'new people', because many had fled to Phnom Penh to escape the fighting.

Svay after the war: the situation upon May Ebihara's return

When Ebihara made her first return trip to Svay in 1989, she found a village devastated by loss—physically, materially and emotionally. Starvation, illness and execution had wiped out 50% of the population that she had studied; in West Hamlet Svay in 1989, 61% of the population was females, and 12 out of the 36 women survivors were widows. These are sad and shocking statistics. Moreover, landholdings of West Svay residents were smaller than they had been before the war. Almost 80% of families had less than one hectare, and some smaller family units had as little as 0.3 hectares, which was insufficient to meet subsistence needs. The equality of poverty and the male–female balance in family units that had characterised village society and economy before the war was no longer evident.

The institution of rural collectives (*krŏm samokki*) in 1979

Svay society, like that of the rest of Cambodia, was devastated after four years of Khmer Rouge rule. Close to starvation and vulnerable to attack after the overthrow of the Khmer Rouge by the Vietnamese-backed revolutionary front in 1979, Cambodians were, nevertheless, desperate to get to their home villages to look for survivors. But the situation was chaotic and the economic situation was grim. With no draught animals, few agricultural implements and tools, and hardly any seed, villagers were in dire need of assistance.

The newly-formed socialist People's Republic of Kampuchea (PRK) instituted a program of rural collectives called *krŏm samokki* (production solidarity groups) to avert famine, catalyse pools of labour and bring about some social order. The *krŏm samokki* were made up of about 10 to 15 families who shared allocated land, labour and whatever farming implements could be found or made. While, in theory, all the agricultural land was the property of the state, the *krŏm samokki* members could occupy land as needed for basic survival needs. Land rights and titles that had been in effect before 1975 were abolished by the PRK, thus making it mandatory for villagers to join the rural collectives in the immediate aftermath of the Khmer Rouge years.

Although little research has been done on the *krŏm samokki*, it has been suggested by some that, without them, many widowed and female-headed families would not have been able to survive. Pooling of labour ensured that those families without able-bodied male relatives could count on other members of the *krŏm samokki* to help out with the arduous tasks of ploughing and harrowing fields. Most significantly, the rights to occupy and use land were tied to the requirement that production from the land be shared among members of the *krŏm samokki*. In this way, a moral dimension of responsibility was instituted, protecting the most vulnerable members of the village society from absolute poverty.

Gender and land redistribution during the PRK

By the mid-1980s, support for the *krŏm samokki* had diminished. Demand for privatisation of property increased as families were reconstituted, became more economically stable, and became able to sell rice and other staples at higher prices than in the PRK state-controlled economic system. Moreover, foreign aid from former Eastern-bloc states practically ceased by the late 1980s, forcing the PRK government to begin implementing free-market system reforms. In 1989, the government introduced the right to own private property, defining it in two respects. The first type of private property was termed 'land for domicile', which was property that people had occupied upon their return to the villages and cities that, in most cases, had not originally been in their possession (Sik 2000). It was a kind of 'finders keepers' solution to the problem of the occupation of properties abandoned or left vacant as a result of internal displacement, war deaths and emigration .

The other type of private property was the agricultural land that was still allocated by the state for peasants to live on and produce what they needed to survive. Land distribution took place on the basis of family size, with large families receiving more land, and according to the availability and quality of land. Under the land privatisation law, agricultural holdings greater than five hectares could be allocated as concessions by the state to private interests, if production from those holdings could be considered a contribution to the overall national economy (Sik 2000).

Land redistribution was implemented by local authorities in consultation with villagers to ensure some transparency in the process, and relative equality. Land plots were also made available for those who had yet to return, a far-sighted legal provision to avert social unrest. As Sik (2000:5) writes, 'Cambodian refugees, overseas returnees, and Khmer Rouge returnees, if returning to a village, were to be provided with land for housing, paddy for farming on land that was free or vacant claimable land'.

The amount of land distributed differed according to population densities and qualitative factors, such as access to water, soil quality and proximity to roads and markets. In theory, the government attempted to ensure fairness by requiring local officials to allocate between one and two hectares of agricultural land to each family, which approximated the average landholdings of more than 50% of Cambodian farmers before the war years. Redistribution efforts, however, did not reflect gender-sensitivity.

The results of three separate socioeconomic surveys of rural Cambodia in the mid to late 1990s indicate a lower rate of land possession by women and female-headed households. The significantly lower rate of female-headed households possessing agricultural land in rural areas might indicate that female-headed households do not have enough adult labour to undertake land preparation or to claim more land. In a 1998 UN World Food Programme survey of 1,040 households including at least one child under five and a mother, randomly selected throughout the country, 87% of male-headed households reported owning agricultural land, as opposed to 83.7% of female-headed households (Sik 2000).

One of Ebihara's later research interests was to track the impact of state property redistribution, in relation to poverty levels among female-headed households, and female strategies to cope without male labourers in their households. Clearly this is extremely important research, and preliminary results of surveys and field work that Ebihara and Ledgerwood conducted together in the mid-1990s indicate that the female-headed households received considerable assistance from extended kin networks whose labour kept the fields productive. The significance of this is that surveys of single households as individual units of production might conclude that female-headed households are necessarily poorer than male-headed households on the basis of labour needs. However, as Ebihara and Ledgerwood noted, widowed or single female household heads rely on nephews, grandsons and other male members of their extended families to undertake the heavy labour, such as ploughing the fields, for example (Ebihara & Ledgerwood 1995).

The revival of traditional village self-help social networks and moral authority of the family is, however, being strained by the growing economic disparities within villages associated with privatisation, by land grabbing by powerful local officials, by the unequal state land reforms of the late 1980s, by globalisation trends and a host of social ills, from domestic violence to child prostitution.

Gendered dimensions of post-war Cambodia

In 1979, women made up between 60 and 64% of the total adult population. The total population in 2001 was 13.1 million, of which 52% were female. Approximately 80% of the population lives in rural areas, with 65% of the rural workforce being female, and 25% of rural families headed by women (UNIFEM 2004). Because of a baby boom in the 1980s, 60% of the population are under 30 years of age, and many in this group are not educated beyond primary school but are now old enough to enter the labour force (NIS 2004).

The gendered dimensions of Cambodia's demographic imbalance are directly attributable to the war years and their devastating carnage. Many more men than women died in battle in the largely male armies during the civil war years (1970–75). Women combatants on both sides tended to serve behind the front as medics, weapons-carriers or propagandists and were, therefore, less likely to be killed in action. During the murderous Khmer Rouge years (1975–79), men outnumbered women as victims of the widespread executions of political rivals in the weeks and months immediately after the regime came to power, because of their professional roles in the male-dominated military, police and government (Shawcross 1979; Chandler 1991). During the internal CPK purges between 1977 and 1978, more men than women were targeted because the party leaders and members at upper levels were predominantly men. Finally, women outlived men under conditions of starvation, malnutrition and disease because of their physical and psychological resilience (Mysliwiec 1988; Ledgerwood 1992).

The many years of conflict have exacerbated other problems, if not created many more, in Cambodia. The society is heavily militarised, with guns and other weapons in homes and vehicles, and carried by people; There are few laws to control guns, and weak enforcement of of those few laws. A culture of violence exists which manifests itself in a large domestic violence problem, mob violence against alleged thieves, acid throwing (often by women) against second wives, drug trafficking and money laundering and political violence. HIV/AIDS and trafficking of persons, particularly women and children, are rampant in Cambodia. Systems are weak, particularly in education, health care and the judiciary. Impunity and corruption are pervasive, and democracy is in its infancy. In spite of this legacy of war, civil society is doing much to combat these problems, and women and women's groups are at the forefront.

Ministry of Education statistics relating to the education of girls and women are particularly disheartening; although approximately 89% of boys enrol in primary school and 83% of girls, the dropout rates are progressively higher for girls, with only 17% enrolment of girls at tertiary level and almost none of these girls coming from rural areas. Adult literacy is reported in the national census as 67.3%, though the rate for rural women is only 54.3%. For those between the ages of 15 and 24, the literacy rate is 81.9% for men and 71.1% for women (MP 2005).There is growing evidence that poverty is more acute for women than it is for men, because of demographic imbalance in various age groups, gender gaps in education and gendered differences in land tenure and ownership patterns. An understanding of the demographic changes between male and females is a helpful entrée to understanding the gendered aspects of poverty and governance in Cambodia.

Gender, demography and poverty

Women's labour is mainly in agriculture where family-run subsistence rice farming or vegetable farming predominates. Women have the triple burden of responsibility for farm work, household management and caring for their children, but in addition to these responsibilities, women typically take on extra work to earn cash income for their families. Most street vendors selling prepared foods such as noodles, rice cakes and sweet breads, are women. Women dominate the open-air fresh produce and meat markets and are often the suppliers of agricultural produce to the markets. Women also dominate the handicrafts industry, typically making, in their homes, woven mats and brooms, or weaving cotton or silk *krâmas* or *sâmpâts* with assistance from the younger females of the household and from older women in the family (UNIFEM 2004). In the urban areas, the main waged employment for women is in the garment factories. The feminisation of labour is of growing concern, as 80% of garment-factory workers are young women who migrate from the provinces and live and work under typical sweatshop conditions, producing designer-label clothing for the export market (WAC 2002).

Women and access to land tenure and ownership

Before the years of war, men and women had equal access to land through inheritance, acquisition through cultivation and recognised rights to land ownership. The post-war period is now characterised by inequalities between men and women in land ownership, access to land and ability to keep land under production. Overall, a distinct pattern is emerging in rural Cambodia, where 80% of the population resides, whereby poorer households that are female-headed have smaller plots of land than do households headed by males. They are not able to enlarge their landholdings through production and are more vulnerable to market forces and indebtedness.

Female-headed households have shown that they are more vulnerable to becoming landless because of three factors: women have higher illiteracy rates than men and, therefore, have little or no knowledge of land titles; women are socialised to look after parents in their old age, spending their savings or selling their assets to buy expensive medicines; and women are vulnerable to being cut off from their assets through divorce.

According to a 2001 social assessment on land use in Cambodia (So et al 2001:20), gender imbalances were clearly marked:

> After the land distribution in the late 1980s, female-headed households could not enlarge their farmland as the male-headed households could due to shortages of labour and draft animals. In general, female-headed households have also been more vulnerable to becoming landless.

In terms of education, literacy rates for adult women are on average 20% lower than for adult men. This is a factor that militates against women's awareness of their legal rights under the law and makes women vulnerable during divorce and separation, when family assets are under dispute.

Generally speaking, women have less knowledge than men about land plot sizes, legal tenure requirements and the new Land Law. Although this stems in part from their lower literacy levels, it is also partly because of the social stigma attached to women engaging directly and equally with men in matters requiring access to local authorities and legal matters (Mehrak, Chhay & My 2008).

A social assessment of land in five provinces (So et al 2001) revealed that, while inherited plots of land are under the parents' names, it is the men and not the women who keep the certificates of entitlement. The study concluded,

'Women especially seem to have less authority in protecting ownership rights over inherited lands, as well as lands that are under shared ownership' (So et al 2001:20).

Female propensity to indebtedness

Female-headed households are also increasingly found to be more vulnerable to poverty and indebtedness than male-headed households. As noted above, a contributing factor has been the costs incurred by daughters for the care of their parents. Caring for elderly parents at home has traditionally been the duty of daughters. For female-headed households, this duty has caused impoverishment and, sometimes landlessness, as women are forced to sell their draught animals or land to pay the high costs of medical treatment.

There is a gendered dimension to their status of the elderly within the family, with elderly men generally more respected than women, which can cause difficulties during illness when resources are scarce. A study by HelpAge International found that:

> This lack of respect causes a particular problem when older women are ill. Because older women hold less formal authority within the family...it is harder for older women to claim family resources for their own care. Although poor older men and women faced the same problem of whether to ask for treatment, or whether to conserve their children's money, it was older women who said that their children were upset or quarrelled over the cost of paying for their treatment (HelpAge International 1998:95).

Elderly women, once the revered bearers of wisdom in the community, are increasingly viewed by themselves and some family members as economic burdens and causes of family impoverishment, even though they continue to contribute much to household management and labour. In fact, the economic contributions of elderly women are hidden in most statistical counts, as these women are not considered active members of the labour force as such and, in household surveys, their work tends to be negatively attributed rather than regarded as contributing to the overall income-generation activities of the household (HelpAge 1998). The HelpAge International study concluded that:

> This belief that women's contribution to the household does not have the same value as men's affects women of all ages. This has an especially significant impact on older women. Older men continue to be respected within the family as the head of the household and the former bread-winner. Yet older women are sometimes considered unproductive once their ability to generate income directly declines, regardless of whether or not they still do unpaid housework (HelpAge Internation 1998:95).

Conclusion

Tracking the social changes of rural Cambodia and one rice-growing village in particular has been a lifelong work of May Ebihara. What stands out today as remarkable about the condition of Svay is how much better-off villagers appeared to be four decades ago, not only in terms that are commonly measured by the Human Development Index, but also in the hermetic ability for villagers to exist with some autonomy and flexibility in how they wished to encounter outside influences. Ebihara did not romanticise peasant life, because she lived with most of the deprivations that peasants had to live with during her year in Svay. Her affectionate and poignant pre-war vignettes of girls and women there, from infancy to elderly years, are one of the few scholarly accounts of how daily life, rites of passage, marriage and marital relations were experienced by ordinary Khmers. Now, the upheavals of the war years have permanently changed social structures, demographic sex ratios and female agency.

Because of the widespread rupture in male–female relations and the grave impact of the demographic imbalance on family and social relations, many women's organisations began operating in the 1990s. They focused on community and media campaigns to educate women and men about domestic violence, prostitution and its link with HIV/AIDS, gendered social constructions of the family, household and work patterns, and equal access to education and civic duties for males and females.

Social empowerment remains one of the most pressing demands of women rural and urban activists in Cambodia. In spite of the tremendous sacrifices women were asked to make throughout the 1980s—giving up sons to the war, taking over agricultural production for the defence of the motherland, supporting the front throughout the war and staffing state institutions—they were left with little status, prestige or dignity after the war.

In view of the sparse anthropological work on pre-war rural Cambodia, Ebihara's work on male–female relations stands alone as a rare and precious contribution to Cambodian studies, because it provides a cultural and historical context for comparison and analysis. Ebihara's lifelong work on Cambodian village culture has achieved the ultimate objective of anthropology—a level of understanding of how Khmer villagers understood their own cultural universe and how their value systems provided some meaning and order to their lives (Ortner 1991:189). Tragically, political and military forces far beyond the control of villagers destroyed this cultural world. We all look forward to the continuation of the story of Svay, to learn how villagers of Svay have regrouped, reorganised their lives and families and responded to the dramatic changes in the relatively 'happy balance' between men and women that existed 50 years ago.

chapter nine

Females and fertility

Jane Richardson Hanks

Editor's note: The reader will note that this essay by Jane Richardson Hanks is different in character from the other contributions. Hanks is of the generation of Southeast Asian anthropologists who preceded Ebihara in the field—a major pioneer in the anthropology of Thailand—and her contribution is that of a mentor as well as a long-term friend. Her contribution could be regarded as a prose-poem; its insights are emotional and intuitive; but it also summarises, succinctly and forcefully, an understanding of gender relationships deriving from a lifetime of careful observation and thought. While this is first and foremost a volume about Cambodia, it also represents, in the chapters by Kirsch and Keyes as well as this essay, the dialogue between anthropologists of Thailand and Cambodia. Cambodianists will recognise the applicability to Cambodia of much of what Hanks writes here.

One of the most spectacular sights in Southeast Asia is Bangkok's fleet of royal barges gliding slowly down the Chao Praya River. On 7 November 1996, His Majesty Bhumipol Adulyadej marked the 50th year of his reign with a procession of 52 of these golden barges, powered by 2,000 red-clad oarsmen. In the old days, however:

> The King and Queen, in separate barges, raced each other down the river to the chants of their oarsmen. Their subjects rooted for the Queen because her victory would signal a plentiful harvest. (*New York Times*, 20.10.1996:3)

Shade of thee, Venus of Wellendorf, ancient symbol of female fertility!

Today in Thailand it is two goddesses, Mae Phosob, goddess of rice, and Mae Thorani, goddess of earth, that assure the fertility of the all important rice fields. On the human side, certain women are called *liangdi* (good nourishers) because they are so amply endowed with breast milk they can nurse another's baby as well as their own. Because their fruitful role is often extended to other arenas, their fertility attracts power.

Both men and women work in the rice fields, but more often than not, the woman sells the crop and takes the money. When husbands and sons work elsewhere for wages, they hand their money over to this woman as head of the household. She then doles it out to those men as requested, or as she sees fit. Today, even an upper-middle-class Thai doctor in Ohio in the United States follows the old custom, regularly giving his pay cheque to his wife. Ultimately responsible for the welfare of the family, Thai women are given the means to carry it out.

From Neolithic times, or before, Thailand has shared matrilineal tendencies in Southeast Asia, first observed by Austrian historians in the late 1800s. However, migration and influences with patrilineal foci have flowed in from India and China. Buddhism is patrilineally biased. In the structure of today's government, Brahmanic and Judeo-Christian forms reflect patrilineality. Relatively few women are selected for posts in the political arena; none, today, at the cabinet level.

In the sequences of reincarnation where meritorious behaviour leads to higher status and sin to lower staus, a Brahman-inspired ladder of life is found with a slot for every being. It leads upwards from the lowly worm to dogs, human beings, gods and goddesses (*thevada*), finally to the peace of Nirvana, when rebirth ceases. The rung of women is below that of men. In daily life this status difference is recognised in the form of the *waj* greeting. To her husband or to any other man a woman bows her head in a gesture of subservience, and clasps her hands high. Nevertheless, many a Thai woman has stated that she does not wish to be reborn to the higher status of men and so lose her female attributes, capacities and power.

A woman's fertility, however, cannot always be implemented alone. Here enters the deep-lying Thai concept of help (*chuaj*). Status differences vanish as a male helps a female to fulfil her procreative function. A wife offers her gratitude for her husband's help with a deep *waj* to him every time she joins him in the marital bed.

The female power through fertility of Neolithic times is recognised elsewhere. In Turkey, archaeologists have recently uncovered a glorious matrilineally focused culture. Across the millennia, Thailand greets Çatolhöyük!

An interview with May Ebihara

John A Marston

The interview was conducted the Friday and Saturday following Thanksgiving, 2004. I took the train in to New York from Connecticut, where I was staying with a friend, riding the subway to her Upper West Side apartment on Riverside Drive. There a uniformed guard buzzed me in, and I took the creaking elevator up to the apartment. May met me at the door and led me through a small hallway to the large living room with windows overlooking a jagged New York cityscape. The room, decorated with semi-abstract art and an eclectic collection of Asian and American Indian artifacts, had to me always typified the lifestyle of the New York intellectual. (The city-struck perspective of a non-New Yorker, but one that, I nevertheless think, had something to do with the way that, without pretension, she and her husband thought of themselves.) The ambience was underlined by a deep open room across the hallway totally lined with bookshelves, where, during part of our interview, her husband Marvin Gelfand sat at his desk, dressed in tennis shoes and a loose-fitting sports outfit. Over the years, my brief conversations with Marvin, a native New Yorker, brought home to me the degree to which, even more than his wife, he cultivated the role of the urban intellectual—an impression perhaps reinforced by his partial blindness, contributing to a slightly distracted air. Their son Adam, also living in the apartment, passed through briefly and greeted us. A second son, Jay, was at the time of the interview stationed as a lawyer with the Judge Advocate General's Corps in Iraq—a source of obvious concern to his parents, even though they expressed some reassurance in the fact that he 'was in the green zone and never left'. May had in recent years required oxygen 24 hours a day, and those of us who were close to her were concerned about her health. I was impressed with how the long tubes attached to the machine gave her great mobility in the apartment and did not seem to cramp her style particularly. We sat at a table in the living room for the interview. She had been hospitalised earlier in the year and had already gone through several difficult periods; I was relieved that she was very much herself for the interview: energetic, alert, and to the point—an image that remains a vivid memory of her.

John Marston

JM: Tell me a little bit about your life.

ME: I was born in Portland, Oregon in 1934 and I was brought up in Portland, except for the war years, when the family was relocated to Idaho. Curiously, to a locale that is not far from where Biff [Charles Keyes], I think, was raised in Idaho. And then we came back to Portland after the war. And I went to public grade school and high school in Portland. Then, I went to Reed College, also in Portland, and I was an anthropology major. All my life I have been kind of interested in archaeology, but they didn't have any archaeology at Reed. There was the one instructor, David French, and one other anthro major, Gail Kelly, who is one of my oldest and closest friends, who just recently retired from teaching at Reed. And it was wonderful in that we got a lot of attention, got first-rate training. And I applied to different schools for fellowships. Columbia made me the best offer, so I went to study anthro at Columbia. Gail went to study anthro at Chicago. And we used to exchange notes during graduate school—lecture notes—so I felt as if I were getting both a Chicago and a Columbia education.

JM: I am curious in general about what it was like to be growing up as a Japanese-American in the US, in Oregon, at that time?

ME: Well, immediately after the war there was still some…Well, let me put it this way, let me start off by saying I was very young when the war broke out; in '42 I would have been about seven or eight, so I wasn't really aware of much prejudice during the war. Also I was in hospitals a great deal when I was young. Then during the war we were of course put away. And I think that children did not really quite understand what the relocation meant. Now after we returned to Portland, shortly after VE Day, the war had not yet ended in the Asia sphere. Then I felt for the first time some prejudice against Japanese, in that people would yell at us on the street and so on, not very frequently, but, you know, it would happen. And when you went into some place like a luncheonette, you were never certain if they would serve you or not, and you knew that you could not buy a house in certain parts of town, etc. Otherwise, I think as time went on I did not feel that much prejudice. But on the West Coast I always felt like a minority, and in a way that I don't in New York, because New York is so polyglot. But I think on the West Coast there is the sense, or at least I always felt it, that Asians are a, quote—minority group—unquote. And when I'm on the West Coast [*laughs*] I feel like a, quote—minority—unquote.

Well, I guess it wasn't really so bad, I mean in the sense that I didn't feel very oppressed or anything. I definitely felt different, and in high school, anyway, one's social life was very much segregated, so to speak. I mean, in school you would have friends who were white, and so on. In terms of going to parties or dances, or whatever, it was definitely segregated, in terms of being with other Japanese-Americans.

JM: Do you think that has affected your interest in anthropology or your approach to anthropology?

ME: I think in the sense that—someone had once said that people who become anthropologists are always, or almost always, marginal people in some way, and I certainly felt marginal, I guess, in more ways than one. So, yeah, that may have brought me into anthropology, ultimately.

Although I often think that the road to anthropology began way back when I was in about the third grade, or whatever, and my older sister brought me a book about dinosaurs. And which fascinated me, as dinosaurs fascinate all kids. And so then I got interested in archaeology, which I mentioned before. Although, then the distinction between archaeology and paleontology, you know, didn't quite get to me; it was all archaeology. And I remember when I was in grade school writing to the Smithsonian, which used to have a wonderful policy of sending out free books if you just asked for them. So I said, you know, 'Dear sirs, I am in fourth grade, and I'm interested in archaeology. And could you send me something?' So they would send me these dry as dust, unreadable, site reports—archeological site reports—which I didn't know from beans about. But I also discovered another wonderful book called *Gods, graves and scholars* [by CW Ceram]. I don't know if you knew that; I still have a copy of it. Oh, and in that, the one chapter in there that really got me, because it's a book about great archeological discoveries, was the one on Chichen Itza. Oh!

JM: I remember that you had an early fascination with Chichen Itza.

ME: Early fascination. Oh God, yes! That chapter was just 'it'! So anyway, that was my interest in archaeology, but as I say when I got to Reed there was no archaeology, and the advisor said, 'Well, take some anthropology, you know, that's the closest thing we have to archaeology'. So I did. But anyway, your initial question was, what was it like to grow up Japanese-American? Well, as I said, I felt like a minority. Then, when I got to Columbia, it was wonderfully liberating in the sense that the whole place was so polyglot, that it made no difference what I was.

JM: You seem very much a New Yorker now. It's hard for me to imagine that you've ever lived anywhere other than New York. What was Columbia like then in the fifties?

ME: Yeah, Columbia I felt was wonderful; I loved it. The faculty was great. I thought they were wonderful. Charles Wagley was chair of the department at that point, and very nice, very welcoming to me. And then there was William Duncan Strong, who was an archaeologist, but he taught American Indians. And he was originally from Portland, or Oregon, somewhere on the West Coast; he was very sweet. Then, in archaeology per se there was Richard Woodbury. In physical there was Harry Shapiro. In theory and linguistics there was Joseph Greenberg, who was astonishing. Oh, so bright and such a great sense of humour! Someone whom I felt very close to on a personal level was Harold Conklin at Yale. I don't know if you've ever met him. I'm sure I'm missing some of the cultural...But, well, the young people—at least they were young then—were Marshall Sahlins and Marvin Harris, who I didn't have classes with. I found him very terrifying. Andrew Vayda was around. Very much on the margins was Ruth Bunzel. And also on the margins was Margaret Mead.

JM: Oh, why were they on the margins?

ME: Well, Mead, because she was very much on the margins anyway, and people—professional anthropologists—looked down on her. I don't know if this is so apparent to those of your generation. Did you know that?

JM: No. I mean, later on there was the whole scandal thing that her first book was...

ME: Oh, the Freeman thing, yeah...

JM: But that was later.

ME: That was later. Earlier on, pretty much through much of her career, the notion that she was a populariser—which she intended herself to be—and she wrote a column for *Redbook* and all that kind of thing—made many professional anthropologists look down on her as being, well, a populariser, and not rigorous, and so on and so on. Now, all I can say is that she was very nice to me. And a couple of incidents, which are my Margaret Mead stories, which I will always remember very fondly. One was when my first draft was due for my dissertation, and I did not have it ready. And I called her up, and said, 'I'm terribly sorry, my first draft is not ready, because I'm accidentally pregnant'. And she yelled—she had this reputation for yelling at people when she was upset—so she yelled over the phone. 'Accidentally pregnant! What do you mean, you're accidentally pregnant,' she said. 'There are no accidental pregnancies,' she said. 'We didn't have the pill back in the 1920s, and we didn't get accidentally...And I said, 'I assure you, Dr Mead, I had no intention of getting pregnant'. She sputtered a bit more and yelled at me. And then—this was also very typical of Mead—then she kind of turned right around and said, 'Oh, well, dear! Take care of yourself, be sure to get enough rest, and eat well,' and blah, blah, blah, and, you know, 'call me when you're ready'. So that was that.

And then, at the other end, the dissertation finally got done, and many years later. She was on the committee, so she had to look at the final draft, and it was New Year's Eve or something like that. And as periodically happens in New York, the subway—the transit system—threatens to strike on New Year's Day. So on New Year's Eve, somewhere in the morning, I got a phone call from Mead, saying, 'If there is a transit strike, you will have to walk over here'. It was snowing, and there was quite a bit of snow. And she lived right north of the museum, which is a bit of a walk from here. She said, 'You will have to walk over here, and it's too far. And so I will be finished reading your dissertation by 4 o'clock. Be here at 4, and I will give you the dissertation'. So I trecked over there. One chapter she made me rewrite. But I thought, well, that's really wonderful of her, you know, given her schedule, which was amazing, on New Year's Eve, to think, 'If there is a transit strike, May will have to walk over to here, so I'm going to read it right now'. And she did. So anyway, I'll always be grateful.

JM: You said your friend was in Chicago and you compared notes between the two. How would you say the two departments were different then? And do you think that your work was significantly different because you were at Columbia than it would have been if you had been at Chicago?

ME: Oh, that is an interesting question. The two were definitely different, and my friend and I could see fairly obviously that they were different. Columbia was still rather Boasian, in the sense that it was still very ethnographic. And you got a lot of ethnography at Columbia, which was great. I love ethnography. Chicago was—the Radcliffe-Brown legacy was still there. And so things were much more social structure, Britishy. Now, that's an interesting question, would my dissertation have been different? Hmmm. I probably would have done more with social system kinds of thing if I've gone to Chicago and maybe less on the descriptive stuff. I tell you, someone else who influenced me at Columbia was Hal Conklin; he was still there at the beginning of my field work—I can't remember when he went to Yale. And you know that he does ecological systems, and so on. So I spent a lot of time on agriculture because of Hal, really. Although once I actually got kind of into the agriculture, once I did it—Judy [Ledgerwood] always kind of laughs, the interest I have in irrigation, for example. So if I hadn't known Hal, I probably would not have spent much time on different varieties of rice, or that kind of thing.

JM: How did you choose Cambodia?

ME: I taught American Indians regularly, Native Americans. But when it came to dissertation, as you well know, you try to find something that someone else hasn't already done. And at that point, I thought, 'Oh, God, American Indians have already been done to death. You know, there's nothing new to be learned from them'. Which was wrong, actually. There've been a lot of good subsequent studies of Native Americans. But at that point it just seemed like this was a dead topic. So, then Southeast Asia seemed interesting, because, well, it just seemed kind of beautiful and, dare I say, strange. Maybe we better not say that. I'm trying to think of a word other than exotic, because we shouldn't say exotic either. And a friend of mine used to talk about Southeast Asia and how marvellous it would be to cruise down the coast or the river or whatever. And I saw a picture of the Temple of the Dawn on the Chao Praya river. And it was beautiful, and I thought, 'Gee, what a lovely place!' And then, when I started to check out Thailand—this is what got a big laugh at that session—I found out that Cornell 'owned' Thailand. (Subsequently, I thought I shouldn't have said that, but it's true in the sense that they had already done quite a bit of research there.) So looking at the map, there is Cambodia right next door. And when I checked on it, I found out that the French had been there, but no Americans had been there, and that there had been next to nothing in term of anthropological work, except for Madame [Eviline] Poree-Maspero, who was not a professional anthropologist. And here I'll make a digression. In my draft dissertation proposal, I'd sent it around to various people to ask their advice and so on and so on. And one of the people I had written to had without my knowing it given it to Bernard Philippe Grolier, who was furious! Did I ever tell you this? He was furious, because, who was this upstart young American anthropologist student who had the temerity to say that there had been no real anthropological work done in Cambodia? So I had neglected all those years of French research in Cambodia. He was really mad at me. And in retrospect, I don't blame him. But anyway, I did not start off on a good foot with him. But that's how I ended up in Cambodia. And I have to say that some of the other French people whom I met, like Madame Poree-Maspero and her husband and [George] Coedes and Francois Martini, who was a linguist...

JM: You met them?

ME: Yes, I was fortunate enough to get one of those Ford Foundation Foreign Area Training fellowships, and I specifically wrote in two weeks in Paris so I could meet these people. Who else did I meet? [Charles] Archimbault, who was a Laotian expert. And I don't know if you know [François] Martini, because he was actually a linguist. He was a metis; he was part Khmer. He was a very, very nice man. And the other person who was really very nice, although at that point I saw him only briefly, is [Georges] Condominas. Whom I also met in Paris. So I have to say the French were very, very pleasant.

JM: So your research in Cambodia was funded by Ford, or just this period in Paris?

ME: Yes, the whole schmere, yeah. They were giving out tons. I think David [Chandler] had one, too. It was because...Let me see, my grant would have been in the late fifties. Well, after the war—World War II—a number of area institutes and also funding agencies like Ford and others were sponsoring knowledge about different parts of the world. Because after World War II, it became obvious that we needed to know about areas abroad. And we needed to have specialists in different areas of the world. So Ford was one of the main funders of this effort.

I think I mentioned at the session in Washington that I really could not find anyone in 1958 or whatever to teach me Khmer, which is a funny story. I went around trying to find someone to teach me Khmer, with no success. And I thought of a place like Berlitz, which claimed they could teach you just about anything in the world, and they were stymied. Finally one language school said they had found somebody who could teach me Khmer. And so this wonderful former Foreign Service officer, very elegant and very charming, very nice guy, came and used to teach me these little phrases and so on in what I thought was Khmer, and I dutifully memorised them and so on. And then I went to see *The Bridge on the River Kwai,* which was filmed in Thailand, and the extras were speaking I presume Thai in the background. And to my great surprise I kind of understood what they were saying to one another. And I thought, 'Wait a second, they're speaking Thai, and I could understand this'. So I told Mr McC about my bewilderment on this point. And he said, 'Oh my God!' He had evidently been a Foreign Service officer in both Bangkok and in Phnom Penh. And after so many years had evidently confused the two languages. So he was teaching me partly Thai along with Khmer. And so that's why I was able to understand the Thai. And our lessons ended because, obviously, it wasn't any use, although we remained friendly with one another. He was such as a sweet, elegant, and wonderful man.

And then I had to pick up Khmer once I got there. There was a linguist in Cambodia at the time named Dale Purtle; I don't know if you ever …

JM: I think he was with the Foreign Service Institute. He was one of the authors of some of these Foreign Service language instruction books.

ME: That's right. He was a linguist attached to the embassy; I guess he was language officer. And it was wonderful knowing him not only because he was an excellent linguist, but because he was particularly interested in vernacular Khmer, and was interested in changes of phonemes. And some other kinds of things that he alerted me to, because he said, once I got into the village I was going to encounter these changes—like 'ch' would become 's', 'sa', or 'sma' or whatever. In many cases, like, *chmar* would become *smar.* Dale would tell me these things in the evening, and then during the day I studied Khmer with a very proper Khmer gentleman, who worked at the embassy, Chea Thong.

JM: How long were you in Phnom Penh before you got to the village?

ME: January, February…About three and a half months, because I arrived shortly after New Year, '59. And then I went to the village around May-ish. I forget what the exact date was—around mid-May.

JM: What was it like in Phnom Penh at that time?

ME: Phnom Penh was very pretty. I've always thought it was a very pretty place. What can I tell you about Phnom Penh? I was staying at the house of the Ecole Francais d'Extreme Orient, which is the house that Eva Mysliwiec lives in now, or at least she used to.

JM: By Calmette hospital?

ME: Yeah, that's right. Anyway, they had a representative in Phnom Penh, Martine Piat, I don't know if you've seen her name around. She killed herself subsequently in Vietnam, I think when she was so distraught over the war and everything. But anyway, Martine was very kind and very sweet, and invited me to come stay there. So I stayed with her for a couple of months until I had to leave because they needed the guestroom for—guess who? [*laughs*] Bernard Philippe Grolier, visiting Phnom Penh. So then, I went to live in Le Royal Hotel. But anyway, Phnom Penh was pretty smallish, in that, effectively, the built-up part of town ended just short of the southern end of the museum. From there on it was all wooden…

JM: Like shantytowns.

ME: I shouldn't say shantytown, but it was all native houses—wooden houses. It wasn't shanty in the sense that these were, like, decrepit, or whatever. They weren't stucco villas..

JM: The more developed part of town was Chinese—Chinese and European.

ME: I was going to say there were different neighbourhoods, so to speak: the Chinese part, sort of, or what I would think of as the Chinese part. I think the East Indians lived in another part. The French. I don't know, did the French congregate in a particular…? I think they were scattered around. The Americans hung out in a couple of complexes, one a big apartment building on the way to the airport. Another bunch lived behind the Royal in those bungalows. And then another bunch lived somewhat to the south, I think, but I was never there, so I can't remember where that was located. So there tended to be little ethnic clumps here and there. Went almost everywhere by cyclo, we did not have motodubs in those days.

JM: What was the political mood? Was there any political mood at all?

ME: Not that I was so aware of. I am sure there was, because we would get word [of things], or the villagers themselves—I think I mentioned this in the dissertation—were afraid of being labelled Sam Sary adherents. So that whole number was going on. The famous Dap Chhuon incident. That happened while I was there, I think. Because one of the American embassy people was accused of having been involved in that. Bopha Devi created a scandal when she ran off with some guy from the airforce, an airforce officer. She was supposed to be married to somebody or the other, and she ran off with this officer in the airforce. So that was a big scandal. So I am sure there were political things going on. But I just wasn't aware of it. My mind wasn't on it. And you know the villagers, as I say in the dissertation, were all—they thought that Sihanouk was just wonderful. And that was it.

JM: Could you remind me how you chose Svay?

ME: ok, I had a list of characteristics that I would like to find in the community that I studied in term of size, in terms of having a temple, if possible, you know, blah, blah, blah. And so I went around looking at different communities, and in the end I chose Svay, for really, I have to confess, kind of subjective reasons. Although it did indeed have some of the characteristics that I wanted. In another way I picked it because it was so pretty. I just sort of fortuitously found Svay.

JM: But it was close to the pedagogical school.

ME: It was close to the pedagogical school, although that always bothered me, in that I wondered to what extent that might have changed village economy, etc. But it was convenient for me.

JM: But was that partly how you found it? Did you go on trips with people? Did foreigners connected with the pedagogical school give you rides?

ME: Yeah, but I didn't...I originally saw Svay not with someone from the pedagogical school, but someone who was working for AID, I think, at the time. The other thing about Svay was that it had this little house which a bachelor— well, he wasn't a bachelor, he was a divorcee; his wife had left or something. So he was living there all by himself. And it was just, you know, a nice little house perfect for me. And he said he'd be happy to rent it to me. Because for him it was an incredible amount of money coming in. So, also, people seemed very kind of nice, and so on. I subsequently found out it was a fool's paradise—which I think I mention also in the dissertation, where I thought everyone was being so sweet and so welcoming, so nice. And then, I found out just before I left that they had been meeting secretly about me, and [*laughs*] some people had wanted to sort of chase me out, because they didn't know what I was doing there, and so on. And Ta Hin, you know, said, 'Well, let's give her a chance, and let's keep an eye on her, and see what she does, and see what kind of character she has, you know, if she has *chĕtt l'â* or not'. And after a while I think the fact that I was young and single and small, and whatever, persuaded them that I was not a threat, and that I really *was* there to study. So they decided to let me stay. So, thank God for Ta Hin. I mean, he was quite extraordinary.

JM: Would you say that what you ended up doing was what you expected to do?

ME: Yeah, pretty much. I think I had said in the original research proposal— I'll have to look it up and find out—that given the fact that no American anthropologist had been there, that something like a general ethnography or community study would be called for—even though, again, community studies were already on the way out at the time I did the study.

JM: But why do you think you felt a particular attraction to the idea of doing a community study?

ME: Because, maybe it was my Columbia upbringing, and I never thought of this before, but it was the idea that it was important to get ethnography, that a lot of what the value of anthropology is, is ethnography. And that, particularly going into an area that hadn't been studied before that it was doubly important to have the ethnography. So I was very conscious of trying to get the lay of the land, as it were, in very general terms. I mean, hitting as many institutions as I could, although inevitably there are certain areas I don't feel I covered very well at all. One is politics or political organisation.

JM: Of course now we wonder whether there was anything that would have given a hint of what would come.

ME: I think I mentioned in the dissertation that one villager said that the communists wanted to share everything, or take from the rich and give to the poor. I forget what he said. Which on the face of it I thought would appeal to him. But on the other hand, any kind of dissidence was being labelled, well, you're a follower of Sam Sary. And, you know, you didn't want to be labeled that, because it was dangerous.

JM: Of course, I remember that Sam Sary was an important and controversial figure, but I'm a little surprised that his case would have even been known in the village. How did people in the village even know? From the radio?

ME: Well, from radio. From—except there was hardly any. Again, as I note in my dissertation, there were only two radios, one of which was mine, in the village.

So they would pick up some stuff from the market town. There were these kind of bulletin boards. And some stuff would be picked up by the guys who worked as cyclos in Phnom Penh and then came regularly back to the village. I suppose some of it was coming maybe through the wat. I don't know.

JM: What do you recall of the challenges of the ethnographic process?

ME: Challenges? The heat! God, the heat! That killed me at times. It was difficult in the sense that I found the heat so debilitating that I just couldn't do that much. And insects. I hate mosquitoes with a passion. I went armed with bottles of insect repellent from an army surplus store. Lack of things like electricity and running water, I coped with, and I didn't grouse too much about, and I managed ok.

JM: You never got sick?

ME: No, surprisingly. I was talking to somebody about this recently. Yeah, a couple of times I got, you know, a bad stomach or whatever. But I was surprisingly healthy. And when I came back I was dumbfounded to find a clean bill of health from the tropical medicine clinic at Columbia. And I do think that living in a village is in some sense cleaner than living in Phnom Penh. Plus I was very careful about things like boiling water. No, I was in surprisingly good health.

JM: How often did you go to Phnom Penh, about every month?

ME: About every ten days, maybe. Some days I'd go in and have a shower, which was a great luxury. I had a good friend who worked for AID, Sandy McCall. She actually had been an anthro major at Barnard. So she was a good friend, and I'd have a shower at her place.

I was going to say that, so far as difficulties in the field go, I am sure that all of us have had experience of days when you could just hardly drag yourself out of bed, as Ruth Bunzel said, or when you'd be homesick, or you wanted to hear English spoken, or that kind of thing. But overall, I would say, as field experiences go, it was probably quite [good]. I think it was a good place to do fieldwork, in that Khmer, generally, are wonderful people to be with. They are very co-operative, they are very welcoming. Once they got over their initial suspicions as to what I was up to, they were really terrific.

JM: I thought maybe we could talk some more about how you ingratiated yourself with the villagers. One story I remember you telling me once—or, well, we joked about this because you're a well-known gossip [*May laughs*]. Your technique for getting information was gossiping with villagers.

ME: Oh, I think that's a technique that any anthropologist ends up using. It wasn't so much a technique as, I love to gossip anyway. No, we talked already about how they decided I was ok. And, you know, I hung out mainly with the other *krâmŏms*, the young women of roughly my age group or younger, and the older people who acted as my parents—surrogate parents or grandparents or *pous and mings,* you know, aunts and uncles and so on. And some of the interviewing was standard directed interviewing, where I'd set out to find out how long men had been at the wat or how many years of education one had or whatever. Other kinds of information, as I think with all anthropologists, you get through gossiping. Or just sitting around and chatting with people.

JM: But you're also following them around and…

ME: Oh, yeah, sure. Classic participant observation. I think that was part of what persuaded them that I was ok, in the sense of, who would want to follow you out to the rice fields? You know, in the hot sun to watch you plough or transplant? Or, you know, who would sit on the dyke with a notebook and camera. And who would do things, you know, follow you to a wedding or whatever? As again, with many anthropologists, it got so very often someone would come and say, well, there's a wedding going on in the next village. Or there's a wedding going on in another part of the village. And do you want to see it?

JM: Were you already engaged when you went into the field?

ME: Yeah, in a sense. So, anyway, I was at Bard [soon after fieldwork], and Marvin subsequently accepted a job at the University of Massachusetts in Amherst. I did not have a job at Amherst, but he did. I was really very much separated from the Columbia department, so I felt that they didn't have much impact on me. We were at Bard for three years and then in Amherst for three years, which I found deadly boring, mainly because I didn't have a job. And I also, at that point had a one-year-old in Amherst. And then we came back in '67, I guess.

JM: Do you think those years at Bard and Amherts changed your thinking a lot?

ME: No. Because I was separated from Columbia. And Hal Conklin went from Columbia to Yale. And the other guys…Well, who else was on my committee? [Conrad] Arensberg, whom we mentioned yesterday, and Mort Freed and Mead, whom we discussed yesterday. None of them really influenced me theoretically. But somehow at Columbia you operated on your own.

Columbia *was* undergoing changes in the late fifties, into the sixties, but I avoided them—or they didn't influence me, because I wasn't around. I was either in the field or I was out of the city. The first [change], which was already getting big when I went off to the field was the whole ecological bit. But ecology in the sense of not just the Hal Conklin ethnoscience and techniques of agriculture [approach], but the whole—interpreting things as having ecological functions. What I would say Roy Rappaport's *Pigs for the ancestors* is often held up as a major example of. Now that just went right by me. And Marvin Harris also began to come to prominence during the sixties. That washed right over me as well, although I knew Marvin. Initially I was terrified of him and found he was really a sweet guy underneath it all, so, you know, I came to know him and like him. Eric Wolf came to Lehman, it is true, and we got to be friendly. But what Eric was interested in was stuff I had long been interested in, especially history. And Marxism, I wouldn't say I rejected it, but I was never a Marxist. So, no, I thought of him as mainly a friend and in some sense a model of intellectual thought, but in no way would I think of myself as a disciple of Eric's, and I don't think he would want me to say that either.

JM: I have the impression that you were not particularly focused on Cambodia or Southeast Asia in your teaching.

ME: No. Because I was at a city school, and when you offered classes your eye was on what would draw students. And I think once or twice I offered a Southeast Asia course, which, you know, got so-so enrolment, where American Indians got excellent enrolment. So I would end up teaching American Indians rather than—in fact, there was no question of doing a Cambodia class, because that would get zero enrolment. And at the Grad Center, there was a problem. Although I said that there were few Southeast Asianists around in New York, there was one at the Graduate Center, Del Jones, who was a Northern Thai specialist. And he was actually hired at the Grad Center itself, so he kind of got dibs, so to speak, on offering Southeast Asia. One year we did a joint course, which was great fun. But normally Southeast Asia—when it was given, which was not that often—was taught by him.

JM: I had the impression when I was looking for grad schools (and it was the impression of other people—maybe David Ablin) that you didn't encourage young anthropologists who were interested in Cambodia to study with you at CUNY. Why not?

ME: No. Why not? Because anybody who's really interested in Cambodia, which means becoming a Southeast Asianist, should go to a place like Cornell, or even UW, where you could get language, where you could have people like Ben Anderson, where you can get courses in Southeast Asian history, language, politics, you know, stuff which you can't at CUNY. And when you can't even if you belong to what is called the consortium, where you're permitted to take graduate courses at other schools in New York, you just would not get the kind of training...At one point I had a letter from Soizick [Crochet]. I didn't know who Soizick was. You know, saying something like, could I come study with you, or could I come to CUNY? And I discouraged her. I think Frank Smith had written to me. I think I never answered him. So, yes, David Ablin was right, I discouraged people. As another friend of mine says, she doesn't believe in having disciples, and she doesn't want disciples. I didn't want disciples.

...We're talking about this interim period. Didn't you have a question about what I was doing during this [time]—I don't know if you meant the seventies or the eighties.

JM: You mean the period when Cambodia was politically...

ME: In upheaval. Ok, well I came back and, as I say, got married almost immediately and then had two kids. So during the sixties I think I wrote a few times to people in Svay, like Ta Hin or others and never got any response. So I thought, well, that's life.

JM: How did you write?

ME: In French. Because I figured they could find someone at the normal school...Or actually I may have written in English. That they could find someone who would translate for them. So then I think I gave up after a bit, writing. But I always thought about them. And then, I'm trying to think, things started to get rocky in Cambodia right around '69, '70, thereabouts when the Lon Nol coup took place. And at that point not only did I have young children, but the whole situation seemed not too good to try to go back. And then, it wasn't too much—well, '75, of course, when Pol Pot happened, and then there was no question about going back. You just couldn't and wouldn't. And I must say that I—so far as Svay was concerned—was very distraught, because *The New York Times*, [Sydney] Schanberg and others, were in Cambodia in the early seventies and were reporting heavy fighting around this market town, Kampong Kantuot, and there were pictures in *The Times*. And also the bombing was going on. I was really distraught. I talk about this, I think, in the *Cultural Survival* article about going back to Svay. You know, I would think, what is happening to Svay? And I just assumed it was just totally bombed, and that people would either have gotten out and/or were killed. Which both ended up true. Fortunately most had gotten out by the time Pol Pot had come in, because they'd gone to Phnom Penh. And again I talk about this in the *Cultural Survival* article, so I won't repeat that. But I really thought the village must have been destroyed, and I really didn't know what had happened to the villagers and how many had survived. So, I can't remember when Judy first went. I asked her at some point, could she sort of check, could she drive by on what used to be a highway not too far away, see if there looked like there were people living there, or whatever. And she managed to find Svay, or what had been Svay, and there were people who had known me. So that was very heartening. Then when SSRC [the Social Science

Research Council] took a trip to Cambodia, I guess it was '89. I think we had gone to, I don't know, Phnom Chisor or somewhere. And we went by Svay on the way and actually stopped. And Biff took me across the rice paddies. We took a kind of shortcut across the rice paddies. And Biff said later that he knew I was anxious to get there, and normally you would have the walk along a dyke and so on, and you have to sort of come around, or you can cut straight across the rice paddies. So he grabbed my hand, and took me across the rice paddies, and we came on to Svay, which was quite extraordinary.

During that period when I was not able to go back to Cambodia, I took a side road, so to speak, into the history of anthropology, which I had also been interested in for a long time. And so for a number of years I worked on this project—[*laughs*] based ultimately on gossip. Of various people's memories of their graduate student years and early professional years. Whom they had studied with, who their friends were. And so on and so on. As a friend of mine said, 'Oh, you're dealing with gossip'. I said, 'Yeah, that's what I'm dealing with'.

JM: I have the impression your connection with SSRC brought a lot of things together for you and connected you with certain people who seem to have stayed connected to you personally and professionally.

ME: I'm glad you said that. Because, yeah, what was very important in bringing me back into the Southeast Asia and Cambodia fold was ISP—Indochina Studies Program [which was affiliated with SSRC]. Well, you know the rationale behind ISP.

JM: I guess so, although when I talked to Gerald Hickey, he seemed to have a different memory than mine. Mine was that since people were not able to go back to these countries, you were doing research among the refugee communities.

ME: Well, in a sense, yes. But in my mind the idea was that there were so many refugees here who had all this wonderful knowledge of various kinds of things, and so why not tap them, since in many cases it was not possible—well, I guess it was at that point pretty much impossible to go to Cambodia or Laos or Vietnam to do research.

JM: How did you happen to be connected with that?

ME: Well, a committee was brought together in which, I think, thanks to Biff, probably, I was one of the members. And David Chandler was also—I can't remember the original committee. Jim Scott was on from the outset. He was important also in organising it. So that was great. In fact, I told Biff that he's really responsible for getting me back into Southeast Asia Studies through ISP. And you and Judy [Ledgerwood] were I think two of our earliest grantees—the earliest batch.

JM: And Kate Frieson.

ME: And Kate.

So anyway, that was a good way back into Southeast Asian Studies. Very, very important. And it allowed me—at some point David and I became good friends. Gerry [Gerald Hickey] I knew from before. And Biff and I became I think good friends after that ISP experience.

JM: Well, the trip to Cambodia, was that ISP connected?

ME: Yes, because we were going to sign agreements with Cambodia. We had a wonderful trip to Angkor. And if you can imagine going to Angkor with Biff and Karl Hutterer, who was also very important on that committee. And other people as well. We had a wonderful time. So, that really—I'd forgotten that, but that was really very, very important. And over time, as I say, you and Judy and others became full-fledged professionals. Another thing that was important was being elected to the Southeast Asia council of the Association of Asian Studies. I can't remember exactly what year that was, but I met a lot of people on that as well. So gradually my Southeast Asia network expanded a lot from both those experiences.

JM: Judy suggested that I ask about the issue of village hierarchy and the issue of community as a community. And these happen to be themes that other people are writing about in the volume, so I thought you might be interested in commenting on also for that reason. You've written about them before. Other themes that are prominent in the book are gender and the relation of spirit practice to Buddhism.

Well, starting with the first one, about village hierarchy?

ME: Ok, hierarchy. I felt that I didn't think deeply enough about—it probably was more hierarchical than I thought, although I am not sure about that. Once I was talking to one of my advisors—Arensberg, in fact. I couldn't get a handle on the social organisation—and it just seemed not to have any real structure to it. I was trying to be—it was a very Radcliffe-Brownian kind of perspective. And he said, 'You are Japanese'. He said, 'Japanese are always looking for neat structure. Did it ever occur to you there is no neat structure'. And my jaw dropped. It was like a revelation to me, that, 'God, he's right, you know!' There certainly have been debates, also, about loose structure, and all that kind of thing. Yeah, it was kind of 'loose'. But on the question of hierarchy, I've often wondered whether I underplayed the [issue]. There was one guy, the one household that had four hectares, right? And then there was Ta Hin and another household that had two hectares. Now those households clearly were the most prosperous. And I had made relatively little of this. Except from the part of I realised that the land holdings gave them a decided advantage economically. But looking back I wonder whether there were subtle—maybe some not so subtle—ways in which that four hectare household and even Ta Hin's household, with two hectares, kind of lorded it over the others. Or maybe 'lorded it over' isn't the right word, at least in the case of Ta Hin's household, because everyone seemed to genuinely love him and think he was you know very egalitarian in some sense

JM: But he was the village chief.

ME: No, he wasn't. He was an *achar* [lay ritual specialist]. But he was not, technically—he was I guess I'd call it the informal chief. Ok, so I think there was probably more hierarchy in Cambodia.

JM: Well, definitely there *are* certain kinds of hierarchy, such as those marked by age...

ME: I was just going to say elder/younger. One could say that there is a gender hierarchy, even though women aren't that badly off. And so on, so there's probably more hierarchy than I had granted or gotten aware of. Then, I guess that maybe partly my perspective, too, as they say about Tepotzlan and the famous Redfield vs Lewis controversy, that I, like Redfield, probably wanted to see a nice harmonious group of people that was fairly egalitarian, etc, etc, and that probably coloured my point of view. So anyway, I think I got that kind of not exactly correctly, if there is such a thing as correctness, which in postmodern times, one could well question, whether there is or not.

JM: But how does the sense of reciprocity relate to issues, for example, of patron–clientism? Do you have any thoughts about that?

ME: The patron–clientage I felt did not really exist that much if at all in the old days, by which I meant my first field work. Although in rethinking the earlier material, maybe that guy that had four hectares or maybe Ta Hin were in some sense patrons. But if so it didn't strike me as being very strong. And in something I've written, I pointed to Jim Scott's assertion or suggestion that patron–clientage was not that strong in parts of Southeast Asia.

JM: Yes, the way he refers to it is in terms of landlordism, and Svay was not that kind of system at all.

ME: Not at all. I think there may have been—well, I don't know, maybe the guy with four hectares or maybe Ta Hin's family did help others in terms of finding employment or whatever. I have no idea again. I don't find it very strong. But, going back in the 1990s, I saw patronage very strong. Especially with relation to this one guy who became a police official in Phnom Penh and later went to work also for the Ministry of Interior and who became very prosperous. And he was clearly getting jobs and giving money and all kinds [of things]—you know villagers were summoned to help out at a child's wedding, and—it's classic patronage stuff.

JM: That's very interesting. It shows a shift in the economic and political relations.

ME: Now the other one was community.

JM: Of course, there's both the question of community at the time you were first doing your research and community in terms of the restoration of community after the Pol Pot period when you went back.

ME: Ok, the one before. Again, this is a question I talk about a little bit in the dissertation, where I said that there were relatively few times when the community acted as a community, but in terms of sentiment rather than action, there was in the sense that people had this feeling about coming from Svay or even from West Svay. Now I hesitate to comment on this question for now, because so many things have happened, and there's also the question of where you live. You know, what the territorial divisions are. The political territorial thing has gotten all screwed up in a way. It's too complex to go into right at this point, but the government reconfigured what was West Svay v. Svay, etc.

[But] the whole issue of whether or not there is a sense of community, whether or not people have this sense of obligation or moral ethic about helping each other which some people say was destroyed during the Pol Pot period. [As I say] people had a sense of community even in the old days, and that there was also along with it a sense of moral obligation to help one other in times of need. Maybe not to help everybody, but certainly to help certain people, and maybe particularly one's own kinfolk, assuming that one was on good terms with them. And I think that continued after the Pol Pot period, at least in my estimation. Again, the community, or Svay as it [was] constituted, mixed up various people, some of whom had lived [together] and knew each other from before, plus some others I suppose who had lived in other parts of the village before. But from what little I could see—and here one would have to live in the village over a period of time to really get firm information on this. But from what I could tell people still felt some sense of obligation to help one another. So in that sense I would say, yes, there is some sense of community at least in the community that I'm familiar with.

JM: I wanted to also talk about gender. Of course, you have the article 'The happy balance', and you said once that that title hadn't actually been yours.

ME: No, that was the editor's title.

JM: Well, what generalisations would you make about gender relations, perhaps gender in relation to community?

ME: Well, I guess I would fall back on this generalisation that used to be bandied about that women in Southeast Asia generally are better off than women in a lot of other places. I remember being at this conference, which was not an anthro conference, it was some other kind of conference, at I think Vassar, and it was mainly on women. Where some Chinese woman got up after I think my presentation. And said she didn't believe it. She said, 'You must be wrong! Women couldn't possibly do what you said they do or have what you said they have'. She was speaking from a Chinese perspective. She just didn't believe that women in Cambodia had these rights. Especially at the village level. I think that women in the city may again be more downtrodden or whatever.

But gender in community, that's something I've never thought of before. I don't immediately see a connection. Gender and work—I am just thinking about work and community—the whole business of co-operative labour. I mean, as you know, at certain times you have to have work [in] teams—especially the transplanting, sometimes for ploughing. Who do you draw the co-workers in your co-operative group from? Which families, which people? There again, you'd have to sit down and draw up lists of the co-operative groups. I mean, they would be mainly from within the community and mainly from—well, in the case of ploughing you don't need as large groups as you do for transplanting. So do you draw from outside the community? No, I think by and large you don't. But I don't know. And also in modern times, this would have changed. And Judy and I talked about widowed—or female-headed households, which have to rent—or have to hire somebody to plough fields for them and so on.

JM: Based on your fieldwork after Pol Pot and before, do you see any difference in gender roles, from what you have been able to observe yourself?

ME: I think that there are more women working outside the home. But that's partly a function of more education, and now within the last few years, which I haven't directly observed, the factories going up. So that Judy says, you walk into Svay now, and during the daytime, there are hardly any young women around at all.

JM: Some of the articles do get into religious issues—and I know you've said that's not your thing. Well, would you comment anything about spirit practice and the relationship to Buddhism. And do you see those as key to community?

ME: All right, as I say in the dissertation and I think elsewhere as well, Buddhism and spirit practice are all part of the same system, really. I mean you can analytically distinguish the two, but for people themselves, it's all part of, in some sense, the same religious system. I mean, this you know yourself. And yes, it is connected to community in the sense that in at least some of the festivals and so on, you sort of contribute as a community, like for *Pchŭm*. Certain days are designated as—you know, you guys in this village are expected to provide the goodies. So, in that sense, the community is defined religiously, and—how would I phrase this?—in terms of the constituency as it were of the particular community. Well, for Wat Svay, clearly the village of Svay was meant to be its constituency: in that sense it defines the community. The other wat, the bigger one, Wat Prey Rum, draws from several villages. So Wat Prey Rum would not be so important in defining village as a village, or in defining the community. Except in the case that we were just talking about, where Svay is designated the village that is supposed to contribute on a particular day.

JM: Do you feel that wats were competing with each other?

ME: Well, I don't know that they were, really, because one is—well, no, maybe that doesn't make any difference—but one, as I told you, was Mohanikay and one was Thommayut. I don't know, that's an interesting question, a sense of competition. There may have been, but Prey Rum is clearly the more prosperous one, because they were drawing from a much bigger base of people. I mean, Wat Svay was always kind of the poor cousin. You know, because it was small and they had less contributors.

JM: But the people who did contribute felt like they wanted to because it was a more local wat?

ME: I don't know if it was locality so much as what their family had [done].

JM: Yes, sometimes it's a question of where your ancestors' ashes are.

ME: One angle on the spirit worship bit is the fact that there is a local *nĕak ta*, who's recognised as being the local [spirit]. And if you want to think in terms of definers of community, I supposed that might be one. Anyway it's funny because they say during Pol Pot time he went away. And then, after Pol Pot he came back. And how did he come back? He came in a cart like everyone else! I love that.

JM: Well, maybe this is the point to ask another question that Judy proposed—do you have any general comment on the place of the anthropologist in the lives of informants and vice versa. Where's the limit? As you said, you became fictive kin with these people. And to what extent is there a border, and when is that border crossed?

ME: Well, it's a difficult situation, as various people have spoken of the relationship of anthropologists to people. Maybe that fictive kin notion is comforting to anthropologists, in that you think you have become like kin, but you haven't really. Or I don't know. But Cambodians are so nice, by and large, that they really do make you feel that you have become in some sense part of their family, sort of. I remember going back and talking to Ta Hin's grand-daughters, you know, who said that Ta Hin cried when he got one of my letters after I'd left, and when I left he carved for me a little model of a plough—he went and chopped this small tree down and he carved this small plough for me, which I have put away now. So in that sense I feel that he had become quite fond of me, and I adored him and his wife and his whole family, in fact. His son and daughter-in-law are still alive and have assumed his position. And so I feel a kind of sense of obligation to them and to certain other families. The two young women who worked as housekeepers for me, I felt some obligation to them. And I think they felt I had some obligation to them as well, similar to family members. And I think for many, many years, all those years I did not go back, I felt this sense of guilt in a way, that they gave me so much, and what did I give them in return? I think precious little, you know, aside from little gifts every now and then which are insubstantial compared what they gave me. And when I went back the first few interviews I did about the Pol Pot years, I was extremely depressed, because I realised that I was able to get up and walk out of there and lead a very comfortable life. They had to stay there and suffered tremendously. So that made me feel really quite terrible. Though the one thing that I feel that I did that I did manage to repay—quote unquote—them to some extent, was the fact that I took back lots of photographs. And I know one woman broke just down in tears when I gave her a photograph of her mother. Many of them had completely lost all the photographs that they had had. So she said I would never have had anything of her without this. And also as the village chief said, you know, 'Our grandchildren would not know what their grandparents looked like without these photographs'. So that I felt was something that in a sense only I could give them—that I was able to give them, and I was very pleased about that. But other than that I think I still have a great debt to them.

JM: Well, just a few more points. I keep trying to coerce you into defining an anthropological school you were in, and you keep resisting. And in our conversation [off tape] just now you mentioned that you have some similarities with Fred Eggans.

ME: Well, I said I turned out to be like Fred Eggans, although he was never my teacher. And I meant that I was like him in that I am a combination of Boasian attention to ethnography, and also interest in history, along with Radcliffe-Brownian interest in structure or social systems. So that I turned out to be like him. And I don't think you can identify me as having been influenced by or as an adherent of a particular school, because I think I'm very eclectic. I was at

Columbia before it turned very heavily ecological and/or Marvin Harris-like. So I escaped all that. When I did my dissertation I consciously made a very detailed ethnography because I thought, well, I'm the first American anthropologist to have studied Cambodia, and I want a lot of this information to be in there so it can be used by subsequent scholars of Cambodia. And it's been tremendously gratifying that that has turned out to be the case. And as John Marston has said, Svay has become a prototypical or the prototypical Cambodian village. Now, I'm not sure whether or not that's a good thing. In fact, there is no typical village, which was a question when I did my fieldwork.

JM: Well, you were just telling me how some Cambodians in Atlanta refer to your dissertation when they're preparing ceremonies and things.

ME: Right. I was saying it turned out to be a resource also for Cambodian refugees in the US, which again is something that is very gratifying to me. But on this question of typicality, which I think I address in the dissertation itself. You know, I said in the dissertation that in some ways Svay is like no other village, you know, in some ways it's like all other villages.

JM: That was nice.

ME: Which I borrowed actually from Kluckholn and Murray—I borrowed it from the discussion of personality of the individual. But in any event, on the question of proto-typicality, it's nice that people can use it as a kind of baseline, as it were, to say what things were like in Svay at least in 1959 or '60.

Timeline

1934	Born in Portland, Oregon
1942–45	Interned with her Japanese-born parents in Minidoka War Relocation Center, Idaho
1955	Bachelor of Arts, Reed College, major in anthropology
1955	Enrols for graduate work in anthropology, Columbia University
1959–60	Fieldwork in Svay, a rice-growing village in Kandal province, Cambodia
1960	Marries Marvin Gelfand; sons Adam and Jeremy born in 1963 and 1967
1961–64	Assistant professor, Bard College
1966	Visiting lecturer, Mount Holyoke College
1967	Moves into apartment in 280 Riverside Drive, New York City; remains there the rest of her life.
1968	PhD Columbia University
1969	Joins Department of Anthropology, Lehman College, City University of New York
1970	Joins doctoral faculty, Graduate Center, City University of New York
1973–88	New York Academy of Sciences, Anthropology Section (Chair, 1976–77)
1980–82	Southeast Asia Council of Association for Asian Studies

1982	Attends mammoth conference on Cambodia at Princeton University and resumes work on Cambodia
1983–88	Member, Social Science Research Council, Indochina Studies Committee
1989-92	Member, Social Science Research Council, Indochina Scholarly Exchange Committee
1989	Social Science Research Council Interim Staff Associate for South Asia and Southeast Asia Program
1989	Re-visits Svay, the site of her field work, on Social Science Research Council trip
1990 (July–August), 1991 (May–June), 1994 (June–July), and 1996 (June)	Field research in Cambodia with Judy Ledgerwood
1991–94	Southeast Asia Council of Association for Asian Studies
2000	Retires from City University of New York
2002	Association for Asian Studies panel in her honour
2005	May Ebihara's death, New York city, April
2010	Marvin Gelfand's death, New York city, August

Publications of May Ebihara

1964   'Khmer (Cambodians)' in LeBar, F, G Hickey and J Musgrave
        (eds), *Ethnic groups of mainland Southeast Asia*, Human Relations
        Area Files Press, New Haven.

1966   'Interrelations between Buddhism and social systems
        in Cambodian peasant culture' in Nash, Manning et al,
        Anthropological studies in Theravada Buddhism, Yale University
        Southeast Asia Studies, Cultural Report Series No 13, New Haven.

1968   *Svay: a Khmer village in Cambodia*, PhD dissertation, Columbia
        University, available from University Microfilms, Ann Arbor.

1974a   'Intervillage, village–town, and village–city relations in Cambodia'
        in LaRuffa, A et al, *City and peasant: a study in sociocultural
        dynamics*, Annals of the New York Academy of Sciences, volume
        220, art 6.

1974b   'Khmer village women in Cambodia' in Matthiasson, C (ed), *Many
        sisters: women in cross-cultural perspective*, Free Press, New
        York.

1977   'Residence patterns in a Khmer peasant village' in Freed, S (ed),
        Anthropology and the climate of opinion, Annals of the New York
        Academy of Sciences, volume 293.

1978   *Papers in anthropology and linguistics* (with R Gianutsos)
        (including 'Introduction' to the papers in anthropology), Annals of
        the New York Academy of Sciences, volume 318.

1981   'Perspectives on sociopolitical transformations in Cambodia/
        Kampuchea: a review article', *Journal of Asian Studies* 41.

1984   'Societal organization in 16th–17th century Cambodia', *Journal of
        Southeast Asian Studies* 15.

1985a   'American ethnology in the 1930s: contexts and currents' in Helm
        J (ed), *Social contexts of American ethnology 1840–1984*, 1984
        Proceedings of the American Ethnological Society, American
        Ethnological Association, Washington.

1985b   'The Cambodian world view: family and community' in
        Bowman, J and E Bruno (eds), *Cambodian mental health: issues
        and alternative approaches to care, conference proceedings*,
        Cambodian Women's Project, American Friends Service
        Committee, New York.

1985c   'Khmer' in Haines, David (ed), *Refugees in the United States: a
        reference handbook*, Greenwood Press, Westport.

1987a   'Khmer religion' in Eliade, Mircea et al (eds), *The encyclopedia of
        religion*, volume 8, Macmillan, New York.

1987b   'Revolution and reformulation in Kampuchean village culture' in
        Ablin, David and Marlowe Hood (eds), *The Cambodian agony*,
        ME Sharpe, Armonk.

1988a   'Biography of Jane Richardson Hanks' in Gacs, U et al (eds),
        Women anthropologists: a biographical dictionary, Greenwood
        Press, Westport.

1988b   'Prospects for the preservation of religion', in Judkins, R (ed),
        *First international scholars conference on Cambodia, selected
        papers*, State University of New York at Geneseo, Department
        of Anthropology, and the Geneseo Foundation, Papers in
        Anthropology, Geneseo.

1988c   'Khmers and Americans: cultural differences' in Judkins, R (ed),
        *First international scholars conference on Cambodia, selected
        papers*, State University of New York at Geneseo, Department
        of Anthropology, and the Geneseo Foundation, Papers in
        Anthropology, Geneseo.

1990 'Return to a Khmer village', *Cultural Survival Quarterly* 14(3).

1993a '"Beyond suffering": the recent history of a Cambodian village' in Ljunggren, B (ed), *The challenge of reform in Indochina*, Harvard Institute of International Development/Harvard University Press, Cambridge.

1993b 'Khmer' in Levinson, D (ed), *Encyclopedia of world cultures, volume 5: Southeast Asia*, GK Hall/Macmillan, New York.

1993c 'A Cambodian village under the Khmer Rouge', in Kiernan, Ben (ed), *Genocide and democracy in Cambodia: the Khmer Rouge, the United Nations, and the international community*, Yale University Southeast Asia Studies and Schell Center for Human Rights, Yale University Law School, New Haven.

1994a *Cambodian culture since 1975: homeland and exile* (ed, with Carol Mortland and Judy Ledgerwood), Cornell University Press, Ithaca.

1994b 'Introduction' (with Carol Mortland and Judy Ledgerwood) in Ebihara, May, Carol Mortland and Judy Ledgerwood (eds), *Cambodian culture since 1975: homeland and exile*, Cornell University Press, Ithaca.

1994c Obituary of David French, *Anthropology Newsletter.*

2002a 'Memories of the Pol Pot era in a Cambodian village', in Ledgewood, Judy (ed), *Cambodia emerges from the past: eight essays*, Southeast Asia Publications, Center for Southeast Asian Studies, Northern Illinois University, DeKalb.

2002b 'Aftermaths of genocide: Cambodian villagers' (with Judy Ledgerwood) in Hinton, Alexander (ed), *Anihilating difference: the anthropology of genocide*, University of California Press, Berkeley.

Reviews

1963   Review of Jean Delvert, *Le paysan cambodgien, American Anthropologist* 65.

1972   Review of Ben Wallace, *Insular cultures of Southeast Asia, American Anthropologist* 74.

1973   Review of WE Willmott, *The political structure of the Chinese community in Cambodia, Southeast Asia* 2.

1976   Review of Harold Conklin film, *Hanuno, American Anthropologist* 87.

1977   Review of Gabrielle Martel, *Lovea: village des environs d'Angkor, Journal of the American Oriental Society* 97.

1978   Review of Charles Keyes, *The golden peninsula : culture and adaptation in mainland Southeast Asia, Journal of Asian Studies* 37.

1979   Review of Melford Spiro, *Kinship and marriage in Burma, Journal of Asian Studies* 38.

1983   Review of Charles Frantz (ed), *Ideas and trends in world anthropology*, American Anthropologist 85.

1984   Review of Ben Kiernan and Chanthou Boua (eds), *Peasants and politics in Kampuchea, 1942–1981, Journal of Asian Studies* 43.

1986   Review of Elman Service, *A century of controversy: ethnological issues from 1860–1960, Science* 233.

1994   Review of Usha Welaratna, *Beyond the Killing Fields, Identities* 2.

ADHOC, Annual Human Rights Report, Phnom Penh, 2006.

American Heritage Dictionary of the English Language 1976, Houghton Mifflin, Boston.

Ang Chouléan 1986, *Les êtres surnaturels dans la religion populaire khmère*, Cedoreck, Paris.

Appadurai, Arjun 1996, *Modernity at large: cultural dimensions of globalization*, University of Minnesota Press, Minneapolis.

Arendt, Hannah 1968, *Totalitarianism*, Harcourt, Brace & World, New York.

Aschmoneit Walter 1995, 'Cambodian pagoda committees and community work', contribution to the workshop 'Traditional Self Help Organizations and Development', Kampong Thom Province, Cambodia.

Aschmoneit, Walter and Jochen Thoma 1995, 'Village population statistics of Cambodia', UNTAC Electoral Data of 1992, Development Planning, Phnom Penh.

Aymonier, Étienne François 1900, *Le Cambodge, Tome I, 'Le royaume actuel'*, Ernest Leroux, Paris.

Baccot, Juliette 1968, *On G'nur et Cay à O'Russei, Syncrétisme religieux dans un village cham au Cambodge*, Thèse pour le doctorat en ethnologie, Ecole Pratique des Hautes Etudes, Paris.

Baldauf, Anette and Christian Hoeller 1998, 'Translocation_new media/art: "Modernity at large", interview with Arjun Appadurai', www.appadurai.com/interviews_baldauf.htm.

Barber, Bernard 1983, *The logic and limits of trust*, Rutgers University Press, New Brunswick.

Bauman, Zygmunt 1989, *Modernity and the Holocaust*, Cornell University Press, Ithaca.

Bayard, D 1980, 'The roots of Indochinese civilization', *Pacific Affairs* 51(1).

Beatty, Andrew 1999, *Varieties of Javanese religion: an anthropological account*, Cambridge University Press, Cambridge.

Becker, Elizabeth 1998, *When the war was over: Cambodia and the Khmer Rouge Revolution*, Public Affairs, New York.

Bellah, Robert 1964, 'Religious evolution', *American Sociological Review* 29.

Benda, Harry 1962, 'The structure of Southeast Asian history', *Journal of Southeast Asian History* 3(1).

Biddulph, Robin 1996, 'Participatory development in authoritarian societies: the case of village development committees in two villages in Banteay Meanchey Province', Cambodia, MA thesis, Australian National University.

—— 1999, 'Ref panel members for the Concept of Community Conference' in Working Group on Social Organization in Cambodia, *Conference on the Meaning of Community in Cambodia*, Volume 1, Phnom Penh.

—— 2000, 'Landlessness: a growing problem', *Cambodia Development Review* 4(3).

Bizot, Francois 1988, 'Les traditions de la pabbajjā' in *Asie du Sud-Est. Recherches sur le bouddhisme khmer 4*, Vandenhoeck and Ruprecht, Göttingen.

—— 1993, *Le bouddhisme des Thaïs*, Édition des Cahiers de France, Bangkok.

Bloch, Maurice 2005, 'Commensality and poisoning' in Bloch, Maurice, *Essays on cultural transmission*, Berg, Oxford and New York.

Bodley, John H 1999, *Victims of progress*, Mayfield, Mountain View.

Boua, Chanthou 1983, 'Observations of the Heng Samrin Government, 1980–1982', in Chandler, David and Ben Kiernan (eds), *Revolution and its aftermath in Kampuchea: eight essays*, Yale University Southeast Asia Studies, New Haven.

Boua, Chanthou and Ben Kiernan 1989, *Oxfam in Takeo*, Oxfam, London.

Bourdieu, Pierre 1977, *Outline of a theory of practice*, Richard Nice (trans), Cambridge University Press, Cambridge.

Bromberger, Christian 1992, 'Monographie' in Bonte, P and M Izard (eds), *Dictionnaire de l'ethnologie et de l'anthropologie*, Puf, Paris.

Brown, E 2007, *The ties that bind: migration and trafficking of women and girls for sexual exploitation in Cambodia*, International Organization for Migration, Phnom Penh.

Caldwell, John Dean 1973, 'Revolution and response: the conflict in northeast Thailand, PhD thesis, University of California at Santa Barbara.

Cambodia–IRRI Rice Project 1989?, *Annual research report*, The Project, Phnom Penh.

Chan Dara 1997, Khmer Women's Voice Center, Interview with author, November, Phnom Penh.

Chandler, David P 1990, 'A revolution in full spate: Communist Party policy in Democratic Kampuchea, December 1976' in Ablin, David A and Marlowe Hood (eds), *The Cambodian agony*, ME Sharpe, Armonk and London.

—— 1991, *The tragedy of Cambodian history: politics, war and revolution since 1945*, Yale University Press, New Haven.

—— 1993, *A history of Cambodia*, Westview Press, Boulder and Silkworm Books, Chiang Mai.

—— 1996, 'Songs at the edge of the forest' in Chandler, David P, *Facing the Cambodian Past, Selected Essays, 1971–1994*, Silkworm Books, Chiang Mai.

—— 1999a, *Voices from S-21: terror and history in Pol Pot's secret prison*, University of California Press, Berkeley and Silkworm Books, Bangkok.

—— 1999b, *Brother Number One: a political biography of Pol Pot*, revised edition, Westview, Boulder.

Chandler, David P, Ben Kiernan and Chanthou Boua 1988, *Pol Pot plans the future: confidential leadership documents from Democratic Kampuchea, 1976–1977*, Yale University Southeast Asia Studies, New Haven.

Chandler, David P, Ben Kiernan and Muy Hong Lim 1976, *The early phases of liberation in northwestern Cambodia: conversations with Peang Sophi*, Centre of Southeast Asian Studies, Monash University, Clayton.

Chatterjee, Partha 1988, 'More on modes of power and the peasantry' in Guha, Ranajit and Gayatri Chakravorty Spivak (eds), *Selected subaltern studies*, Oxford University Press, New York, Oxford.

Clifford, James 1983, 'On ethnographic authority', *Representations* 1(2).

Coedès, George 1963, *Angkor: an introduction*, Oxford University Press, New York.

—— 1966, *The making of Southeast Asia*, University of California Press, Berkeley.

—— 1968, *The Indianized states of Southeast Asia*, East–West Centre Press, Honolulu.

Collins, William 1998, *Grassroots civil society in Cambodia*, Center for Advanced Study, Phnom Penh.

Copans, Jean 2002, *L'enquête ethnologique de terrain*, Nathan, Paris.

CPT (Communist Party of Thailand) 1978, 'A brief introduction to the history of the Communist Party of Thailand (1942–1977)' in Turton, Andrew, Jonathan Fast and Malcolm Caldwell (eds), *Thailand: roots of conflict*, Spokesman, Nottingham.

Criddle, Joan D and Teeda Butt Mam 1987, *To destroy you is no loss: the odyssey of a Cambodian family*, Doubleday, New York.

Curtis, Grant 1998, *Cambodia reborn?: The transition to democracy and development*, Brookings Institution Press, Washington.

D2183, Srei Ha, Srei Hun 1976, 'The Revolutionary principles of Marxism-Leninism', Documentation Center of Cambodia archive document, Phnom Penh.

Davis, Sara 2005, *Song and silence: ethnic revival on China's southwest borders*, Columbia University Press, New York.

de Beer, Patrice 1978, 'History and policy of the Communist Party of Thailand' in Turton, Andrew, Jonathan Fast, and Malcolm Caldwell (eds), *Thailand: roots of conflict*, Spokesman, Nottingham.

de Bernon, Olivier 1998, 'L'etate des biblioteques dans les monasteres du Cambodge' in Sorn Samnang (ed), *The Socio-Cultural Research Congress of Cambodia*, University of Phnom Penh, Phnom Penh.

Debre, François 1976, *Cambodge, la révolution de la forêt*, Flammarion, Paris.

Delvert, Jean 1961, *Le paysan Cambodgien*, Mouton and Co, The Hague and Paris.

Demaine, Harvey 1986, '*Kanpatthana*: Thai views of development' in Hobart, Mark and Robert H Taylor (eds), *Context, meaning, and power in Southeast Asia*, Cornell University Southeast Asia Program, Ithaca.

Derks, Annuska 2005, *Khmer women on the move: migration and urban experiences in Cambodia*, Dutch University Press, Amsterdam.

Derks, Annuska 2008, *Khmer women on the move: exploring work and life in urban Cambodia*, University of Hawai'i Press, Honlulu.

DPC (Direction Provinciale de la Culture) 1996, February. Figures from a stencilled report translated and communicated by Mr Oum Sokh, Director of Kompomg Thom Culture and Information Department.

Douglas, Mary 1990, 'No free gifts' in Mauss, Marcel (ed), *The gift*, New Fetter Lane, London.

Du Bois, Cora 1959, *Social forces in Southeast Asia*, Harvard University Press, Cambridge.

Dufosse, M Dr 1918, *Monographie de la circonscription de Kompong Thom*, Imprimerie de l'Union, Saigon.

Ebihara, May 1966, 'Interrelations between Buddhism and social systems in Cambodian peasant culture' in Nash, Manning et al, *Anthropological studies in Theravada Buddhism*, Yale University Southeast Asian Studies, New Haven.

—— 1968, *Svay, a Khmer village in Cambodia,* PhD thesis, Department of Anthropology, Columbia University.

—— 1974a, 'Intervillage, village–town and village–city relations in Cambodia', *New York Academy of Sciences* 220(6).

—— 1974b, 'Khmer women in Cambodia: a happy balance' in Matthiasson, Carolyn J (ed), *Many sisters: women in cross-cultural perspective*, The Free Press, New York.

—— 1977, 'Residence patterns in a Khmer peasant village' in Freed, Stanley (ed), *Anthropology and the climate of opinion, annals of the New York Academy of Sciences* 293.

—— 1987, 'Revolution and reformulation in Kampuchean village culture' in Ablin, David and Marlow Hood (eds), *The Cambodian agony*, ME Sharpe, Armonk.

—— 1990a. 'Revolution and reformulation in Kampuchean village culture' in Ablin, David A and Marlowe Hood (eds), *The Cambodian agony*, ME Sharpe, Armonk and London.

—— 1990b, 'Return to a Khmer village', *Cultural Survival Quarterly* 14(3).

—— 1993a, '"Beyond suffering": the recent history of a Cambodian village' in Ljunggren, Borje (ed), *The challenge of reform in Indochina*, Harvard University Press, Cambridge.

—— 1993b, 'A Cambodian village under the Khmer Rouge 1975–1979' in Kiernan, Ben (ed), *Genocide and democracy in Cambodia: the Khmer Rouge, the United Nations and the international community*, Yale University Southeast Asia Studies, New Haven.

—— 2002, 'Memories of the Pol Pot era in a Cambodian village' in Ledgerwood, Judy (ed), *Cambodia emerges from the past: eight essays*, Southeast Asian Publications, Northern Illinois University, DeKalb.

Ebihara, May M and Judy Ledgerwood 1995, 'Economic transformations and gender in a Cambodian village', unpublished manuscript.

—— 2002 'Aftermaths of genocide: Cambodian villagers' in Hinton, Alexander (ed), *Annihilating difference: the anthropology of genocide*, University of California Press, Berkeley.

Edwards, Penny 2007, *Cambodge: the cultivation of a nation, 1860–1945*, University of Hawai'i Press, Honolulu.

Eisenbruch, Maurice 1992, 'The ritual space of patients and traditional healers in Cambodia, *Bulletin de l'Ecole 'Française d'Extreme-Orient* 79(2).

Em Phally 1997, domestic worker, interview with author, Phnom Penh.

Embree, John F 1950, 'Thailand: a loosely structured social system', *American Anthropologist* 52.

Erikson, Erik H 1995, *Childhood and society*, Vintage, London.

Evans, Grant 1998, 'Secular fundamentalism and Buddhism in Laos' in Oh Myung-Seok and Kim Hyung-Jun Seou (eds), *Religion, ethnicity and modernity in Southeast Asia*, Seoul National University Press, Seoul.

FAO (Food and Agriculture Organization) 1991, *Cambodge, Évaluation de la situation agricole, Rapport de la mission FAO*, Bureau des Opérations Spéciales de Secours, OSRO 01/91/F, Rome.

—— 1999, 'National Food Security and Nutrition', paper presented at the National Seminar on Food Security and Nutrition in Cambodia, April, Phnom Penh.

Fordham, G 2006, *As if they were watching my body: a study of pornography and the development of attitudes towards sex and sexual behaviour among Cambodian youth*, World Vision, Phnom Penh.

Forest, Alain 1980, *Le Cambodge et la colonisation française, histoire d'une colonisation sans heurts (1897–1920)*, L'Harmattan, Paris.

Foucault, Michel 1979, *Discipline and punish: the birth of the prison*, Alan Sheridan (trans), Vintage Books, New York.

—— 1980, *Power/knowledge: selected interviews and other writings 1972–1977*, Colin Gordon, Leo Marshall, John Mepham and Kate Soper (trans), Pantheon, New York.

Frieson, Kate 2001, *In the shadows: women, power and politics in Cambodia*, Center for Asia-Pacific Initiatives, University of Victoria, June.

Frings, K Viviane 1993, *The failure of agircultural colletivization in the Peoples Republic of Kampuchea*, Centre of Southeast Asian Studies, Monash University, Clayton.

—— 1994, 'Cambodia after decollectivization 1989–1992', *Journal of Contemporary Asia* 24(1).

—— 1997, *Le paysan Cambodgien et le socialisme*, L'Harmattan, Paris.

Fukuyama, Francis 1995, *Trust: the social virtues and the creation of prosperity*, Hamish Hamilton, London.

Gambetta, Diego 1988, *Trust: making and breaking cooperative relations*, Basil Blackwell, New York and Oxford.

Garbett, GK 1967, 'The restudy as a technique for the examination of social change' in Jongmans, DG and PCW Gutkind (eds), *Anthropologists in the field*, Van Gorcum, Assen.

Garfinkle, Harold 1956, 'Conditions of successful degradation ceremonies', *American Journal of Sociology* 61(5).

Garrigues-Creswell, M, JL Jamard and FR Picon 2000, 'Terrains retrouvés', *Gradhiva* 28.

Geertz, Clifford 1961, 'Studies in peasant life: community and society', *Biennial Review of Anthropology* 2.

—— 1973, *The interpretation of cultures*, Basic Books, New York.

Gellner, Ernest 1988, 'Trust, cohesion and the social order' in Gambetta, David (ed), *Trust: making and breaking cooperative relations*, Basil Blackwell, New York and Oxford.

Geschiere, Peter 1997, *The modernity of witchcraft: politics and the occult in postcolonial Africa. Sorcellerie et politique en Afrique: la viande des autres*, University Press of Virginia, Charlottesville.

—— 1999, 'Globalization and the power of indeterminate meaning: witchcraft and spirit cults in Africa and East Asia' in Geschiere, P (ed), *Globalization and identity: dialectics of flow and closure*, Blackwell Publishers, Oxford and Malden.

Ghasarian, Christian 1996, *Introduction à l'étude de la parenté*, Editions du Seuil, Paris.

Giddens, Anthony 1990, *The consequences of modernity*, Polity Press and Blackwell, Cambridge.

—— 1991, *Modernity and self identity: self and society in the late Modern Age*, Polity Press and Blackwell, Cambridge.

Girling, John 1981, *Thailand: society and politics*, Cornell University Press, Ithaca.

Grunewald, François 1990, 'The rebirth of agircultural peasants in Cambodia', *Cultural Survival Quarterly* 14(3).

Guillou, Anne 1994, 'La question foncière', in FAO/PNUD, *Cambodia. Agricultural Development Options Review*, rapport, Phnom Penh/Rome.

Gyally-Pap, Peter and Michael Tranet 1990, 'Notes on the rebirth of Khmer Buddhism' in Thai Inter-Religious Commission for Development and International Network of Engaged Buddhists, *Radical conservatism: Buddhism in the contemporary world—articles in honour of Bhikkhu Buddhadasa's 84th Birthday Anniversary*, Sathirakoses-Nagapradipa Foundation, Bangkok.

Haing Ngor 1987, *A Cambodian odyssey*, Warner Books, New York.

Hall, Stuart, David Held, Don Hubert and Kenneth Thompson (eds) 1995, *Modernity: an introduction to modern societies*, Polity, Cambridge.

Hansen, Anne Ruth 2007, *How to behave: Buddhism and modernity in colonial Cambodia 1860–1930*, University of Hawai'i Press, Honolulu.

Harris, Ian 1999, 'Buddhism *in extremis*: the case of Cambodia' in Harris, Ian (ed), *Buddhism and politics in twentieth-century Asia*, Continuum, London and New York.

—— 2005, *Cambodian Buddhism: history and practice*, University of Hawai'i Press, Honolulu.

—— 2008, *Buddhism under Pol Pot*, Documentation Center of Cambodia, Phnom Penh.

Hauff, Edvard 2001, 'Kyol Goeu in Cambodia', *Transcultural Psychiatry* 38(4).

Haysahi Yukio 2002, *Practical Buddhism among the Thai-Lao: religion and the making of a region*, Kyoto University Press, Kyoto and Trans Pacific Press, Melbourne.

Headley, Robert K Jr, Kylin Chhor, Lam Kheng Lim, Lim Kah Kheang and Chen Chun 1977, *Cambodian–English dictionary*, Catholic University of America Press, Washington.

Heder, Stephen R 1980, *Kampuchea, occupation and resistance*, Institute of Asian Studies, Chulalongkorn University, Bangkok.

—— 2004, *Cambodian Communism and the Vietnamese model. Volume 1: Imitation and Independence, 1930–1975*, White Lotus, Bangkok.

Hefner, Robert (ed) 1998, *Market cultures: society and morality in the new Asian capitalism*, Westview Press, Boulder.

HelpAge International 1998, *Summary report on the situation of older people in Cambodia*, Phnom Penh, May.

Hinton, Alexander Laban 1997, *Cambodia's shadow: an examination of the cultural origins of genocide*, PhD thesis, Emory University.

—— 2001, 'Begrudgment, reconciliation and the Khmer Rouge: in search of truth', *Journal of the Documentation Center of Cambodia* 20(August).

—— 2002a, 'The dark side of modernity', in Hinton, Alexander Laban (ed), *Annihilating difference: the anthropology of genocide*, University of California Press, Berkeley.

—— 2002b, 'Purity and contamination in the Cambodian genocide' in Ledgerwood, Judy (ed), *Cambodia emerges from the past: eight essays*, Northern Illinois University Press, DeKalb.

—— 2005, *Why did they kill? Cambodia in the shadow of genocide*, University of California Press, Berkeley.

Hinton, Devon, Khin Um and Phalnaraith Ba 2001a, '*Kyol goeu* [Wind Overload] Part I: A cultural syndrome of orthosstatic panic among Khmer refugees', *Transcultural Psychiatry* 38(4).

—— 2001b, '*Kyol goeu* [Wind Overload] Part II: Prevalence, characteristics, and mechanisms of kyol goeu and near-kyol goeu episodes in Khmer patients attending a psychiatric clinic', *Transcultural Psychiatry* 38(4).

Hughes, Caroline 2001, *An investigation of conflict management in Cambodian villages: a review of literature with suggestions for future research*, Centre for Peace and Development, Cambodian Development Resource Institute, Phnom Penh.

Hughes, Caroline and Joakim Öjendal 2006, 'Reassesing tradition in times of political change: post-war Cambodia reconsidered', *Journal of Southeast Asian Studies* 37(3).

Hyden, Goran 2004, 'Informal institutions, the economy of affection, and rural development in Africa', *Tanzania Journal of Population Studies and Development* 11(2).

Jackson, Karl D ed 1989, *Cambodia, 1975–1978: rendezvous with death*, Princeton University Press, Princeton.

Janzen, John M 1995, *La quête de la thérapie au Bas-Zaïre*, Karthala, Paris.

Jit Poumisak 1987, 'The real face of Thai Saktina today' in Reynolds, Craig, *Thai radical discourse: the real face of Thai feudalism today*, Cornell University Southeast Asia Program, Ithaca.

Kamala Tiyavanich 1997, *Forest recollections: wandering monks in twentieth-century Thailand*, University of Hawai'i Press, Honolulu.

Kant, Elise 1993, *Comparing poverty to poverty, internally displaced persons and local villagers in Kompong Svay. Results of a baseline survey in Kompong Svay district, Kompong Thom province, Cambodia*, Church World Service.

Kapferer, Bruce 1988, *Legends of people, maths of state: violence, intolerance and political culture in Sri Lanka and Australia*, Smithsonian Institution Press, Washington.

Kemp, Jeremy 1988, *Seductive mirage: the search for the village community in Southeast Asia*, Foris Publications, Dordrecht-Holland and Providence.

Kent, Alexandra and David Chandler (eds) 2008, *People of virtue: reconfiguring religion, power and moral order in Cambodia today*, Nordic Institute of Asian Studies, Copenhagen.

Keyes, Charles F 1964, 'Thailand, Laos and the Thai northeastern problem', *Australia's Neighbours*, 4th Series, 17.

—— 1966a. 'Peasant and nation: a Thai-Lao village in a Thai state', PhD thesis, Cornell University.

—— 1966b, 'Ethnic identity and loyalty of villagers in northeastern Thailand', *Asian Survey* 6(7).

—— 1967, *Isan: regionalism in northeastern Thailand*, Data Paper No 65, Southeast Asia Program, Cornell University, Ithaca.

—— 1968, 'Cotmāi cāk īsān' [Letter from the northeast], *Social Science Review* 6(1), Bangkok (in Thai, published anonymously under the by-line of 'Our Special Correspondent').

—— 1975, 'Kin groups in a Thai-Lao village' in Skinner, G William and A Thomas Kirsch (eds), *Change and persistence in Thai society: homage to Lauriston Sharp*, Cornell University Press, Ithaca.

—— 1976, 'In search of land: village formation in the Central Chi River Valley, northeast Thailand', *Contributions to Asian Studies* 9.

—— 1977, 'Millennialism, Theravāda Buddhism, and Thai society', *Journal of Asian Studies* 36(2).

—— 1982, *Socioeconomic change in rainfed agricultural villages in northeastern Thailand*, (Report for the United States Agency for International Development), Thailand Project, Department of Anthropology, University of Washington, Seattle.

—— 1983, 'Introduction' in Keyes, Charles F (ed), *Peasant strategies in Asian societies: perspectives on moral and rational economic approaches*, *Journal of Asian Studies* 42(3).

—— 1984, '*Mother or mistress but never a monk: Buddhist notions of female* gender in rural Thailand', *American Ethnologist* 11(2).

—— 1994, 'Communist Revolution and the Buddhist past in Cambodia' in Keyes, Charles F, Laurel Kendall and Helen Hardace (eds), *Asian visions of authority: religion and the modern states of East and Southeast Asia*, University of Hawai'i Press, Honolulu.

—— 1995, *The Golden Peninsula, culture and adaptation in mainland Southeast Asia*, University of Hawai'i Press, Honolulu.

—— 1999, 'Buddhism fragmented: Thai Buddhism and political order since the 1970s', keynote address presented at Seventh International Thai Studies Conference, Amsterdam.

—— 2002a, 'Migrants and protestors: 'development' in northeastern Thailand', Keynote address, 8th International Thai Studies Conference, Nakhon Phanom, January.

—— 2002b, 'Weber and anthropology', *Annual Reviews in Anthropology* 31.

—— 2006, 'Migration, development and the persistence of a rural community : a northeastern Thai village through four decades', unpublished research proposal.

Keyes, Charles F, Helen Hardacre and Laurel Kendall 1994, 'Contested visions of community in East and Southeast Asia' in Keyes, Charles F, Helen Hardacre and Laurel Kendall (eds), *Asian visions of authority: religion and the modern states of East and Southeast Asia*, University of Hawai'i Press, Honolulu.

Khy, Ven Sovanratana 2008, 'Buddhist education today: progress and challenges' in Kent, Alexandra and David Chandler (eds), *People of virtue: reconfiguring religion, power and morality in Cambodia today*, Nordic Institute for Asian Studies, Copenhagen.

Kiernan, Ben 1979, '1970 peasant uprising in Kampuchea', *Journal of Contemporary Asia* 9(3).

——, *How Pol Pot came to power. A history of Communism in Kampuchea, 1930–1975*, Verso, London.

——, *The Pol Pot regime: race, power and genocide in Cambodia under the Khmer Rouge, 1975–79*, Yale University Press, New Haven.

Kiernan, Ben and Chanthou Boua (eds) 1982, *Peasants and politics in Kampuchea, 1942–1981*, Zed Press, London and ME Sharpe, Armonk.

Kim Sedara 2001, 'Reciprocity: informal patterns of social interactions in a Cambodian village near Angkor Park', MA thesis, Northern Illinois University, Dekalb.

Kirsch, A Thomas 1973, *Feasting and social oscillation*, Cornell Southeast Asia Program Data Paper Series, Ithaca.

—— 1976, 'Kinship, genealogical claims, and societal integration in ancient Khmer society' in Cowan, CD and OW Wolters (eds), *Southeast Asian history and historiography: essays presented to DGE Hall*, Cornell University Press, Ithaca.

—— 1977, 'Complexity in the Thai religious system: an interpretation', *Journal of Asian Studies* 36(2).

Kitahara, A 1996, *The Thai rural community reconsidered*, Chulalongkorn University Press, Bangkok.

Komai, Hiroshi 1997, 'The role of Buddhism in the reconstruction of the Cambodian rural village: a case study in Tropeang Veeng, Takeo', unpublished paper presented at the University of Phnom Penh.

Laplantine, François 1996, *La description ethnographique*, Nathan, Paris.

Larcom, Joan 1983, 'Following Deacon, the problem of ethnographic reanalysis, 1926–1981' in Stocking, George W (ed), *Observers observed, essays on ethnographic fieldwork*, University of Wisconsin Press, Madison.

Leach Edmund R 1954, *Political systems of highland Burma*, Harvard University Press, Cambridge.

Leclere, Adhémard 1917, *Cambodge, fêtes civiles et religieuses*, Imprimerie Nationale, Paris.

—— 1984, *Cambodge, contes, légendes et Jatakas*, Cedorek, Paris.

Ledgerwood, Judy 1990, *Changing conceptions of gender: women, stories*, PhD thesis, Cornell University.

—— 1992, *Analysis of the situation of women in Cambodia: research on women in Khmer society*, UNICEF, Phnom Penh.

—— 1995, 'Khmer kinship: the matriliny/matriarchy myth' *Journal of Anthropological Research* 51(3).

—— 1998, 'Rural development in Cambodia: the view from the village' in Brown, Frederick and David Timberman (eds), *Cambodia and the international community: the quest for peace, development, and democracy*, Institute of Southeast Asian Studies, Singapore.

—— (ed) 2002, *Cambodia emerges from the past: eight essays*, Center for Southeast Asian Studies, Northern Illinois University, DeKalb.

—— 2008, 'Buddhist practice in rural Kandal Province 1960 and 2003: an essay in honor of May Ebihara' in Kent, Alexandra and David Chandler (eds), *People of virtue: reconfiguring religion, power and morality in Cambodia today*, Nordic Institute for Asian Studies, Copenhagen.

Lederwood, Judy, May M Ebihara, and Carol A Mortland 1994, 'Introduction' in Ebihara, May, Carol A Mortland and Judy Ledgerwood (eds), *Cambodian culture since 1975: homeland and exile*, Cornell University Press, Ithaca.

Ledgerwood, Judy and John Vijghen 2002, 'Decision making in rural Khmer' in Ledgerwood, Judy (ed), *Cambodia emerges from the past: eight essays*, Center for Southeast Asian Studies, Northern Illinois University, DeKalb.

Lemarquis, Bruno 1992, *Hydraulique villageoise. Pratiques paysannes et interventions des projets. Reflexions pour une meilleure prise en compte des contextes*, (Mémoire) En vue de l'obtention du diplôme d'ingénieur des techniques agricoles en régions chaudes. Multigraphié, GRET/CINAM/CNEARC, Paris, Montepellier.

Lewitz, Saveros 1967, 'La toponymie khmère', *Bulletin de l'École française d'Extrême Orient* 52.

Linton, Ralph 1955, *The tree of culture*, Knopf, New York.

Locard, Henri 2004, *Pol Pot's Little Red Book: the sayings of Angkar*, Silkworm, Chiang Mai.

Long, Jancis F, Millard F Long, Kamphol Adulavidhaya and Sawart Pongsuvanna 1963, *Economic and social conditions among farmers in Changwad Khonkaen*, Kasetsart University, Bangkok.

Long, Pov 2004, 'History of a Kreung village in Rattanakiri province', fellow's thesis, Centre for Khmer Studies, Phnom Penh.

Mabbett, Ian W 1977, 'Varnas in Angkor and the Indian caste system', *Journal of Asian Studies* 36(3).

Madge, Charles 1957, *Survey before development in Thai villages*, United Nations Series on Community and Development, New York.

Malinowski, Bronislaw 1922, *Argonauts of the Western Pacific: an account of native enterprise and adventure in the archipelagoes of Melanesian New Guinea*, Routledge and Kegan Paul, London.

Mam, Kanyanee E 1998, *An oral history of family life under the Khmer Rouge*, Yale Center for International and Area Studies, New Haven.

Mann, Michael 2004, *The dark side of democracy: explaining ethnic cleansing*, Cambridge University Press, New York.

Marcus, GE 1990, 'Imagining the whole. ethnography's contemporary efforts to situate itself', *Critique of Anthropology* 9(3).

—— 1995, 'Ethnography in/of the world system: the emergence of multi-sited ethnography', *Annual Review of Anthropology* 24.

Marston, John 1994, 'Metaphors of the Khmer Rouge' in Ebihara, May, Carol A Mortland and Judy Ledgerwood (eds), *Cambodian culture since 1975: homeland and exile*, Cornell University Press, Ithaca.

—— 1997, 'Cambodia 1991–1994: Hierarchy, neutrality and etiquettes of discourse', PhD thesis, Department of Anthropology, University of Washington.

—— 2002a, 'Democratic Kampuchea and the idea of modernity' in Ledgerwood, Judy (ed), *Cambodia emerges from the past: eight essays*, Northern Illinois University Southeast Asia Publications, DeKalb.

—— 2002b, 'Khmer Rouge songs', *Crossroads: An Interdisciplinary Journal of Southeast Asian Studies* 16(1).

—— 2002c, 'La reconstruccion del budismo 'antiguo' de Camboya', *Estudios de Asia y Africa* 37(2).

—— 2008a, Reconstruction of 'ancient' Cambodian Buddhism, *Contemporary Buddhism* 9(1).

—— 2008b, 'Wat Preah Thammalanka and the Leged of Lok Ta Nen' in Kent, Alexandra and David Chandler (eds), *People of virtue: reconfiguring religion, power and morality in Cambodia today*, Nordic Institute for Asian Studies, Copenhagen.

Marston, John and Elizabeth Guthrie (eds) 2004, *History, Buddhism and new religious movements in Cambodia*, University of Hawai'i Press, Honolulu.

Martel, Gabrielle 1975, *Lovea village des environs D'Angkor: aspects démographiques, économiques et sociologiques du monde rural Cambodgien dans la Province de Siem-Réap*, École Française D'extrême-Orient, Paris.

Martin, Marie-Alexandrine 1997, *Les Khmers Daeum, 'Khmers de l'Origine', Société montagnarde et exploitation de la forêt. De l'écologie à l'histoire*, Presses de l'École française d'Extrême-Orient, Paris.

Martini, Francois 1955, 'Le bonze cambodgien', *France-Asie* 12.

Marx, Karl 1958 [1869], 'The Eighteenth Brumaire of Louis Bonaparte' in *Karl Marx and Frederick Engels: Selected Works*, Foreign Languages Publishing Houses, volume I, Moscow.

Matras-Troubetzkoy, Jacqueline 1983, *Un village en forêt. L'essartage chez les Brou du Cambodge*, Selaf, Paris.

Mauss, Marcel 1967, *The gift: forms and functions of exchange in archaic societies*, Norton, New York.

—— 1970, *The gift: forms and functions of exchange in archaic societies*, Cohen & West, London.

—— 1990 [1950], *The gift: the form and reason for exchange in archaic societies*, WD Hall (translator), New Fetter Lane, London.

McAlister, John Jr and Paul Mus 1970, *The Vietnamese and their revolution*, Harper and Row, New York.

McAndrew, John 1998, *Interdependence in household livelihood strategies in two Cambodian villages*, Cambodian Development Resource Institute, Phnom Penh.

—— 1999, *Interdependence in household livelihood strategies in two Cambodian villages*, Cambodia Development Resource Institute, Phnom Penh.

McGrew, Laura 1999, 'On the record - women of Southeast Asia fight violence', Advocacy Project International Seminar, Phnom Penh, 18–22 January, www.advocacynet.org.

McGrew, Laura, Kate Frieson and Chan Sambath 2004, *Good governance from the ground up: women's roles in post-conflict Cambodia*, Women Waging Peace, Hunt Alternatives, Boston.

Meas Nee 1995, *Towards restoring life: Cambodian villages*, Krom Akphiwat Phum, Phnom Penh.

Mehrak, M, K Chhay and S My 2008, *Women's perspectives: a case study of systematic land registration in Cambodia*, Gender and Development for Kampuchea, Phnom Penh.

Migozzi, Jacques 1973, *Cambodge, faits et problèmes de population*, Éditions du CNRS, Paris.

Mills, Mary Beth 1999, *Thai women in the global labor force: consuming desires, contested selves*, Rutgers University Press, New Brunswick.

Misztal, Barbara A 1996, *Trust in modern societies: the search for the bases of social order*, Polity Press, Cambridge.

Morell, David and Chai-anan Samudavanija 1981, *Political conflict in Thailand: Reform, Reaction, Revolution*, Oelgeschlager, Gunn and Hain, Cambridge, NY.

Moura, Jean 1883, *Le royaume du Cambodge*, Ernest Leroux, Paris.

Moyer, Nancy 1991, *Escape from the Killing Fields*, Zondervan Publishing House, Grand Rapids.

MP (Ministry of Planning), 2005, National Poverty Reduction Strategy 2003–2005, Ministry of Planning, Royal Government of Cambodia, Phnom Penh.

MRC (Ministry of Religion and Cults) 1999, *Statistics 1998–1999*, mimeo.

—— 2002, *Statistics 2001–2002*, mimeo.

—— 2003, *Statistics 2002–2003*, mimeo.

Murdock, George Peter and SF Wilson 1972. 'Settlement patterns and community organization: cross-cultural codes 3', *Ethnology* 11.

Mus, Paul 1952, *Viêt-Nam: sociologie d'une guerre*, Editions de Seuil, Paris.

MWA (Ministry of Women's Affairs) 2005, *Violence against women: a baseline survey*, Phnom Penh.

—— 2008, *A fair share for women. Cambodia gender assessment*, Phnom Penh.

Mysliwiec, Eva 1988, *Punishing the poor: the international isolation of Kampuchea*, Oxfam, London.

Népote, Jacques 1992, *Parenté et organisation sociale dans le Cambodge moderne et contemporain*, Ed Olizane, Genève.

—— 1995, 'Compte-rendu de Jennar, Raoul M, Les clés du Cambodge', *Péninsule* 31.

Nhiek Neou 1962, *Khmer customs and traditions*, Phnom Penh.

NIS (National Institute of Statistics) 1994, *Cambodia socio-economic survey 1993/94*, Ministry of Planning, Royal Government of Cambodia, Phnom Penh.

—— 1998, *General population census of Cambodia 1998*, Ministry of Planning, Royal Government of Cambodia, Phnom Penh.

—— 1999, *General population census of Cambodia 1998*, Ministry of Planning, Phnom Penh.

—— 2004, *Cambodia inter-censal population survey general report*, Ministry of Planning, Royal Government of Cambodia, Phnom Penh.

O'Leary M et al 1995, 'Reflections: a record of training from the evolution of Krom Akphiwat Phum', Overseas Servive Bureau, Phnom Penh.

Ollier, Leakthina Chau-Pech and Tim Winter (eds) 2006, *Expressions of Cambodia: the politics of tradition, identity and change*, Routledge, London, New York.

Ortner, S 1991 'Reading America: preliminary notes on class and culture' in Fox, Richard G (ed), *Recapturing anthropology: working in the present*, School of *American* Research Press, Santa Fe.

Oum, Dr S 2003, personal communication, February.

Overing, Joanna 2003, 'In praise of the everyday: trust and the art of social living in an Amazonian community', *Ethnos* 68(3).

Ovesen, Jan, Ing-Britt Trankell and Joakim Öjendal 1995, *When every household is an island, social organization and power structures in rural Cambodia*, Sida, Phnom Penh.

—— 1996, *When every household is an island: social organization and power structures in rural Cambodia*, Department of Cultural Anthropology, Uppsala University, Uppsala.

Parmentier, Henri 1927, *L'art khmer primitif*, Paris.

Peters, Heather 1990, 'Buddhism and ethnicity among the Tai Lue in the Sipsongpanna' in Proceedings of the 4th International Conference on Thai Studies, 11–13 May 1990, Institute of Southeast Asian Studies, Volume 3, Kunming.

Phillips, Herbert P 1965, *Thai peasant personality: the patterning of interpersonal behavior in the village of Bang Chan*, University of California Press, Berkeley.

Pijpers, Bert 1989, *Kampuchea: undoing the legacy of Pol Pot's water control system*, Trócaire, Blackrock.

Pin Yathay 1987, *Stay alive, my son*, Touchstone, New York.

Pol Pot 1977, 'Long live the 17th anniversary of the Communist Party of Kampuchea', speech delivered 29 September, Ministry of Foreign Affairs, Phnom Penh.

Polanyi, Karl 1944, *The great transformation*, Farrar & Rinehart, New York.

Ponchaud, François 1977, *Cambodge Année Zero*, Julliard, Paris.

—— 1978, *Cambodia, Year Zero*, Holt, Rinehart and Winston, New York.

—— 1989, 'Social change in the vortex of revolution' in Jackson, Karl D (ed), *Cambodia 1975–1978: rendezvous with death*, Princeton University Press, Princeton.

Prak, Bonamy 2004, 'Changing lifestyles of female garment factory workers,' fellow's thesis, Centre for Khmer Studies, Phnom Penh.

Quinn, Kenneth M 1976, 'Political change in wartime: the Khmer Krahom Revolution in southern Cambodia, 1970–1974', *US Naval War College Review* Spring.

Rabasa, José 2001, 'Beyond representation? The impossibility of the local (notes on subaltern studies in light of a rebellion in Tepoztlán, Morelos)' in Rodríguez, Ileana (ed), *The Latin American subaltern studies reader*, Duke University Press, Durham.

Rahula, Walpola 1996, *What Buddha taught*, Buddhist Cultural Centre, Dehiwala, Colombo.

Redfield, Robert 1955, *The little community*, University of Chicago Press, Chicago.

—— 1956, *Peasant society and culture*, Chicago University Press, Chicago.

—— 1960, *The little community/peasant society and culture*, University of Chicago Press, Chicago.

Rubin, Herbert J 1973a, 'A framework for the analysis of villager–official contact in rural Thailand', *Southeast Asia* 2(2).

—— 1973b, '"Will and awe". Illustrations of Thai villager dependency upon officials', *Journal of Asian Studies* 32(3).

Rudasill, Kate 2004, 'Alms round traditions in Cambodia', paper for Undergraduate Research Apprenticeship Project, Northern Illinois University, Spring.

Sahlins, Marshall David 1972, *Stone Age economics*, Aldine Atherton, Chicago.

Sam, Yang 1987, *Khmer Buddhism and politics, 1954–1984*, Khmer Studies Institute, Newington.

Satoru, Kobayashi 2005, 'An ethnographic study of the reconstruction of Buddhist practice in two Cambodian temples: with the special reference to Buddhist Samay and Boran', *Tonan Ajia Kenkyu [Southeast Asian Studies]* 42(4).

—— 2008, 'Reconstructing Buddhist temple buildings: an analysis of village Buddhism after the Era of Turmoil' in Kent, Alexandra and David Chandler (eds), *People of virtue: reconfiguring religion, power and morality in Cambodia today*, Nordic Institute for Asian Studies, Copenhagen.

Sauer, Carl O 1952, *Agricultural origins and dispersals*, American Geographical Society, Cambridge.

Scarry, Elaine 1985, *The body in pain: the making and unmaking of the world*, Oxford University Press, New York.

Schimmel, Annemarie 1975, *Mystical dimensions of Islam*, University of North Carolina Press, Chapel Hill.

Schrauwers, Albert 2003, Through a glass darkly: charity, conspiracy and power in New Order Indonesia' in West, HG and Todd Sanders (eds), *Transparency and conspiracy: ethnographies of suspicion in the New World Order*, Duke University Press, Durham and London.

Scott, James C 1976, *The moral economy of the peasant: rebellion and subsistence in South-east Asia*, Yale University Press, New Haven.

—— 1985, *Weapons of the weak: everyday forms of peasant resistance*, Yale University Press, New Haven.

—— 1986, 'Gender: a useful category of historical analysis', *American Historical Review* 91(5).

——— 1998, *Seeing like a state: how certain schemes to improve the human condition have failed*, Yale University Press, New Haven.

Shanin, Theodor 1966, 'The peasantry as a political factor', *Sociological Review* 14.

Shapiro(-Phim), Toni 1994, *Dance and the spirit of Cambodia*, PhD thesis, Department of Anthropology, Cornell University.

——— 2002, 'Dance, music, and the nature of terror and Democratic Kampuchea' in Hinton, Alexander Laban (ed), *Annihilating difference: toward an anthropology of genocide*, University of California Press, Berkeley.

Sharp, Lauriston 1962, 'Cultural continuities and discontinuities in Southeast Asia', *Journal of Asian Studies* 22(1).

Sharp, Lauriston and Lucien M Hanks 1978, *Bang Chan: social history of a rural community in Thailand*, Cornell University Press, Ithaca.

Sharp, Lauriston, Hazel M Hauck, Kamol Janlekha and Robert B Textor, with the assistance of John Brohm, J Marvin Brown and Singto Metah 1953, *Siamese rice village: a preliminary study of Bang Chan, 1948–1949*, Cornell Research Center, Bangkok.

Shawcross, William 1979, *Sideshow: Nixon, Kissinger and the destruction of Cambodia*, Simon and Shuster, New York.

Sik, B 2000, *Land ownership, sales and concentration in Cambodia*, Cambodia Development Resource Institute, Phnom Penh.

Skidmore, Monique 1996, 'In the shade of the bodhi tree: Dhammayietra and the re-awakening of community in Cambodia', *Crossroads* 10(1).

Sliwinski, Marek 1995, *Le génocide khmer rouge, une analyse démographique*, L'Harmattan, Paris.

Sluka, Jeffrey A (eds) 2000, *Death squad: the anthropology of state terror*, University of Pennsylvania Press, Philadelphia.

Smith, Frank 1989, *Interpretive accounts of the Khmer Rouge years: personal experiences in Cambodian peasant world view*, Center for Southeast Asian Studies, University of Wisconsin-Madison, Madison.

Smith Hefner, Nancy 1999, *Khmer-American identity and moral education in a diasporic community*, University of California Press, Berkeley and Los Angeles.

Smith, HE 1979, 'The Thai rural family' in Das, MS and PD Bardis (eds), *The family in Asia*, George Allen & Unwin, London.

So Savannarith, Real Sopheap, Uch Utey, Sy Tathmony, Brett Ballard and Sarthi Acharya (eds) 2001, *Social assessment of land in Cambodia, a field study*, CambodiaDevelopment Resource Institute, Phnom Penh.

Solheim, WG 1969, 'Reworking Southeast Asian prehistory', *Paideuma* 15.

Sovannarith, So, Rea Sopheap, Uch Utey, Sy Rathmony, Brett Ballard and Sarthi Acharya 2001, *Social assessment of land in Cambodia, a field study*, Cambodia Development Resource Institute, Phnom Penh.

Speigel, Susan 2006, *The role of the monk in Cambodian Buddhism: crisis, change and continuity*, MA thesis, Northern Illinois University.

Spiro, Melford E 1967, *Burmese supernaturalism*, Transaction, New Brunswick,.

Srinivas, Mysore Narasimhachar 1978, *The remembered village*, Oxford University Press, Delhi.

Suárez-Orozco, Marcelo 1990, 'Speaking of the unspeakable: toward a psychosocial understanding of response to terror', *Ethos* 19(3).

Suchit Bunbongkarn 1987, *The military in Thai politics, 1981–86*, Institute of Southeast Asian Studies, Singapore.

Suthep Soonthornpesuch (ed) 1968, *Sangkhomwitthayā không mūbān phāk tawanôk chiang nüa* [Sociology of northeastern villages], Faculty of Political Science, Chulalongkorn University, Bangkok.

Tambiah SJ 1970, *Buddhism and the spirit cults in north-east Thailand*, Cambridge University Press, Cambridge.

—— 1976, *World conqueror world renouncer*, Cambridge University Press, New York.

Tannenbaum, Nicola 1984, 'Chayanov and economic anthropology' in Durrenberger, Paul (ed), *Chayanov, peasants, and economic anthropology*, Academic Press, Orlando.

Taylor, Christopher C 1999, *Sacrifice as terror: the Rwandan genocide of 1994*, Berg, Oxford and New York.

Taylor, JL 1991, 'Living on the rim: ecology and forest monks in northeast Thailand', *Sojourn* 6(1).

—— 1993, *Forest monks and the nation-state: an anthropological and historical study in northeastern Thailand*, Institute of Southeast Asian Studies, Singapore.

Thayer, Nate 1994, 'Morale low on front lines', *Phnom Penh Post*, 14 – 27 January.

Thích Nhất Hạnh 2005, 'Retour De Thich Nhat Hanh Au Vietnam', www.tnh2005.com/, last accessed 21 March 2006.

Thion, Serge 1983, 'Chronology of Khmer Communism, 1940–1982' in Chandler, David P and Ben Kiernan (eds), *Revolution and its aftermath in Kampuchea: eight essays*, Yale University Southeast Asia Studies, New Haven.

—— 1990, 'The pattern of Cambodian politics' in Ablin, David A and Marlowe Hood (eds), *The Cambodian agony*, ME Sharpe, Armonk and London.

—— 1999, 'Summary and concluding remarks' in Working Group on Social Organization in Cambodia, *Conference on the meaning of community in Cambodia*, Volume 1, Phnom Penh.

TIC (Thailand Information Center) 1980, 'The Communist Party of Thailand and the conflict in Indochina', *TIC News* 4(1), 31 October, Sweden.

Tichit, Lucien 1981 *L'agriculture au Cambodge*, Agence de Coopération Culturelle et technique, Paris.

Tuot, Sovannary 2003, *Type of female-headed households in Cambodia*, Centre for Population Studies, Royal University of Phnom Penh, Phnom Penh.

Turner, Victor 1969, *The ritual process: structure and anti-structure*, Cornell University Press, Ithaca.

Turton, Andrew 1978, 'The current situation in the Thai countryside' in Turton, Andrew, Jonathan Fast and Malcolm Caldwell (eds), *Thailand: roots of conflict*, Spokesman, Nottingham.

Tyler, Stephen A 1986, 'Post-modern ethnography: from document of the occult to occult document' in Clifford, James and George E Marcus (eds), *Writing culture: the poetics and politics of ethnography*, University of California Press, Berkeley.

Ung Vanna 1998, 'Gender in writings', Khmer Women's Media Center, Phnom Penh.

UNHCR 1992, 'Cambodia looking to the future', information bulletin No 7, 28 October, Phnom Penh.

—— 2003, 'Forced marriages; whether forced marriage is currently practised; protection available from the government; consequences for a woman who refuses a forced marriage', UNHCR and the Immigration and Refugee Board of Canada, Cambodia, 9 December.

UNICEF 1990, *Cambodia: the situation of children and women*, Phnom Penh.

—— 1996, *Towards a better future, an analysis of the situation of children and women in Cambodia*, Phnom Penh.

UNIFEM 1974, *A fair share for women: Cambodia gender assessment*, World Bank, Asian Development Bank, and Department of Foreign Investment for Development/ UK with Ministry of Women's Affairs, Phnom Penh.

van de Put, Willem 1997, 'An assessment of the community in Cambodia', draft, TPO, Phnom Penh.

Van Liere, WJ 1982, 'Was Angkor a hydraulic society?', *Ruam Botkhum Prawatsat* [Collection of Historical Articles], Silpakorn University, Bangkok.

Vickery, Michael 1983, 'Democratic Kampuchea: themes and variations' in David P Chandler and Ben Kiernan (eds), *Revolution and its aftermath in Kampuchea: eight essays*, Yale University Sourtheast Asia Studies, New Haven.

—— 1984, *Cambodia 1975–1982*, South End Press, Boston.

Vijghen, John 1991, 'Community diagnosis Psar Trach and Traopean Somrong in Kampong Chhanang, Cambodia', Assignment of the American Friends Services Committee, Phnom Penh.

Vijghen, John and Sareoun Ly 1996, *Customs of patronage and community development in a Cambodian village*, Cambodian Researchers for Development, Phnom Penh.

WAC (Womyn's Agenda for Change) 2002, *Labels wear out: a social study of women workers in the Cambodian garment industry*, Oxfam, Cambodia, Phnom Penh.

Wakeman, Frederic E 1996, *Policing Shanghai, 1927–1937*, University of California Press, Berkeley.

Watkins, Huw 1996, 'Land ownership "a real mess"; courts backed up', *Phnom Penh Post*, 14–27 June.

Wedel, Yuangrat Pattanapongse 1981, 'The Communist Party of Thailand and Thai radical thought', *Southeast Asian Affairs 1981*, Institute of Southeast Asian Studies, Singapore.

Wedel, Yuangrat and Paul Wedel 1987, *Radical thought, Thai mind: the development of revolutionary ideas in Thailand*, Assumption Business Administration College, Bangkok.

West, Harry G and Todd Sanders 2003, *Transparency and conspiracy: ethnographies of suspicion in the New World Order*, Duke University Press, Durham and London.

WGSOC (Working Group on Social Organization in Cambodia) 1999, *Conference on the meaning of community in Cambodia*, volume 1, Church World Service, Phnom Penh.

White, Joyce C, Pisit Charoenwongsa, Ward H Goodenough 1982, *Ban Chiang: discovery of a lost Bronze Age*, University of Pennsylvania Press, Philadelphia.

Wikan, Unni 1990, *Managing turbulent hearts: a Balinese formula for living*, University of Chicago Press, Chicago.

Willmott, William E 1966, 'History and sociology of the Chinese in Cambodia', *Journal of Southeast Asian History* 7(1).

Wittgenstein, Ludwig 1992, *Leçons et conversations*, Gallimard, Paris.

Wolf, Eric R 1969, *Peasant wars of the twentieth century*, Harper and Row, New York.

Wolters, OW 1982, *History, culture, and region in Southeast Asian perspectives*, Institute of Southeast Asian Studies, Singapore.

Yatsushiro, Toshio (ed) 1968, *Studies of northeast villages in Thailand*, US Agency for International Development, Bangkok, September.

Zucker, Eve Monique 2006, 'transcending time and terror: the re-emergence of Bon Dalien after Pol Pot and thirty years of civil war', *Journal of Southeast Asian Studies* 37(3).

—— 2007, *Memory and (re)making moral order in the aftermath of violence in a highland Khmer village in Cambodia*, PhD thesis, London School of Economics and Political Science.

—— 2008, 'The absence of elders: chaos and moral order in the aftermath of the Khmer Rouge' in Kent, Alexandra and David Chandler (eds), *People of virtue: reconfiguring religion, power and morality in Cambodia today*, Nordic Institute for Asian Studies, Copenhagen.